D1146172

Wendy Richard . . . No 'S'

Wendy Richard... No 'S'

My Life Story

Wendy Richard

with Lizzie Wiggins

SIMON & SCHUSTER
A VIACOM COMPANY

First published in Great Britain by Simon & Schuster UK Ltd, 2000
A Viacom Company

1 3 5 7 9 10 8 6 4 2

Simon & Schuster UK Ltd
Africa House
64–78 Kingsway
London WC2B 6AH

Simon & Schuster Australia
Sydney

A CIP catalogue record for this book is available
from the British Library

ISBN 0-7432-0280-5

Typeset in Granjon by SX Composing DTP, Rayleigh, Essex
Printed and bound in Great Britain by
Butler & Tanner Ltd, Frome & London

I dedicate my book to Mr Gilmore, my surgeon, and Dr Carmel Coulter, my oncologist, without whose skills, I would not be here today.

And to my dear friend Joy Barry, for being there when I needed her.

And to my partner John Burns, whose love and encouragement got me through my darkest days.

And always my thanks to Julia Smith and Tony Holland for giving me Pauline.

Contents

Foreword

As soon as I heard that cheeky, cockney voice on Mike Sarne's 'Come Outside', I was determined to find a suitable place for it in one of my programmes.

The first opportunity came in *Hugh and I* starring Terry Scott and Hugh Lloyd where I was looking for someone to play 'The Girl Next Door' who was, incidentally, the daughter of the next door neighbours played by Molly Sugden and Wallace Eaton. Wendy came up to my office and nervously read the part. I don't think she had much experience as an actress but I thought she had a completely natural talent. She read the part perfectly.

That was the start of a long, happy association. She played an outrageous tart for me in *Up Pompeii* and managed to get on with Frankie Howerd which was no easy task. She played Private Walker's girlfriend in *Dad's Army* and, in Captain Mainwaring's opinion, was 'quite the wrong class of girl'.

Next came her incomparable playing of Shirley Brahms in the television series *Are You Being Served?* which continued for twelve years and included a record breaking summer season on the stage of the Winter Garden Theatre in Blackpool.

After a number of years break, she joined the staff of Grace Brothers during their retirement when they ran a small country hotel in *Grace and Favour*.

Above all, she sparkled, she was fun and in all the ridiculous things she was called upon to do, she was a truthful performer. I will always love her.

David Croft, OBE

Preface

It is May 1962. A record by previously unknown UK male vocalist Mike Sarne enters the British charts for the first time. By 28 June his increasingly persistent attempts to lure a young lady away from the dance hall and outside into the moonlight for 'a bit of slap and tickle', take the record, 'Come Outside', to the Number 1 spot. 'Come Outside' was only the second comedy record ever to go top of the pops since charts began (the first being Lonnie Donegan's 'My Old Man's a Dustman'). Written and produced by Charles Blackwell, the record went on to sell over half a million copies and remained in the British charts for a total of nineteen weeks.

At the height of its success, I was walking down a London street with my mother. A fan approached us and asked me for my autograph. Yes, for the record, I *WAS* the female voice on 'Come Outside'. My interjections of 'Get Lost' 'What For?' and 'Give Over', to the eventually compliant: 'Oh, All Right, Then' seemed to have fixed my 'voice' firmly in the limelight.

'So, Mummy, what is it like to have a famous daughter?' I asked as the fan left.

I remember my mother just gave me one of her withering looks. Obviously, she was very chuffed about the autograph

1

hunter but at the same time, she wanted to keep my feet firmly on the ground. Despite the glare I knew she was indeed truly proud of her only daughter. Proud that I had achieved some measure of fame and recognition at such an early stage in my career. Proud also because it had been a financial struggle for her, as a widow, to help get my foot on the first few rungs of the ladder of success. My mother encouraged me as much as she could in my aspirations to become an actress. It was she who worked unceasingly to earn the money to pay for my drama classes but she was never a typically forceful 'showbiz mother'. She was a quiet woman and certainly not at all pushy. But she took great delight in the parts that came my way.

In that London street, on that June day in 1962, little did either of us realize it had been more than worth all her hard work and the sacrifices she'd made – because those initial accolades for the record were but only a small beginning.

I'd already had a few 'bit parts' and modelling jobs during the previous two years but what Mummy and I didn't know then was that later I would become an established household name, as one of the best-known actresses on British television. My face and voice invariably recognized wherever I went . . .

CHAPTER ONE

Just the Three of Us

OK, so I wasn't exactly born with a silver spoon in my mouth but when I was only an hour and a half old, my father put a silver spoonful of champagne to my lips for good luck. It must have done the trick because, looking back, I've had a pretty lucky life. Forty years as a working actress have brought me the kind of experiences I would never have dreamt of as a child and – even with the ups and downs – I wouldn't swap them for anything. That silver spoonful was probably the moment I first developed my love of champagne – now my favourite and only tipple, apart from an occasional glass of wine with a meal. I really do love a glass or two of Moët Chandon when I have a chance to relax – but then I also enjoy tea too and believe you can't beat a good cuppa!

Be honest, I bet you think I'm a Cockney don't you? It's the accent, I'm sure. I've no idea where 'the voice' came from – it just appeared when I was young. My mother was forever nagging me about the way I spoke. But I took no notice and told her 'Mummy, one day my voice will earn me a lot of money,' – and it has.

No, I'm not a Cockney, far from it. In fact I was born Wendy Emerton, a long way away from the sound of Bow Bells, up in the north east of England, at Middlesbrough. I changed my stage name to Richard for the sole reason it was short and neat. A decision that proved to be right, for I remember one of my earliest showbiz bosses, David Croft remarking 'Never choose a long stage name should you want your name in lights – they won't like paying for all the bulbs!'

My parents, whom I adored, worked in the licensed trade. They met in the 1930s in a pub called The Bedford, at Balham in South London. My dad was running the place and Mum came down from the North East to work as a trainee manageress there. They fell in love, eventually married in London and held their wedding reception at The Cumberland Hotel, opposite Marble Arch. I appeared eight years afterwards.

By the time I was born they'd moved on in the trade away from London and Daddy was manager of the Corporation Hotel in Middlesbrough but it, like a lot of other traditional old buildings, has now been demolished to make way for a shopping centre. So no blue commemorative plaque for Wendy Richard there!

My father, Henry William Emerton – who was always known as Harry – was over 50 when I arrived on the scene. He'd been married before but was divorced by the time he met my mother. He and his first wife had a daughter who, ironically, also became an actress. Mummy and I never had any contact with my half-sister whom, I think was called Kay, nor for some reason with Daddy's own family either. All Mummy and I knew about his relatives were that they came from a military background. To this day I have never met my half-sister or made any attempts to trace her. Daddy had been divorced in the 1930s and divorce was not widely talked about then, certainly not in front of me as a young child. As far as I was concerned, Daddy's former marriage had been a completely separate life to ours and he chose not to refer to it in front of me.

Daddy originated from St Albans. He was an extremely handsome man and very tall too, well over 6ft in height. Mummy was born on Tyneside – in Newcastle, 'the Holy City' – and was in her late thirties when she had me. She was a genteel, petite woman, only five feet tall and had lovely brown hair and beautiful blue eyes. Although she was called Beatrice, she was usually referred to as 'Bea,' until later, when it was always: 'Wendy's Mum' – much to her annoyance!

Mummy came from a family of girls and, though they were not a very close family, I do remember some of my aunties from when I was a child. One, my Aunty Elsie, was always very good to me. She was a wonderful needlewoman and made lovely little silk dresses for me which, I remember, always had lots of decorative smocking. I was lucky enough to have some beautiful clothes as a youngster, many of them produced by Aunty Elsie. Second was Aunty Betty of whom I was very fond too. Betty had a twin brother called Alfie, although for some reason or another I only ever met him a couple of times. There was also a third sister: Aunty Bobbie.

To be honest, I was a bit of a Daddy's girl really. Of course I loved both my parents equally but he spoiled me most of the time and I could get away with anything as far as he was concerned. As a small child I longed to have a brother for company instead of being completely on my own. When I was six years of age I thought my prayers had been answered – Mummy became pregnant. Sadly though, she miscarried and lost the baby; it was obviously destined that I should be an only child.

We left the North East when I was a babe in arms and lived in various places over the ensuing years, including Bournemouth and the Isle of Wight. It was nice being by the seaside in Bournemouth but with both my parents occupied with work, they had little time to take me to the beach. I do remember though one particular outing in Bournemouth and that was when Mummy took me shopping for clothes. We went into Bobby's, which was a rather exclusive department store in The Square. I tried on a lovely coat and thought that I looked the bee's knees wearing it. However, Mummy decided otherwise and told me to take it off immediately. In a fit of pique I ran off, screaming that I wanted the coat, whatever she thought. Well, unfortunately, I had whooping-cough at the time and as a result of my coughing, I ended up being violently sick right down the front of the coat. Mummy had no option but to buy it for me then!

My parents were reasonably strict in my upbringing. Little things seemed to count a lot to them. For instance, I was never allowed coats with pockets. Mummy said it would encourage me to put my hands in my pockets and that was not considered lady-like. One day in Bournemouth I was out playing with my friend, Janey Hill, whose parents owned a hotel nearby. Janey had a coat with pockets, so I asked her if we could swap. That afternoon Janey and I were out walking and, as children do, we decided to try and climb the cliffs.

Half-way up we got stuck and couldn't move any further up . . . or down. A passer-by called the fire brigade who came out to rescue us. Next thing I knew, Mummy was at the bottom of the cliff too, shouting out instructions to the firemen.

'Quickly!, Quickly! Bring her down first, the one in the green coat.'

As the firemen obliged, she suddenly realized the first child being rescued wasn't me at all and that Janey and I were wearing each others' coats.

'No! No! Not her, the other one,' she called up frantically. Fortunately the firemen brought us both down safely at the same time and no doubt had a little chuckle afterwards about the incident.

Another trip I remember is Daddy taking me up to Blackpool. He went there to have a look at the hotel they were thinking of moving into. While we were there he took me on a tram ride along the prom. He'd bought me an ice-cream before we got on but after I'd eaten it I began to feel queasy.

'Daddy, how much does it cost if you are sick on one of these trams?' I asked him.

'Oh a lot of money, Wendy,' he fibbed.

'Well then Daddy, I think we'd better get off please ... QUICKLY!'

It was while we were living on the Isle of Wight that Daddy entered into what turned out to be a disastrous business partnership. He and another man bought a hotel but Daddy ended up losing all the capital he'd sunk into the venture. So we had to move back to the mainland and he then started work for Carrs, a major pub chain.

It was through his job – when my parents took over Carrs' flagship pub: Shepherds Tavern, in Shepherd Market, at the back of Park Lane – that, at the age of five, I had my first taste of life in London. I think my parents were very happy to be back there again too. I was brought up in Shepherd Market until I was 10 and I absolutely adored it around there. In fact, I've always loved the capital ever since those days and there is nowhere else but London that I would even consider living.

We visited my aunts when we made occasional trips back up North but my mother's family was not a particularly close one. It was difficult to get together regularly anyway because my parents were always fully occupied with their work.

I started my first primary school in London: St George's in Mount Street and it's still open today. I especially remember St George's school trips, when we spent a fortnight at Hopton on sea, in Suffolk. We were taken on long flower-spotting walks and although it is unlawful to pick wild flowers these days, at that time we did. We took them back to school to press into our exercise books and wrote floral prose to match each specimen. It was always good fun going on the school holiday, except I always became homesick. Mummy would have to visit on the middle weekend in order to placate me!

Life in London was great and I didn't have a care in the world. A couple of my school friends lived within Shepherd Market too, which was handy because we could play out in the market and it was totally safe to do so in those days. One of the girls – Jacqueline Dunn – and I went ice-skating to the rink in Queensway. Jacqueline's mother was a widow and the pair of them lived above Lambs, the appropriately named butcher's shop. When I started ice-skating seriously, Mummy had some smashing skating outfits made for me. In fact, I enjoyed ice-skating so much, at one stage I even had notions of becoming a famous ice-skater.

Shepherds Tavern, where we lived, was very nice. The walls were covered with oil paintings and in the bar there was a sedan chair, which had been converted into a telephone box and was a big talking point among the customers. Naturally, I was never allowed to mix with the customers. I had to walk straight through the bar to the upstairs, where we had a lovely flat.

One of our regulars was Elizabeth Taylor, during the days she was with Michael Wilding. Another notable was Anthony Armstrong Jones, long before he married Princess Margaret and became Lord Snowdon. Daddy had a house rule that men could not be served with a drink unless they were wearing a tie. Whenever Anthony Armstrong Jones came in he never wore a tie, only a cravat. However, Mummy insisted that it counted just the same because he had such a pleasant, friendly smile!

Daddy also had a 'No Dogs' rule in the bar. I remember coming home from school for lunch one day to find him in a bit of confusion. A customer had brought in a tortoise and was feeding it greens on the carpet! I think it was allowed to stay.

There were a considerable number of prostitutes about in the market in those times. They were referred to as the 'Messina girls' because they worked for a couple of Maltese brothers whose surname was Messina. The women were always wonderfully dressed and little did we kids realize that they were prostitutes. Daddy always wore an Anthony Eden-style hat and I recall on one occasion when he was walking through the market with me, one of the girls walked past us.

'Hello Wendy', she called out.

Of course my father, being a gentleman, had to raise his hat to her, which he no doubt found an amusing tale to relate to the regulars back at the pub!

In the main, the pub was frequented by business clientele. My parents ran a very busy restaurant on the first floor, where they had three chefs working for them and it was always particularly hectic at lunchtimes.

As they were so occupied in the business, I was brought up by a series of nannies who spent a lot of time with me. My favourite was a Dutch girl called Wilhelmina, because she played cowboys and Indians with my friends and I in Hyde Park and Green Park. Wilhelmina also knitted lovely cardigans and sweaters for me to wear to school. Mother was a great believer in school uniform and even to this day, I have to say it's good to see St George's pupils still wearing the same red and white uniform that I once wore.

We were living in Shepherd Market at the time of the Coronation in June 1953. I know a lot of people bought a television for the first time especially for the occasion but I thought we were very grand because we had one long before then. I loved watching the Children's Hour series, particularly *Bill and Ben the Flowerpot Men*, *Andy Pandy* and *The Wooden Tops*.

On the Coronation Day Mummy made me go to Down Street to watch Queen Elizabeth ride past in her golden coach pulled by eight grey horses. I didn't particularly want to go. I remember a chap lifting me up on his shoulders so that I got a better view of the coach going past but I couldn't have cared less quite frankly and was unimpressed by the whole spectacle. I'd much rather have stayed indoors playing than watch the Queen out in the street. Funny really, considering I've turned out such a Royalist.

The sedan chair/phone box in our bar came into its own once again at the time of the Coronation. One of the national newspapers photographed Mummy sitting inside it and included the picture in a special supplement they produced which portrayed the 'flavour of London' at the time of the Coronation.

I did very well for family holidays in those days, in addition to the breaks I had with the school. Daddy always took me to Jersey for a week and I have some very fond memories of our times spent together there. We always stayed at The Grand Hotel, which is in a prime position on the esplanade in St Helier. I usually palled up with other children of my age who were staying in the hotel and we'd go off to the beach together. Daddy had friends living in Jersey who worked for Mary Ann, the island brewery; so a trip around the brewery was sometimes on our holiday itinerary. Aside from that we visited the usual tourist venues, such as the German Military Underground Hospital and the Neolithic tomb.

We spent most of our time though visiting the various beautiful bays around the island. Daddy didn't drive so we'd either go by taxi and spend the whole day in one particular bay, or on other occasions we booked a coach trip which took in several places. My favourite bay was always Greve de Lecq, the rock pools there were a veritable treasure trove for children to explore.

Whenever Daddy took me to Jersey for our week's holiday Mummy refused to come with us because she hated flying. As soon as we returned though it was Mummy's turn to take me away for her week's holiday. Her choice was Monkey Island at

Bray, near Maidenhead, an island with an exclusive hotel built in the middle of it. The hotel was rather snooty but I enjoyed being with my mother and having her undivided attention. We lazed around, reading and chatting and sometimes we took a punt down the River Thames.

One of my godparents was a French woman called Tina Voller. She was a widow and lived in Nice with her daughter Vivienne. My parents thought it would be good for me to go and stay with her for awhile, with a view to my eventually attending school there. Off I went, in the care of the airline stewardess. I quite enjoyed my stay, visiting Monte Carlo on one occasion. It would be nice to go back now that I am probably more appreciative. I think it might have been around about then that Daddy's health began to decline because I was called home early and my plans for schooling there abandoned.

I only ever had one holiday with both my parents at the same time and that was during the summer of 1954, a few months before Daddy died. I don't know whether she had any premonition, or what but oddly enough, that year we were able to persuade Mummy to come to Jersey with us, for what turned out to be the first – and last – holiday the three of us ever spent together.

CHAPTER TWO

Tragedy Strikes

After that holiday we had to leave Shepherd Market because my father was appointed manager of the Valentine Hotel, at Gants Hill in Essex. When Mummy broke the news to me that we were moving on I was terribly upset because I loved living there.

'Is there anywhere else you would like to live instead?' she asked, just to take my mind off our imminent departure.

'Yes, Ambridge,' I replied instantly.

Then Mummy had to tell me, Ambridge was not a real place and – worse still – *The Archers* were fictional characters. Do you know, that realization upset me far more than when I later discovered that Santa Claus was really Daddy.

After our move to Essex it was awfully difficult for me to get back to Queensway. So my skating boots were given away and my dreams of an ice-skating career melted away too.

The Valentine Hotel was a typical suburban establishment which catered mostly for business customers. There was one compensation for my loss of ice-skating and that was that at the back of the hotel there was a large restaurant where a local drama group frequently staged amateur plays and I was fascinated watching them perform. The actors were superbly dressed, often in period costume. My parents allowed me to invite a few school friends to watch the plays and it was probably at that point I first had the idea of becoming an actress. Maybe the lure was the costumes. I know I was very impressed by the way the actors and actresses were dressed when they appeared on stage. After the performances I'd go off and dress up in my mother's clothes, imagining I was all sorts of different characters.

Daddy loved the theatre – which was probably what influenced me (and my half-sister) to become actresses – and he sometimes took me to the theatre with him when he had a day off work. We always saw at least one pantomime each Christmas. He'd become pally with Chesney Allen, as a result of doing the catering for one of his family functions and so he often took me to see The Crazy Gang shows at the Victoria Palace. We also saw Max Miller at the Palladium and a load of other good turns. I count myself lucky because for one so young I was fortunate to see a host of excellent performers. Mummy liked the theatre too but probably to a lesser extent. I do remember her going to see Kenneth Williams in the West End in a review called *Pieces of Eight*, which she thought was very funny and enjoyed tremendously.

The three of us were all keen radio listeners too. Archie Andrews was a firm favourite of ours every Sunday in *Educating Archie* on the Light Programme. I remember being taken to see him live, in the *Archie Andrews' Christmas Show*. Among the other programmes we particularly enjoyed were *Life With The Lyons* and *Take It From Here* with Jimmy Edwards.

Sunday was always a good day on the radio. That day was sacrosanct to us anyway because the bar was closed longer and I saw more of my parents. My mother was a good cook and even though we couldn't always eat together as a family during the week, on Sundays – without fail – the three of us sat down together at the table for a traditional Sunday roast, no matter how busy my parents might otherwise be.

Overall, I had a happy childhood. Despite the fact my mother and father worked long hours, they each regularly made time for me whenever they could. Neither of them ever hit me but if I was rude to a member of staff, then they made me apologize immediately. It was a good lesson to learn in life – to be able to say 'Sorry' when you are wrong and it has always stood me in good stead.

In the licensed trade it was usual practice for managers to be moved around frequently from one establishment to another. After Gants Hill our next move was to Streatham, where my parents took over the management of a pub called The Streatham Park Hotel, which was a busy place with bars, restaurant and an off-licence. I don't know what it was about the hotel but right from the beginning none of us were ever really happy there. There must have been a sense of foreboding, for it was in Streatham, on 12 December 1954 that Daddy died.

That dreadful December day was one of the saddest and also one of the most frightening days in my life. I was only 11 years old and it was I who discovered him.

It was early on Sunday morning when I found him. I hadn't been awake for long when I decided to get up and have some breakfast. I walked through into the lounge and saw Daddy lying in front of the gas fire. He wasn't moving at all and I thought he was asleep but I felt sure he must be uncomfortable laying there. I ran through to Mummy and told her 'Daddy is asleep in the lounge and I can't wake him up.'

Mummy jumped out of bed and rushed down the hall into the lounge. I still recall her dreadful screams. She kept crying, murmuring the same words over and over again: 'Oh no! Oh no! Please, dear God, don't let this be true . . .'

A member of staff called the police. When they arrived, one of them tried to comfort Mummy but there was no consoling her. The man she loved had died by taking his own life. 'My Daddy' had left us both. His death was like a bolt out of the blue. I'd had a very happy childhood up to that point in time and hadn't been aware that anything was wrong. However, after he died Mummy discovered letters from a Harley Street doctor among his personal effects, which made it clear my father was a very sick man. Apparently, Daddy had been suffering from depression.

In the time leading up to his death, Mummy might have realized that he was not himself but I never heard anything discussed between them to that effect. If she was aware that things were not right, she never intimated anything to me and certainly, I never noticed anything different about my father.

To me, he was just 'My Daddy' as he always had been – and now he was gone and I would never see him again. It was unbearable.

My mother would not let me go to his funeral. She said I was too young and she didn't want me to be even more upset by the occasion than I already felt and I believe she made the right decision. Funerals are not the place for children. Naturally, I was not allowed to attend the inquest either.

To this day I do not know for certain what really happened. According to the post mortem there was a bump on Daddy's head. Mummy thought he might have got up during the night, turned on the fire to warm himself but over-balanced and banged his head. I know he was extremely unsteady on his feet. He had fought in the First World War, surviving mustard gas and many other disturbing experiences. Unfortunately, the effects of the mustard gas left him partially paralyzed in his feet, so it's true that his balance was not good. He could walk but he couldn't run.

Although my mother was a strong woman in so many ways, after my father's death she really went to pieces. The pity was none of her family were supportive, at all.

Also, due to the wide age gap between my parents, we didn't know any of Daddy's family. They had all passed on, we believed. So Mummy and I had no one to stand by us. We only had each other.

It is true, I was a Daddy's girl. He spoilt me with whatever I wanted: books, clothes, toys, the lot. Both my parents made a big fuss of me but a child always knows when they can get around one more than the other – and I could twist my Daddy around my little finger. He was a wonderful man and I adored him. After his death I missed him desperately. One thing I am sure about and that is, that the insecurity I have suffered all my life dates back to the time of his death. The only way I knew how to deal with it was to blot the memory of this time from my mind.

CHAPTER THREE

Boarding School Beckons

For Mummy and I, Daddy's death was the turning point in our lives. Life was never easy after that for either of us. Mummy was not one to shirk from hard work and I felt extremely sorry for her because she was immediately relegated from being the boss's wife, in charge of others, to becoming an ordinary member of staff. The company Daddy worked for suggested we moved to one of their places in Southend where Mummy could be under-manageress, but she was not happy working in Southend at all.

In the early 1950s, when the child of a Freemason lost one or both parents, an assisted place could be made available for the daughter at The Royal Masonic School for Girls, located at Rickmansworth in Hertfordshire, on the outskirts of London. My father had been a Master Mason and as a result I qualified to attend the Masonic school but with places at a premium, I had to wait until they had a vacancy for me.

In the interim, Mummy decided that she would send me to a boarding school at St Neots, in Cambridgeshire and the Masons agreed to pay the fees. I think she chose that particular school because she and Daddy had once lived nearby to it. Of course, I didn't want to leave Mummy and go away but it was a bleak time for her, she had no fixed home and employers didn't want a young child around the place. The truth was that I was in the way.

She took me to St Neots by train and I was utterly miserable throughout the journey, dreading our arrival. The only light moment came when she leaned forward in the railway carriage, to caution me: 'When you go to church, there will be choir boys there.'

'Yes, Mummy?'

'Well, stay away from them! You know what boys can do to you don't you?'

Quite honestly, I hadn't the faintest clue. So I sat there meekly and whispered: 'Yes,' still having no idea what on earth she was talking about.

We said our goodbyes amid floods of tears. I was terribly homesick straightaway. I pined for Mummy and also missed having my toys, books and other personal possessions around me. I was an avid reader of Enid Blyton's *Famous Five* books and also enjoyed comics such as *Dandy* and *Beano* but comics were forbidden at school, they were contraband.

For some reason, pupils were not allowed even telephone contact with their parents. The only life line was in being able to write two letters to home each week but the letters were read by the principal before being posted and if she didn't like any of the contents, they had to be re-written.

How I hated that school, I was incredibly unhappy there. We had to wear three different uniforms: one for weekdays, another for Saturdays and a different one on Sundays. In the summer when we attended Sunday service we also had to wear white gloves; leather ones in winter. Although Mummy had some financial help from the Masons for my fees, she had to pay for my uniform and all those changes of clothing made it terribly expensive for her.

My mother left Southend while I was at St Neots and took managerial positions wherever she could find suitable employment, including at one stage in Wales. It was not an easy time for her because she had no support from anyone, apart from the Masons. In those days when a widow was left alone looking after a child, a close family friend was usually appointed as guardian to help out. As bad luck would have it, my appointed guardian, Mr Waddington, died from cancer a few months after Daddy's death. So Mummy and I were totally on our own yet again, which is why some of Daddy's brother masons had rallied round and paid my boarding school fees at St Neots. Eventually they managed to make a place available for me at their own school – the Royal Masonic at Rickmansworth – but once again, I had to attend as a boarder and could not be with my mother, as I would have much preferred.

The Royal Masonic School for Girls was founded in 1788 and is set in 315 acres of grounds, overlooking the Chess valley. When I arrived there everything was provided for me: from shoes to hairbrush, comb and toothbrush, down to three sets of underwear and even sanitary towels. The combs were beautiful bone ones, although we girls wanted the brightly coloured plastic combs which were all the fashion then. When I think of how much money you would have to pay for a bone comb nowadays! We were also given a wooden pencil box each, containing everything we needed for school work. However, we were not allowed to use fountain pens until we were 13 years of age, so until then we all used a dip-in pen instead.

Unless you already had long hair when you arrived at Rickmansworth, special permission from the headmistress was required to grow your hair. Otherwise, it had to be kept short and could not touch your collar. My hair was short when I started there and that's the way it had to stay. By my teenage years my hair had turned quite brown in colour, even though I was light blonde when I was a little girl.

At Rickmansworth I became friendly with a girl called Mary Boyce, who lived in Birmingham. She had very nice short dark brown hair but I remember when she returned after one school holiday she had plonked loads of peroxide on the front of her hair to make it blond. God, she was nearly crucified by the staff for that.

School rules at the Masonic were excessively strict. For entertainment we were only permitted a radio, the *Radio Times* and the daily *Times*. My mother asked if I could have my portable record player at school and surprisingly, permission was granted. I often played a selection of Bill Haley and Elvis Presley records, which the teachers frowned upon. They considered me some-what of a rebel because of my choice in music! Anyway their opinions didn't bother me because we had a great time in the Common Room at night, listening to Bill and Elvis and teaching each other to jive. I say 'at night' but by 7.30p.m. we had to be in bed, so there wasn't all that much jiving tuition – unfortunately – because it could have come in handy. Such as when I was home from school on holiday and one of the regulars in the pub where Mummy worked in London asked if I'd like to go dancing with her daughter and some friends? Despite the jiving lessons, I was still not a very good dancer and because of attending a girls-only boarding school, I had become used to leading anyhow. I went to the dance but I cringe when I remember Jerry Lee Lewis' 'Great Balls of Fire' being played and a chap invited me on to the dance floor. He was obviously deeply disappointed with my dancing prowess because he sat me down almost straightaway and that was that, me left as a wallflower for the rest of the evening!

Aside from pop music, as a teenager I loved the cinema too, especially the new film releases from Elvis Presley, Tommy Steele and Cliff Richard. I also still enjoyed the Charlie Chaplin and Laurel and Hardy cartoons and Pathé newsreels.

I wasn't all that sporty at school, although I was a good hockey player and a reasonable swimmer. I hated lacrosse because I was terrified of being hit by one of the cradles. Neither did I much care for tennis or rounders and I absolutely loathed athletics. When I saw how athletics had developed the leg muscles of some of the older girls, I was certain that I definitely didn't want legs like those when I grew up.

My mother changed jobs again and in 1956 became house-keeper to a nice gentleman who had a pub called the Sir John Falstaff, immediately opposite the Drury Lane Theatre in Covent Garden. It was fun returning there during school holidays because Covent Garden was such a busy, noisy market, with lots happening. There was a permanent traffic jam and constant honking of horns from the fruit and veg lorries. The bustle reminded me in part of our days at Shepherd Market. Somebody told me that the ghost of Nell Gwynn walked outside the Drury Lane Theatre at midnight. The pity was though that at that age I was always asleep by midnight, so I never saw her!

After the Sir John Falstaff, in 1958 Mummy went to work for a chap called Harold Ive, who ran a pub in Eden Grove, off Holloway Road. She did all the cooking there for him. Harold was a very kind man and he and Mummy remained friends throughout their lives.

Apart from school holidays I saw very little of my mother and I missed her so much. We were allowed only three parental visits per term: two had to take place in school and on the third we could go out. Mummy and I usually went into Watford on our outings.

Although to others it might have appeared as if Mummy was coping OK, I was worried because I suspected that she had started drinking heavily. Her behaviour changed and I guess she became partial to having a drink to help abate her loneliness.

She never took up with another man after Daddy died. Perhaps it was because she knew I still missed my father so much. No one could ever love me as much as Daddy had done and she probably felt it was not right to introduce another man into the situation. I know from other people's experiences, it is often difficult for a man to accept someone else's child. So Mummy kept herself to herself but the loneliness must have been made worse for her with me being away at boarding school for long periods. If circumstances had been different, I could have been living with her and we could have kept each other company, which I would have much preferred.

As it was I was no great scholar. I was pretty much of a daydreamer, who sat in class staring out of the window most of the time. There was a beautiful cedar tree outside, which especially transfixed me. I imagined it had steps going up to heaven and wondered what it would be like up there. I'd daydream about all sorts of other things too, anything not to have to concentrate on school work. Unfortunately, I only worked for teachers I really liked. Boy, did we get worked hard at Rickmansworth. As well as classes every day of the week, we had prep each evening and classes on Saturday morning too. We didn't go short on religion either – on Sundays we were expected to attend church for Communion, Morning Service and Evensong. In addition to which, we also had weekday morning and evening assembly in school, so one way or another we were up to our ears in religion – not such a bad thing, I suppose.

Looking back and realizing the amount of money spent on my education, well, I suppose I wasted much of it really. As a result, my school reports were never brilliant. There were always comments like: 'could do better,' 'should show more discipline', which far from pleased my mother.

Many years later when I was invited back to school to speak at an old girls' reunion, I looked through some of the reports for inspiration for my talk. In my speech I told a story about our art mistress, Miss Funnel, who, in her report on me, claimed: 'Her paintings and drawings are all affected – rather like herself.' As I told the tale I looked down into the audience and there was Miss Funnel, sitting in the front row, turning a very pleasant shade of pink.

Reading through the reports reminded me also that I was absolutely terrified of our French mistress, Miss Vickridge. Her entire class was conducted in French and although I'd started to learn the language when I was six years old, I couldn't keep pace with her. She was strict beyond belief and so, I started daydreaming in her classes too. Miss Vickridge was at the reunion but after my talk I felt awkward about approaching her. For courage I urged Diana Fawkes, who'd once been our head girl, to come and speak to her with me. I duly apologized to Miss Vickridge for wasting time during her French lessons and for the fact I still could not speak French fluently.

'It matters not a jot, my dear. You have the ability to make people laugh and that's far more important than speaking French.' Much to my surprise, I think I was exonerated.

I saw through, rather than enjoyed, my education at the Royal Masonic. I didn't have any career aspirations they would have approved of because all I could imagine myself being was an actress. I briefly flirted with the idea of becoming an archaeologist after we had some lessons on Egyptology but that idea didn't last long. My mother had long chats with my house Matron, Miss Birchette. These were usually held in the linen room of my school house, Sussex House, and they tried to persuade me that I could have a good career in commerce – the last thing on my mind!

For those girls with the aptitude, the Masons were prepared to pay for them to attend University. Similarly, if any of the girls had foreign language potential, then they would send them to language school. Me? Well, I was put in the commercial form to learn shorthand and typing from Miss McColl, who was also my house mistress and my goodness, did she make my life a misery. She was an overbearing disciplinarian who never seemed happy unless she was making us girls unhappy. A Scottish spinster, her idea of good health was to ensure we kept every other window in the dormitory open all night. As a result, our dormitory ended up with the worst record in school for coughs and colds.

She seemed to pick on me more than most so, in the end, my mother made an appointment to complain to our headmistress, Audrey Fryer, who was a rather 'jolly hockey sticks' 1930s lady. 'Miss McColl is making Wendy very unhappy. I certainly don't think she knows much about young people,' Mummy pointed out.

'Oh, I am sure she must do because she goes out twice a week . . . to the library,' came the innocent reply.

That's the sort of genteel naiveté that abounded in our school because most of the teachers were either spinsters or War widows. Anyway, I continued with Miss McColl's shorthand typing course but became even more determined to leave school as soon as I could.

I maintained my secret ambition to become an actress and grew more determined in my resolve as the time approached for me to leave school. Not that I told any of the teachers about my ambition – acting would have been considered a totally unsuitable vocation for a Royal Masonic girl. Instead, I pretended I wanted to be a continuity girl in films.

When girls left the Royal Masonic they were helped to prepare for the outside world by either being given a cheque for £50, which was a lot of money in those days, or, they were taken to Marshall and Snellgrove and bought a raincoat, a winter coat, a suit, a dress, a hat, gloves, shoes and underwear. The whole point being that when they went out into the world, as ex-Royal Masonic pupils, they were supposed to be smart and as well dressed as the best.

Eventually because my mother didn't want to see me so unhappy, she gave in to my pleadings and said she would allow me to leave school just before my sixteenth birthday. When I finished at the Royal Masonic it was with the equivalent of a public school education. Although it might be considered I didn't make the most of mine I do, however, have a lifelong gratitude to the Freemasons for what they did for me.

Those leaving school had a final meeting with the headmistress, Miss Fryer. At ours she warned us 'Girls, when you go out into the world, you will probably be invited to a cocktail party. One may have one drink, perhaps two, but never three.' Miss Fryer also cautioned us: 'Remember, your virginity is the highest card you can ever play.'

Years later, Diana Fawkes and I chuckled at the memory of Miss Fryer's warning, with her adding: 'I don't know about you, Wendy but I learned you can still have a jolly good game . . . long after you've played your highest card!'

CHAPTER FOUR

My First Job . . . In a Department Store

After finishing school at Easter I thought I'd relax and enjoy myself during the holidays and start work sometime later. But oh no, my mother had completely different ideas! She only allowed me one week off and then sent me to Fortnum and Mason for a job interview. I was taken on as a junior in the fashion department, earning the princely sum of £3 eight shillings and four pence per week – no Luncheon Vouchers or any perks like that, mind you.

The fashion buyer there was a woman called Miss Whiteside. Looking back, I swear she was the prototype for Mrs Slocombe in *Are You Being Served?* Miss Whiteside wore brightly coloured eye shadow, her blonde hair was solidly lacquered into place (although, fortunately, not dyed different colours each week, like Mrs Slocombe's!). She had the same build as Mrs Slocombe and was always dressed in the latest of fashion. There was something in her demeanour that made us all terrified of her. Anyway she was a true doppleganger for Mrs Slocombe, the only thing I didn't know was whether or not she had a pussy at home! I was a junior and those were the sort of questions you simply did not ask of a senior member of staff!

It was jolly hard work all day at Fortnum and Mason and after work I had to attend evening classes. My mother had paid 25 guineas – a large sum then – to send me to a modelling school. I honestly don't think the classes did me much good, particularly as the principal of the modelling school told Mummy I was not photogenic.

A few months after I started at Fortnum and Mason, Mummy took over the running of a small bed and breakfast hotel in Argyle Street, opposite St Pancras Station. Thankfully, this meant that I could finish at the store and start work at the hotel with her instead. In due course, we were able to scrape up enough money to buy our own B & B business, a few doors down from the one she had managed. We bought the property from a man called Mr Allcock. There was a sign outside the hotel: 'Allcock bed and breakfast' but it just shows how naive Mummy and I were – it was a long time before we made the connection as to why people found the sign amusing!

We inherited several of Mr Allcock's regular holidaymakers. In those days many people came to London for their fortnight's holiday because cheap package holidays abroad were not widely available as they are today. Most of our guests travelled from Yorkshire and I must say they were a good crowd.

One was a rather rotund Reverend, whose wife was a tiny mouse-like creature. He usually wore a black beret on his head and carried a satchel across one shoulder. For some unknown reason, when he went out for the day he left his wife alone in their bedroom. Mummy and I used to make up stories to amuse ourselves, imagining he probably visited all the bookshops and dives in Soho. No wonder he didn't want her with him according to our reckoning!

The reverend was in the habit of spending ages in the WC and one night he complained to my mother: 'Mrs Emerton, there is something wrong with your lavatory.'

With that brief announcement, he disappeared. Mummy went up to the toilet to find out what had happened, only to discover it was not the seat that the reverend had broken, he'd cracked the pan.

'You can claim on the insurance,' I reassured her . . . 'After all, it was an Act of God, Holy wind broke that!' From then on he became known, to Mummy and I, as 'The Farting Vicar'.

Mummy and I often sat up late into the night, in case anyone called to take one of our vacant rooms. To while away the time we would sit and watch old black and white movies, which were great favourites of ours. Going to bed very late meant it was hard getting up early next morning to cook breakfast for the guests. We virtually lived on egg and bacon ourselves and it was several years before I was ever able to face eating them again. Once, I suggested kippers for breakfast, as a change. However, a lot of guests didn't fancy them – so Mummy, the cat and I ended up eating loads of kippers, until I was sick of the sight of those as well. Mummy ribbed me for sometime over the kipper episode. 'If you have any more bright ideas about changing the breakfast menu, keep them to yourself,' she told me in no uncertain terms.

It was while we were at our B & B that Mummy saved up sufficient money to send me to the Italia Conti Stage Academy, which was then based in Soho. It was famous for having trained the likes of Sir Noel Coward, Anthony Newley and Jack Hawkins. Italia Conti was a large place with a number of rehearsal halls and dance studios, where they taught tap and ballet. We students had to sit in long rows of seats in front of the teacher, just like at school!

In the beginning I lapped up every minute. We spent our days learning all aspects of acting but particularly elocution, which seemed to take up a lot of our time. Our elocution teacher, a well-spoken woman in her forties was forever urging me to change my accent, in readiness for my new career. I took no notice and pressed on regardless.

Comedy was my favourite subject. Our comedy classes largely featured the works of Noel Coward, which I enjoyed very much. When it came to dancing classes, I displayed my usual prowess . . . none! I was absolutely hopeless. As for singing classes, well, I've never had a voice, so it's just as well I've not had to earn my living from a singing role. The founder, Miss Ruth Conti, a descendant of Italia, was still alive in those days and she took the acting classes. I must admit though I just could not get on with Shakespeare, certainly not with an accent like mine!

It was while I was at Italia Conti that I started to make up time for a lot of things I felt I'd missed out on in life. Angela Reading, a girl I made friends with, introduced me to the wonders of the Lyceum Ballroom in the Strand. I'd never been to a place like that before and coming from a relatively sheltered background, the Lyceum was an education to me. The buzz of the music, the flashing lights, but most of all the boys! As far as I was concerned, it was a fantastic place, compared to anything I'd known before.

Instead of attending our Friday afternoon dancing classes at drama school, we bunked off and went to the Lyceum to dance around our handbags. It was much more fun than at Italia Conti because of the array of boys there. Of course Mummy didn't know about my secret sessions at the Lyceum and I'm not sure how but unfortunately for me she discovered that I was disappearing from drama school on Friday afternoons. From then on I was banned from the Lyceum! Every Friday afternoon someone from the academy had to ring Mummy to confirm that I was present in class.

Another of our favourite haunts – after class! – was Le Grand Coffee House in Soho, where we idled away many hours, talking and lingering over a cup of coffee.

I did not qualify for a grant from the education authorities and with my mother being a widow, it was quite a struggle for her to pay my drama school fees. So then, and also in the earlier years of my career, I worked in some of London's biggest department stores such as Selfridges, D.H. Evans, Dickins and Jones and Fenwicks, in order to help pay my way.

I lasted precisely a day and a half at Fenwicks. In the short time I was there they held a coat sale but I couldn't seem to sell anything. The final straw came when one customer tried on a coat and asked my opinion. I told her, truthfully, it did not suit her and for my honesty, I ended up being fired on the spot. As I know what it's like to be on the receiving end of rude customers, to this day, I always ensure I'm polite to sales people who look after me.

While I was at drama school I was sent to have a set of photographs taken by a wonderful showbiz and fashion photographer called Michael Barrington-Martin, who took what I considered to be an excellent set of pictures of me. I did quite a bit of advertising work with Michael and before I was 17 I picked up a few modelling jobs for magazines like *Woman* and *Woman's Own*. It just goes to show how wrong that principal of the modelling school turned out to be! Anyhow, Mummy was overjoyed to see pictures of me in some of the top national women's magazines and they were shown around with great pride.

Things were just beginning to look good for me when Italia Conti relocated from Soho to larger premises at Clapham North. It was at that point my career nearly came to a premature end. On my first day at the new site, I was run over. What happened was three of us had been trying to cross the road, looking for a café. Maybe it was the excitement of being at a new school site because all I can remember saying was: 'I think there's a café over there'. . . The next thing I knew was waking up in hospital. The accident looked so bad, someone even telephoned my mother and told her I was dead.

My head injuries were serious, necessitating thirty-three stitches in my head. My mother sat at my bedside and said, 'They might not take you back at the drama school.' 'Why not?' I asked. 'Well, these theatricals are very superstitious, and they might regard you as a bad omen!' Thanks a lot Mummy! I was in hospital for forty-eight hours before they discharged me but on returning home I started to suffer dizzy spells and feel generally unwell. It took me a long time to recover. Mother tried to pursue the issue, to find out if I could sue for damages but nothing ever came of it. Anyway, at the end of the day, I guess I was lucky to escape with my life.

We had a great group of students at drama school and had a lot of fun, besides working hard in order to be able to carve out a career for ourselves. Actress Sandra Payne was one of my contemporaries and I was reunited with her in *The Newcomers*. So too was David Griffin, who has been in *Hi De Hi* and played the next door neighbour in *Keeping Up Appearances*. Graham Harper, who went on to become a director, was a fellow student. Another classmate was Jackie Jerome, whom I have worked with since. So too was Peter Fernell, who subsequently gave up acting and become a school teacher, which I considered to be a great shame, as he was good. Of course there was also Angela Reading, who introduced me to the wonders of the Lyceum. Angela eventually gave up acting too, her mother owned several hairdressing salons and she went to work for her instead. One would-be actor at Italia Conti was a guy named Bill Lyons but after a while he stopped acting to become a scriptwriter. After a few years I saw Bill again when I worked on a film he'd written for the Duke of Edinburgh award scheme, which starred John Hurt and Pauline Collins. Little did I realize at the time but Bill's and my paths were to cross yet again many years later, for Bill ended up being one of the early scriptwriters on *EastEnders*.

CHAPTER FIVE

'Come Outside'

While I was still training at Italia Conti, I made my very first television appearance – with none other than the legendary Sammy Davis Jr. Sammy was appearing at the Prince of Wales in his one-man show and while he was in Britain he did a show for ATV called *Sammy Meets The Girls*. I got the work as a result of buying a book called *Contacts* which is a 'Bible' for every budding actor and actress because it lists all the theatrical agents. I wrote to one of the agencies listed, the Bill Watts Agency, which was famous for glamorous girls. God knows why he took me on but anyway he did and one of the first bookings Bill obtained for me was work with Sammy.

When I arrived for the audition Sammy Davis was there with his producer and Lionel Blair. By then I had dyed my hair blonde and when Sammy first saw me I think I reminded him of his wife, May Britt. I overheard Sammy comment to the producer: 'This girl has fantastic bone structure, I must have her on the show.'

I was the second youngest girl on the programme, the youngest being Mandy Rice Davies, who later became renowned for her role in the Profumo affair. At the time Mandy was a model and she turned up for rehearsals wearing an orange coloured designer dress and a big green hat. I remember the costume designer coming into the rehearsal room, asking: 'Where's that other girl gone? The one who looks like a carrot!'

Sammy Davis was marvellous to all of us who worked with him on the programme. He was a really lovely man, so well-mannered, a complete gentleman. At the time, he was also appearing at the Prince of Wales Theatre and he gave each of us tickets to see his show. I took my mother backstage afterwards and Sammy was delightful to her, even telling Mummy 'You have a very charming daughter.'

On the way home, I remarked to her that she'd now met one of the world's greatest entertainers. Never mind about personally meeting a top international performer, I think Mummy was more impressed that her daughter knew him and had actually appeared on television with him.

More than a decade later I was to meet Sammy again, at the Trattoria Restaurant in Dean Street, Soho. I was dining there with two gay friends of mine, who were visiting from Blackpool. Sammy was at the next table with Lionel Blair. By then I'd already started doing *Are You Being Served?* and Lionel must have obviously reminded him that I'd been one of his 'girls' in the ATV show. Sammy came across to our table.

'Hello, Wendy. I hear you are doing very well for yourself nowadays and I am really pleased for you.'

It was a smashing compliment. He didn't have to go out of his way to come over and speak. My friends were dead impressed, I can tell you.

My first speaking part on television was also in 1960 in an episode of the popular police drama series *Dixon of Dock Green*, which starred Jack Warner in the title role. We went *en masse* from Italia Conti for auditions. I was chosen for the main girl's part – a runaway teenager. Several other girls were taken on as extras and some of the boys obtained parts too, so it was nice for us all to be in it together. When I told her the news about my part, Miss Conti warned me: 'I hope you will learn your lines.'

'I most certainly will. After all, I am being paid for it,' I insisted.

'That is most definitely not the right attitude, Wendy,' she countered – and she was right I soon realized.

While I was still at drama school an opportunity also arose for me to take part in another police drama series, this time *No Hiding Place*. I was in an episode with Pamela Cundell (who later went on to play Mrs Fox in *Dad's Army*) and she and I had to share a dressing room. I met Pamela again very recently and she reminded me that at the time when we did *No Hiding Place* Italia Conti were trying to persuade me to take extra elocution lessons so that I could get rid of my accent. Pamela's advice to me then was 'Stay as you are, you'll be all right with that accent, mark my words.' How right she proved to be!

Although I was happy at Italia Conti, I stayed for only three terms. I could have remained longer but when I started to get acting work, I decided to grab the opportunities as they arose. Maybe I left before I should have done but in reality, life is a university. I think I was learning more from life's experiences than drama school could have ever taught me. As an actress, you either have natural timing, or you don't.

I nearly landed a job with Alfred Marks, which would have been great on the CV but it was not to be. He had a regular weekly TV show running called *Alfred Marks Time* and for one of his sketches the producers wanted a few girls, dressed in 1930s gear, who would look as if they were part of the audience. We were supposed to just sit there and look pretty. I went along with a few other girls to be made up and dressed up. Then, they decided they had too many and I was one of the too many. So that was me out! I was naturally disappointed but that kind of rejection is part and parcel of an actress's career and it wasn't a bad lesson for me to learn early on.

I also wrote to various other theatrical agents, hoping to be taken on for work. One was Robert Stigwood, who I thought might get some television commercial work for me. What I didn't realize at the time was that Robert Stigwood was the manager of several pop singers. Eventually, I was called to see him and after a couple of weeks they rang to say they wanted me to be 'the voice' in the background on a pop record. The song was about a chap in a dance hall who wanted to persuade a young girl outside for a spot of canoodling. I was told I'd have to come in at the end of the chorus with a few smart answers. It was only to be three or four lines, which I had to make up myself. Off I went with the singer, Mike Sarne, to the recording studio off Baker Street. I was called back again to do two verses, then back again for the third.

When all the recordings were completed I went home and told my mother I'd made a pop record. She was quite dismissive of the whole affair. Until one morning, when we were out shopping together and on the way back stopped off at our local for a light ale and cheese roll. Sam Costa was on the radio in the pub and played a record called 'Come Outside'. The landlord's daughter, Janice piped up: 'Wendy, that doesn't half sound like you.' When I revealed it was indeed me, my mother went hysterical! She just could not believe it. The record went to Number One in the Hit Parade and various television appearances followed. The irony was, it was Mike Sarne being promoted by Robert Stigwood but it was me who ended up receiving all the publicity. People constantly wanted to know who the mystery girl was on the record.

I don't know whatever happened to Mike Sarne (whose real name was Michael Scheur). After our record he did a follow-up with Billie Davis, entitled 'Will I What?' The song was on fairly similar lines to 'Come Outside' but it wasn't a big hit. Later he turned to film directing. One of his films was *Myra Breckinridge*, starring Raquel Welch but that was not a great success. Since then I've heard nothing of him.

But I was very excited to be in the public eye. In one way that was a turning point in my career, my first real brush with fame. Though, not fortune: I made a £15 flat fee for my work on the record that sold over half a million copies. The record was so catchy that today, nearly forty years on it is still played on the radio occasionally – and a lot of people remember all the words! And, not many will know that until my screen nephew, Wicksy – Nick Berry – had a hit with 'Every Loser Wins' in 1986, I was the only member of the *EastEnders* cast to have had a No 1 hit!

CHAPTER SIX

Jigsaws

Life has a pattern. It's almost like a jigsaw. You collect various pieces along the way, even though you cannot always foresee how they will fit in.

So it was with 'Come Outside'. I might not have made a lot of money from the record but on the strength of its success I was taken to meet Terry Owen and Bernard Hunter, who ran Lom Artists. They eventually became my agents and were to guide my career for the next nineteen years.

Mother had to sign the original contract on my behalf, as I was under 21 years of age. While she was signing, Terry asked her if there had ever been any other actresses in her family.

'No,' she replied 'but my husband was always falling in love with actresses.'

Hardly the sort of remark I would have expected from my mother. I tell you, I could have dropped through the floor! She didn't mean it literally, of course but it's true Daddy was often infatuated with the likes of Dorothy Ward and Bebe Daniels when he'd seen them acting.

One of the first jobs Lom Artists obtained for me was ten days work with Granada Television, in Manchester on a series called *The Bulldog Breed*, a single-series sitcom which gave Amanda

41

Barrie her first major TV role. It meant leaving home for the first time but Terry told my mother not to worry. He'd booked me into Mrs MacKay's, where he'd lived during the time he was Head of Casting at Granada. Anyone in the business, who has worked at Granada at some time or another, has stayed at Mrs MacKay's. She was the most amazing woman. She had a double-fronted property called Astra House, in Daisybank Avenue. In one part she put all her clubs and 'turns' and in the other, all her television people. There were two separate lounges – and the two sets of people were never allowed to mix.

Peter Butterworth and Ronald Leigh Hunt were in the show I was doing. At that time I'd never eaten curry in my life, so one evening the two of them turned up to take me out for an Indian meal. I was in my room finishing dressing when suddenly Mrs MacKay appeared at the end of the corridor: 'Leave that child alone! She is in my care and she is not going anywhere. I speak to her mother every night on the telephone.'

Well, that was something I certainly didn't know about. I'd no idea she was in contact with Mummy. I had to laugh though, two nicer gentlemen and a more innocent evening out you could not find anywhere. However, there was no way Mrs MacKay would allow me out. I was furious.

It was while staying at Mrs MacKay's I met Val Doonican for the first time. He'd just started out on his career and was playing club dates in Manchester. I used to enjoy sitting and chatting with his wife, Lynne, in the evenings when Val was out working.

Shortly after my stint in Manchester, I celebrated my twentieth birthday. I had a wonderful surprise on the day because out of the blue, my mother bought me a toy poodle, whom I called Tottie. I'd always loved animals and we'd had cats at home but never dogs, so it was a lovely new experience to have a young puppy. In due course, one of the local ladies recommended a young girl who came to the house to groom my dog. She was called Lydia and she and I became close friends. We are still firm friends today, despite the fact that my dog, our common contact, died in the late 1970s.

Lom Agency then got me my first television series: *Harpers West One*, which was set in an upmarket West End department store – more Harrods than Grace Brothers. 'Shopping with the lid off,' was how the TV Press Releases described it at the time. Created by John Whitney (who went on to become IBA director-general) and Geoffrey Belman, it was made by ATV at Elstree Studios in Borehamwood which, coincidentally, is now where the BBC makes *EastEnders*.

Harpers West One starred Gordon Rattan, Graham Cowden, Jan Holden, Philip Latham and Bernard Horsfall. It was a thrill for me to be in a series. It makes such a difference for an actress to have regular work, as opposed to 'one-off' appearances, not just financially but in terms of the public getting to know your face. I was lucky to be in that position so early on in my career.

I played Susan Sullivan, a receptionist in the offices of the department store and shudder when I remember seeing my first episode go out. God, I was dreadful. You couldn't hear my voice properly; I just whispered, without projecting. I wasn't the only one to notice and after a few 'guiding words' from the director and producer I improved immensely as the series progressed.

The drama ran for two series until 1963 and was, coincidentally, responsible for John Leyton's biggest hit: 'Johnny Remember Me'. John was in the series, playing the character Johnny St Cyr.

Inspired by my own previous record success on 'Come Outside', in 1963 my girl friend, Diane Berry and I made a record entitled 'We Had A Dream'. Like me, Diana had also attended Italia Conti but she'd since given up the business and become a hairdresser, which is how we first met. Our record was produced by Leslie Cohn, who worked for Melcher Music in Soho. I don't recall how we first met Leslie but it was in the days when 'everyone' seemed to be making records. Decca released our disc, which was really just a list of disc jockeys' names, with a few nonsensical words stringing them together (pretty much like many other records at the time!).

I'm no singer and Diana? – well, she was a good hairdresser! We didn't actually do any shows together as a duet but we did appear in some of the music papers, to – shall we say – 'mixed reviews'. Anyway it was a bit of fun – and that was all. I don't think either of us received any royalties from it!

We were doing *Harpers West One* as my twenty-first birthday approached. I decided it was high time I should learn to drive. I hate to admit it but my driving lessons were a total disaster and I ended up failing my driving test . . . OK let me be honest . . . six times. On one test I well, not exactly hit a pedestrian, it was more just a question of him giving up and throwing himself on to the bonnet of the car! Mummy bought me a car for my twenty-first birthday but there was still no sign of me passing my test. By the time of my twenty-second birthday she had given up all hope, sold the car and that was the end of my attempts to learn to drive.

I enjoyed my role in *Harpers West One* but my real inclination was towards comedy, which I loved. One thing seemed to lead to another and I started to obtain spots on several TV comedy shows. I was thoroughly enjoying my new life as an actress. On one day I was working at ATV and when we had a break for lunch I went for a meal in the canteen. Two chaps came along and asked if they could sit at my table. Unbeknownst to me they were Michael Caine and Johnny Speight.

Michael nudged Johnny and remarked: 'She would be good to have in "*the*" show.'

They used to say in those days that I could be haughty. Anyway, I remained dismissive, thinking the two fellas were just trying to chat me up. Eventually, one of them asked me: 'What is your name and what is your availability?'

I remained on my high horse and replied grandly: 'You will have to speak to my agent about that.' Then, as an afterthought, I enquired: 'Who are you, anyway?'

'I am Johnny Speight and I write *The Arthur Haynes Show*. This is Michael Caine and he is playing a burglar in one of our episodes.'

My mother absolutely adored Arthur Haynes. His series of sketch shows had been running regularly on ITV since 1957 and were hugely popular. He had recently also started a successful series on radio, recorded before BBC audiences. Arthur was a wonderful comedian, who could portray characters brilliantly through his natural ability to mimic actions and mannerisms. So I can tell you, I was excited about the possibility of appearing on one of his shows.

Johnny Speight kept his word and did contact my agent. I was duly booked for *The Arthur Haynes Show* which went out live from the Golders Green Hippodrome. Arthur, who was a lovely man, used to adopt that certain 'look' in his eyes which was enough to make anybody laugh. In the sketch I was Arthur's daughter and Nicholas Parsons played the posh boyfriend whom I brought home. We had a truly dreadful set, including newspapers scattered all over the table and a plate of winkles in front of us – like a real naff Cockney tea party. Towards the end, Arthur started with 'that look' and made me laugh so much, I couldn't speak my lines any more. Nicholas had to do them for me. That was my ordeal by fire with Arthur Haynes!

It was a great pity because later Nicholas told me Johnny Speight wanted Arthur to progress from sketches to doing a sitcom. Johnny already had the idea for the sitcom, a development from the sketch we'd done. The cast would comprise the bloke with the pretty daughter, her upper class boyfriend and her mother. Unfortunately, Arthur refused to entertain the idea. He wanted to stay with his tried and tested formula of sketches.

After Arthur had a heart attack and died at 52 years of age, Johnny Speight shelved the scripts. Soon afterwards though, he decided to resurrect them and changed the characters slightly. The belligerent socialist father had become a right-winger and the upper class twit of a boyfriend had been changed into a Scouse son-in-law. It became *Till Death Us Do Part* with Warren Mitchell and Dandy Nicholls. Una Stubbs took the part of Rita, the daughter that I had once played. Her husband Mike was played by Anthony Booth. Obviously, my involvement was not meant to have been because of Arthur's premature death but it would have been a fabulous opportunity for me, judging by the success that *Till Death Us Do Part* enjoyed.

Nevertheless, I firmly believe in fate and there's no point in thinking about what might have been. To this day I've remained grateful to Michael Caine for suggesting me for the part in the first place. I met Michael again in Le Grand Coffee House in Soho when he was appearing at The Criterion in a play called *Next Time I'll Sing To You*. He used to sit with our crowd to have a chat and a laugh. One day he came in and told us he'd just returned from an audition for a film. We were so excited for him and wanted to know all about it. Michael confided: 'It's called *Zulu* and I hope I get the part. I think it will do me a bit of good.' For Michael, with all the wonderful roles he has subsequently played in films – and now a twice-winning Oscar actor, with a knighthood to boot – that comment turned out to be somewhat of an understatement.

My first comedy series was in the long-running BBC suburban domestic sitcom *Hugh and I* which starred Terry Scott and Hugh Lloyd. It was set in Lobelia Avenue, Tooting, south London where Terry Scott lived with his screen Mum (Vi Stevens). Hugh Lloyd played the family's lodger.

It was another turning point for me. One, was in meeting Mollie Sugden for the first time. She was playing Mrs Crispin, the Scott's neighbour and I was cast as her daughter. It was a joy to meet Mollie because we got on so well together, right from the start. Who could have imagined then that pairing would form the strong foundation for a much longer working relationship yet to come in *Are You Being Served*? It just goes to show, you never know what will happen and who you'll meet up with again in our business.

As well as palling up with Mollie, *Hugh and I* was vital to me in that was how I first met David Croft, who would eventually become my governor on many other shows. David was producing the series and I assure you, he gets to know his actors well. I have tremendous respect for all producers and admire the track records of those I've worked with but David has a special knack of remembering people and their various acting strengths and abilities. When a new part comes up he is very loyal to those who have worked with him in the past. He is a lovely man, who has an easygoing approach to his work and is, similarly, very easy to get on with. So *Hugh and I* was my introduction to David – and how very important that would be, as I was to find out later.

I progressed nicely in a few other bits and pieces, including an episode of the BBC comedy sitcom *The Likely Lads*, which starred James Bolam and Rodney Bewes. I played alongside Wanda Ventham and we were two demonstrators in a shop. I worked with James Bolam again when I took the part of an office worker in a TV play for Rediffusion called *The London Wall*, in which Helen Cherry and Jane Asher also appeared.

My first tentative venture into films was in 1964 with a small part in The Beatles' second feature film *Help!*. I did a scene with John, Paul, George and Ringo, which also starred Frankie

Howerd. The Beatles were brilliant to work with, really nice lads. Frankie was fantastic too. He played the proprietor of the SAM AHAB (Bahamas, spelt backwards) drama school and my role was as one of his drama students. The boys were supposed to be hiding out there, in their efforts to escape from an Eastern princess, played by Eleanor Bron.

Frankie, bless his heart, was suffering with a bad back at the time and was in constant pain. The hundreds of screaming girls outside the studios certainly didn't help his condition at all. The filming job occupied three days. On the second day John Lennon asked if I had any of their records at home. Like most young women of my age, I had loads of Beatles records and I told him I also had a copy of his book *A Spaniard in the Works*.

'Bring the records in; I'll get the boys to sign them and I'll do the book too,' he offered.

I was thrilled and John did as he had promised when I took the records and book to work next day. I still have them all now and value them tremendously.

When *Help!* was due for release in 1965 I wasn't sent an invitation for the premiere. I was utterly devastated. It turned out my scene ended up on the cutting room floor – one of the biggest blows of my entire career. Someone later told me the producers had an uncut version of the film, including my scene, how I would have loved to have seen it!

The first film I made, which actually ended up being shown as my screen début, was *Doctor in Clover* in 1966. I spoke precisely four words: 'Yes, Matron.' and 'No, Matron.' It was during the shooting of that film I met British actor and scriptwriter, Jeremy Lloyd, for the first time. He played one of the doctors. Jeremy would later play an even more important role in my professional life, for it was he who would go on to create *Are You Being Served?*

Jigsaws

As I said at the beginning of this chapter, life has a pattern and without realizing it, I had already come into contact with three important pieces of my career jigsaw: Mollie, David and Jeremy but it would be the 1970s before I would be able to see the connection.

CHAPTER SEVEN

My First BBC Soap

Aside from comedy, an early opportunity arose for me to try my hand at something more serious. In 1965 the BBC launched one of its earliest soaps called *The Newcomers*. It was created by Colin Morris and was intended to rival ITV's *Coronation Street* in realism, by taking a group of London families out of the capital and re-locating them in a fictitious Suffolk dormitory town called Angleton (Haverhill, in real life). Some of the plots were considered quite daring for their time, including an exposé on witchcraft.

The soap went out live, twice a week. I had a friend working in it, who had told me all about the pressures of live television in that situation. Although I'd done some live TV, I really couldn't imagine how the cast could possibly learn a host of lines and then perform two live shows, every single week.

Anyway, some months later I found myself doing exactly that. I played Joyce Harker, the daughter of the new family who moved into the estate. June Bland played my mother, Robert Brown my father and David Janson my little brother. Maggie Fitzgibbon was the leading lady in the series. She played Vivienne Cooper. The late Alan Browning – who was a lovely chap and of whom I was very fond – played her husband, Ellis Cooper, a supervisor at the local computer parts factory. Vanda Godsell, who was a very glamorous blonde and had been in the film *This Sporting Life* with Richard Harris and in the BBC sitcom *I Didn't Know You Cared* was also in it, along with another actor called Gerald Cross, who looked just like the Pope of the time.

My character – the teenage daughter – ended up being the manageress of the local supermarket. My boss was a fine old English actor called Campbell Singer, another really nice man. In due course, Maggie left and Heather Chasen took over as the leading lady, with Robin Bailey playing her husband.

When I joined the series, it still went out live from Lime Grove, and it had been there for years. But a few months later they moved it to Birmingham where they could pre-record shows. Despite having to commute from London to Birmingham each day, which became tedious and extremely tiring, we all had a great time doing *The Newcomers*. And I learned a great deal during that period, particularly about memorizing lines. You had to be word perfect and know exactly where to stand on the set because there was a lot of pressure doing two weekly live TV performances. Of course, any performer can dry up or make the wrong moves but if you did and they had to do a retake, nobody would speak to you!

In one scene, Joyce was in the family room and was supposed to walk upstairs. As I left, I turned to walk down the side of the set between the backcloth and the kitchen door. I was just lighting a fag when I heard Robert Brown, playing my father, remark 'It's a lovely evening, you can see clear down to the bottom of the garden.' Well, you couldn't; all you could see was Joyce smoking her cigarette! I was not all that popular, I can tell you.

When you work on a series – as I was also to learn much later from *Are You Being Served?* and *EastEnders* – the cast, crew and

Aged about two, with Mummy and Daddy in Bournemouth. (Author's Collection)

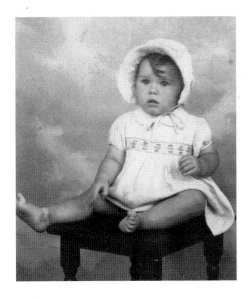

A budding model. (Author's Collection)

Mummy and Daddy – a handsome couple. (Author's Collection)

Mummy and Daddy behind the bar in the Shepherds Tavern. (Author's Collection)

The famous sedan chair in the Shepherds Tavern. Some of my happiest memories are from this time. (Author's Collection)

Outside the Shepherds in Hertford Street. Then, aged about six and (below) now. It was here that I began my love affair with London. (Author's Collection)

My first modelling pictures taken by Michael Barrington-Martin. Things were beginning to happen for me.

A Sixties look. (Sunday Mirror)

A still from *Gumshoe* autographed by Albert Finney. A small but good part that got me noticed. (Columbia Pictures)

My scene from *Help!* may have ended up on the cutting room floor, but it was still great to work with people like Paul McCartney and Frankie Howerd. (Apple)

It was also good to work with people like Dora Bryan, which for me was the best thing about my stint on *Both Ends Meet*.

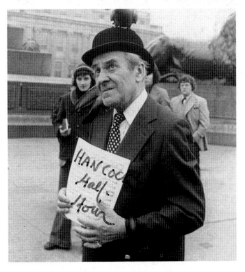

My dear friend John LeMesurier

I appeared in a few episodes of *Dad's Army*. Here are me and Arthur Lowe in *My British Buddy*. (Don Smith, *Radio Times*)

Me and the cast of *Are You Being Served?* in the episode *The Hold Up*. (Don Smith, *Radio Times*)

This picture was from the episode called *Big Brother*. I appear with Nicholas Smith and Trevor Bannister. (Don Smith, *Radio Times*)

Mollie and Wendy. German Week. (Don Smith, *Radio Times*)

A cast shot of my favourite cast, including my favourite director, David Croft.

Pauline with Arthur Fowler. (BBC)

A shot of the cameramen at *EastEnders'* first photo call – they all look pretty relaxed but that was far from how we all felt in the early days. (Author's Collection)

production become like a tight-knit family. You strive to get on well because you have to spend a lot of time together and each has a common goal – the success of the programme. So you take an interest in each other's real lives, away from the studio: how's the husband? how's the wife? how are the kids doing at school? what's the garden looking like this year? – all the little things that families talk about. As the relationships develop you grow to share each other's highs and lows.

I became especially close to Robert Brown (who played my father) and his family. My friend Lydia (the girl who groomed my dog) and I often used to visit Bob, at his house in Cookham at weekends. He held the most brilliant parties there. One of Bob's neighbours had a young brother called John, who was without a girlfriend. Bob told him he'd invited two young ladies down from London and he had the choice of a blonde or a brunette. Well, John and Lydia hit it off straightaway. They've been married for many years now, have two beautiful children and still live in Cookham. At least that is one happy marriage I am responsible for . . .

When we were working together on the series I frequently went away on holiday with Bob, his wife and their two children. Bob had been in the Royal Navy and was at one time stationed in Gibraltar, where he'd established a water polo team. He still had loads of friends in Gib and I went there two or three times a year, with him and the family.

The work kept coming and I continued to live at home in the bed and breakfast hotel with Mummy, helping her whenever I could. It meant I had no real major financial responsibilities of any kind. For the first time in my life I began to build up a nest egg in the building society, which allowed little luxuries such as holidays. My mother never wanted me to pay her keep, so I always made sure I treated her whenever I could. Once I took her to Weatheralls in the Burlington Arcade and bought her a new suit, coat, silk blouse and hat. Another time I bought her a fur coat and on several occasions got her items of jewellery. She was pleased and equally, I was thrilled, to be able to do it after all she had done for me in my life.

It was just before *The Newcomers* finished that my mother became very unwell. I realized she was drinking even more heavily than ever and eventually her stomach started to distend. One day at the studio when we were working on The Newcomers I mentioned to Bob that Mummy's tummy was becoming considerably bloated. I saw him give someone a knowing look. It was at that point I realized it must be something really serious and I became very worried. But there was only so much I could do. I wanted to help Mummy but didn't know how to help her get over the loneliness of losing Daddy. So, in the end, things just carried on as they were.

The Newcomers was a good show to be in but it finished in 1969 when the BBC moved into transmitting in colour, because they were not prepared to change all our sets. Of course, in those days, you could wear any combination of colours when working on TV because it was all black and white anyway. There was a great deal of sadness when we stopped working together but I have remained friends with Robert Brown and his wife, Becky, to this day.

As one door closed another opened, for in 1970 I renewed my acquaintanceship with David Croft, whom I'd first worked for in *Hugh and I* a few years previously. David had teamed up with Jimmy Perry, who created the comedy series *Dad's Army* which had been running on BBC since 1968. They co-wrote the scripts and David also produced and directed the shows. Jimmy's idea centred around the misadventures of a group of men who, through old age or their various infirmities, hadn't been able to enlist but had instead enrolled in the Home Guard. Jimmy's inspiration for the series had come from his own experiences in the Home Guard on Barnes Common in London. David was interested in the project because he had been in the services and was at one time the youngest major in the Army.

Dad's Army was set in Walmington-on-Sea, an imaginary seaside town on the Kent coast not far from Dover where, in a series of highly amusing exploits, the local Home Guard helped form part of Britain's last line of defence against the Germans. What a wonderful cast Jimmy and David had gathered together, including Arthur Lowe (Capt Mainwaring), John LeMesurier (Sergeant Wilson), Clive Dunn (Lance-Corporal Jones), John Laurie (Private Frazer), Arnold Ridley (Private Godfrey), Ian Lavender (Private Pike) and Bill Pertwee (Air Raid Warden Hodges).

David remembered my previous work for him in *Hugh and I* and suggested me for a part in two episodes of the fourth series. In one of them, entitled *The Two & A Half Feathers*, I played Edith Parish, a cinema usherette, who was the tarty girlfriend of Private Walker, played by Jimmy Beck. The story revolved around Lance-Corporal Jones, whose history came under a cloud when an old comrade of his dragged up their service record in the Sudan. In the second one, *Mum's Army* I was cast in the character of Edith again, in an hilarious episode in which Captain Mainwaring enlisted the help of the ladies of Walmington-on-Sea, in order to recruit a woman's auxiliary for the platoon.

Of course I didn't realize at the time that I was taking part in the making of a piece of television history. The series was to run for a total of eighty episodes over nine years until 1977. Even now, thirty years later, it is still regarded affectionately as one of the best ever comedy programmes on TV – and probably will continue to do so for the next thirty years as well! *Dad's Army* was also adapted into a stage musical, a long-running radio series and a full-length feature film, made by Columbia Pictures. Some of its catch phrases, like : 'You stupid boy!' and 'Don't panic' will I'm sure never be forgotten.

When we had finished rehearsing one of our episodes John, Jimmy, Clive and I went off on one of our sorties. We were sat chatting over a glass or two, when Clive leaned over and said to me 'You are going to be famous one day, a real star!' I had a good laugh at that but asked him why? 'Well because you have a long thigh bone,' was the reply. I guess there was just no answer to that!

Being in the cast of *Dad's Army* was like being part of an exclusive gentleman's club. They were all, without doubt, the loveliest people I have ever worked with. There are only a couple of other people, outside that series, whom I would place in the same category. All of the regulars were absolute sweethearts and I adored them all but became particularly pally with John Le Mesurier. One day in the studios, I told John Le Mes the story about the 'Farting Vicar' from our B&B hotel and it amused him greatly. He gave me a signed photograph of himself, writing on it: 'What is to become of us all? As the vicar said when he cracked your pan.' I'll never forget the advice he gave me on acting: 'Always give the same performance and, if possible, wear the same suit.'

Despite my few appearances in *Dad's Army* I remember it fondly as an important part of my working life. In fact, I had a happy reunion with the surviving members of the cast at the recent opening of the *Dad's Army* museum in Bressingham. There was Clive Dunn and I swear he looks younger today than he did when the series was made.

After working in *Dad's Army* in 1970 I also renewed my earlier acquaintance with Frankie Howerd and made an appearance in

Up Pompeii!, (also a David Croft show). The Roman farce had only been launched by the BBC that year but based in old Pompeii and full of innuendo and double entendre, it made a fantastic platform for Frankie's brand of humour. I was really pleased to see him again, so many years after our first contact on The Beatles film. Frankie was a wonderful man but, like most comics, was very subdued off stage. Although I was to work with Frankie again later in Belfast during 1972, I never met up with him socially. He was a very private person whom, I believe, didn't go out very much.

Away from comedy, I made an appearance in the MGM film *No Blade of Grass*, which was produced and directed by former Hollywood star, Cornel Wilde. He had adapted the film from a brilliant book about ecology and industrial pollution, called *The Death of Grass*, which was way ahead of its time. I played Clara, the flashy, sexy wife of cold-blooded killer, Pierre (played by Anthony May). They wanted me to wear see-through tops in the film but I wouldn't agree, although I did concede to wearing a black wig.

The storyline was about a terrible famine which threatened civilization. It was filmed entirely on location in London and the Lake District. We all enjoyed working in the Lake District because it made a pleasant change to get out of London. Nigel Davenport was the star and the young female lead was played by Lynne Frederick, who later married Peter Sellers. Lynne was only about 15 at the time and her mother, Iris, who had been head of casting at Thames TV, asked me to look after her daughter while we were away. It turned out to be a nightmare trying to control Lynne because she was a very headstrong young lady. I wanted to make sure she was OK but she was away from home for the first time and was obviously intent on making the most of it!

The whole crew were lovely, especially the guys who were lighting the film, Lee Electrics who were great but unfortunately they grew to dislike Cornel because he had no understanding of their Cockney sense of humour. Cornel's wife Jean Wallace who, like him, had acted in Hollywood, co-starred. Jean was not supposed to drink but one of the crew gave her some scrumpy and told her it was apple juice. Not only did she get off her head on it but she also gave some to their small child.

Cornel was a keep-fit fanatic and would often bait Dennis, the camera grip, who was a big guy: 'Big Den, how many press-ups have you done today?'

'About 100, sir.'

'Is that all?' Cornel would reply dismissively.

'Yes, but I do them on one hand!' Dennis would counter.

Cornell had no answer, would just swallow and walk away.

Apart from one or two ructions, making *No Blade of Grass* was a truly enjoyable experience for me. As it was the last film MGM made at Borehamwood – I suppose you could say I closed that studio down!

It was also while making the film that I met a young actor named Derek Keller. We have remained friends to this day and indeed Derek was also part of the John Mahoney Agency who in due course became my agent and represented me for many years. Derek also introduced me to the medium and clairvoyant, Don Galloway, who later was to be such a help to me when my mother died.

Rounding off 1970 I also did an ITV special for Thames: *Carry On Again Christmas: Carry On Long John*. Thames had persuaded the *Carry On* cast and crew to move from the big to the small screen and do some special made-for-TV productions. The sixty-minute Christmas one I appeared in was a parody on *Treasure Island* and was where, I think, I met Barbara Windsor for the first time. She was blond, bubbly and full of fun. Immediately we struck up a rapport and had lots of laughs together. Yet again, Barbara was a person I would work with regularly, later in my career. It is such a small world.

Bits and pieces of work came along and I got used to the life of a working actress. I went from one thing to the next and doing this variety of roles was fun and challenging. But after a taste of playing a regular character such as I had in *The Newcomers*, I was hoping for a new series to come along.

Meantime comedy was to the fore again in 1971. I played a clippie in a couple of episodes of London Weekend Television's popular sitcom *On the Buses*. The production starred Reg Varney (who was previously best known for his role in *The Rag Trade*) as Stan Butler, the driver; Bob Grant was his conductor, Jack Carter and Stephen Lewis played the tetchy Inspector Blake.

I was also in the Hammer film production of *On The Buses*. It was Hammer Films' first comedy for ten years. As fate would have it, I was cast as a customer in a launderette in Borehamwood High Street. Borehamwood is where the *EastEnders* studio is located – and now I'm working in a launderette – so nothing much has changed, even after all these years!

I worked for London Weekend Television again in an episode of their comedy sitcom *Please Sir!* which was set in a tough south London school. It starred John Alderton as the naive teacher, who soon came to be respected by his unruly class. I played the so-called 'niece' of one of the school's governors but was really his bit of stuff on the side! He was played by Arnold Peters who is now Jack Woolley in *The Archers*.

Later I was also in its follow-up series: *The Fenn Street Gang*, which traced the lives of the teenagers after they left school. I was a beauty queen in an episode based around a beauty contest: one of the other contestants was Sandra Bryant, an old mate of mine from Italia Conti. I can't remember much else about it except that it was bloody freezing cold the day we did the filming!

I was working, I was having great fun and, though of course I didn't know it, the best (and worst) was yet to come.

CHAPTER EIGHT

(Are You Free, Miss Richard?)

In the New Year of 1972 I was summoned to LWT to accompany Richard Price, who was head of casting, to meet Michael Grade. At the time, Michael was LWT's Head of Light Entertainment and Director of Programmes. They were casting for a new TV series starring Dora Bryan. When I went in with Richard Michael asked him: 'How long have you known Wendy?' I was about to open my mouth and say I'd never met Richard before when he piped up:

'I've known her for years and her work is excellent.' Well, although he did not know me personally, it was obviously his job to watch as much television as possible in order to spot new talent, so that was that . . . I was in!

However, the new programme *Both Ends Meet*, which started in February 1972 and was based in a sausage factory, turned out to be not the funniest of sitcoms. It was written by a series of writers and was not greeted with a great deal of acclaim, which was a pity because Dora Bryan is a great performer. I was disappointed it was not more of a success.

For me the saving grace about *Both Ends Meet* was working

alongside a wonderful actor called Ivor Dean. At that time I was still extremely worried about my mother's health and one day at work Ivor came up to me and said: 'You are a believer aren't you?' I told him yes, I did believe in the Spirit world. (The interest probably stemmed from my mother, who had always been interested in clairvoyancy and Spiritualism and I had felt the same for a good many years). Ivor continued: 'I was travelling home on the train last night when your father appeared to me.' He then gave me a totally accurate description of Daddy and warned me that one evening, soon, I would return home to find Mummy in a collapsed state.

'It is not her time to pass yet,' he assured me. 'However, you must be prepared and you must ensure she is admitted to hospital.'

I returned home that night with a heavy heart. It seemed what I feared most – losing my mother – would soon become a reality. A reality, I just did not know how I could face. I was frightened, wondering what would happen to Mummy and highly nervous about how I would cope without her. Ivor Dean had not been specific in his message about when I was to expect the inevitable, so each day was like a living death. Seeing my mother getting worse, wanting what was best for her but not bearing to be able to let her go.

Work, fortunately, was my salvation. As with so many things in my life, I've discovered that when one door is about to close, another door opens. While I was making the series of *Both Ends Meet* I received a call from David Croft, asking me to do a *Comedy Playhouse* for the BBC. The *Comedy Playhouse* series were half-hour one-off playlets, designed to give a potential sitcom a public airing on television and if it proved popular, it might be turned into a series.

Ours was a comedy, set in an antiquated department store and was to be called *Are You Being Served?* David had teamed up with Jeremy Lloyd, whom I'd worked with in *Doctor In Clover*. Apparently, Jeremy had recently returned from the States where he'd been writing *Rowan and Martin's Laugh-In*. He came up with the idea of *Are You Being Served?* based on his own two years experience of working at top London store, Simpson's, in Piccadilly. The pair of them had written a pilot and were quietly confident of its chances of success.

Once again, David's loyalty to actors he's worked with in the past helped me out and from his observations of my work in *Hugh and I* and *Dad's Army*, he thought I would be right for the character of Miss Brahms.

Shirley Brahms was to be the assistant saleswoman in the ladies separates and underwear department. Jeremy described her as: 'Typical of girls of her time: great figure, lots of lipstick, high heels, looking for love but thinking they're too good for most men they meet – and being right in that.' Exemplified by Shirley's remark in one episode: 'I'm looking for *Dallas* and all I'm getting is *Coronation Street*.'

David trusted me sufficiently to deliver the character of Miss Brahms as I saw fit, by instinct. Whilst she might have been the target of sexist remarks, she was certainly no bimbo. In fact I think she was the most sensible of the characters in the cast because she excelled at pertinent one-liners, with quips such as: 'If your brains was dynamite you still wouldn't 'ave enough to blow your ears off.' Or, 'What a pity your ear'oles aren't a bit bigger . . . because then you could shove a toothbrush in and clean out that filthy mind of yours!'

Whenever some far-fetched scheme was being conjured up among the Grace Brothers staff, it was always Shirley who seemed to put the stamp of sensibility on the situation.

What a fabulous surprise when I turned up for rehearsals for the *AYBS?* pilot because it was like being at a party for old friends. The only person I didn't know was John Inman. Most of the others – such as Frank Thornton, Trevor Bannister, Mollie Sugden, Nicholas Smith – I'd worked with before. Mollie and I just picked up from where we had left off on *Hugh and I* and continued to get on like a house on fire. During rehearsals the two of us were standing by a table where David Croft had placed his script covers with the titles for the various *Comedy Playhouse* series written down. There was a gap at the bottom. 'There is just enough room there to put *Are You Being Served?* on that list,' Mollie remarked to me.

Anyway, we made the pilot and kept our fingers crossed. With anything of David's you knew you were on to a winner. All we needed was luck, firstly to find a slot for it to be broadcast and subsequently for it to be well received by the public.

Shortly after making the *Comedy Playhouse* pilot I went out with a girlfriend of mine to Gerry's, the actors' club in Soho. The pair of us got absolutely plastered. Sir Stanley Holloway's son Julian, whom I knew, was there that evening with a mate of his. We all had rather a boozy time together and then went our separate ways.

Next day my girlfriend phoned me and asked: 'Was that Albert Finney we were with last night?'

'I don't think so,' I replied.

'Well, I think it was,' she insisted.

About a week later I had a call to audition for a day's work on a Columbia Pictures film called *Gumshoe*, written by a young actor called Neville Smith with whom I'd worked before on a play called *The Making of Jericho* which also starred John Thaw. *Gumshoe* was to star none other than Albert Finney. I went along to the location and was told to wait in the unit car. I asked the driver if any other girls had auditioned for the part and what they were like.

'A few; they were all dolly birds.'

So I thought well, I probably don't stand a chance. The director, Stephens Frears and Finney then came out of a house where they had been filming. Finney looked at me and I introduced myself.

'But we have met before, haven't we?' he asked

I said: *'NO!'* emphatically.

He simply stared at me. Later I was to learn that, unfortunately for me, Finney has total recall. I was convinced that meant I would definitely never get the part if he remembered our first boozy meeting. Anyhow, I read for it but in a most diabolical Liverpudlian accent and was completely hopeless.

Finney looked at me and enquired: 'Would you be thrown if you had to quickly study lines?'

'No, quick study artist me, not a problem,' I insisted, thinking it didn't matter what I said because I'd blown it anyway.

'OK,' he mused.

Anyway, the script was delivered that same night and by the following morning I was doing the film! Michael Medwin (remember him from the long-running ITV comedy series *The Army Game* and films too numerous to mention?) had teamed up with his old friend Finney and was the co-producer on the film.

As it turned out, Michael was very pleased with my day's work. Finney and I had to do an important scene in a one-camera movement action. It was based on Humphrey Bogart and Lauren Bacall's famous semi-romantic scene in the 1944 film *To Have and Have Not*. If anything had gone wrong, we would have had to go right back to the beginning and start again, which would have been costly and time-consuming. Anyway, I managed the scene with Finney, without any problem.

Albert Finney, who gave a marvellous performance as small time private eye, Eddie Ginley, could not have been any more

charming or helpful to me. He was obviously a generous man –
some friends of mine, Nita and Roger Hulme moved into
Finney's old mews house in Marleybone. The dustmen came to
introduce themselves and Nita gave them two half-crowns. 'Mr
Finney used to give us a fiver!', he complained. 'Well I'm not on
Mr Finney's wages,' she retorted.

When the film came out I was delighted to receive exceedingly
good reviews. I met the Press after their preview screening and
they were all very good to me. Billie Whitelaw was the female
lead but nevertheless, publicity-wise I did well out of it too.

Also, importantly, shortly before my mother died, I was able to
take her to The Odeon in Leicester Square, where a large colour
promotional picture of me in *Gumshoe* was lit up on display
outside the cinema. I felt relieved that, at long last, she was at least
able to see some return for her hard-earned investment in me.

CHAPTER NINE

Death and Marriage

My mother's health continued to deteriorate. It transpired she had cancer of the liver. She started drinking even more, in order to try and kill the pain but obviously the alcohol only aggravated her condition.

The final months leading up to her death in May 1972 were a terrible time for both of us. I cooked meals for her but she would not eat. She'd lock herself in her room and I would have to break in, only to discover stale food in there which she had not touched. She had become incontinent too and I had that to deal with. The furniture was ruined, so much so that after she died it all had to be thrown out.

Although I'd always continued to help Mummy in our bed and breakfast business in Argyle Street, the main responsibility for keeping the business on the go then fell on to my shoulders, on top of my work as an actress. It was a very traumatic time.

As she grew worse, I suggested to Mummy that maybe she would be better off in a nursing home, where she could be looked after twenty-four hours a day but she would not hear of it. There was nothing I could do to persuade her otherwise; you certainly can't take a person screaming and kicking to somewhere they don't want to go. In the end it was too late for the suggestion to be taken up anyway because one night I came home to find my mother collapsed on the floor, as Ivor had predicted. I phoned for an ambulance and she was immediately taken to University College Hospital. I went with her in the ambulance but when they took her into a ward, I had to sit outside. I waited for ages, frantic with worry about what was happening. Ultimately a very nice young doctor came to see me and broke the sad news: 'I'm awfully sorry but you know your mother is not going to leave hospital, don't you?'

'Yes, I do know. I have faced up to that,' I admitted. However, she lingered on for some time.

A few months previously I had become acquainted with a chap called Len Black. He was a music publisher and we met through friends in Gerry's club. Len was not particularly good looking but he was pleasant and charming. I suppose it was the typical older man syndrome. He was more than twenty years older than me and at the time I guess I became attached to him because I was feeling vulnerable. Len knew of my fears of being alone and when Mummy went into hospital, he proposed to me. Out of the blue, I agreed to marry him. I have to be honest, my sole reason was that I was frightened of being on my own. I didn't really love Len but I knew my mother was about to die and I wanted to have someone around to help alleviate the pain of her passing. I thought I wouldn't be able to cope otherwise.

So I took Len to the hospital to meet Mummy but she didn't seem that keen on him and she certainly wasn't pleased when I told her about our forthcoming marriage plans. By then she was in such a state that she couldn't take it all in properly.

On Sunday 28 May I was preparing to leave the house and visit Mummy when Matron telephoned to say my mother had passed away. Although I knew her death was imminent, the reality of it was something different. I felt completely numb, empty, the grief was almost too much to bear. Now I really was alone, both my parents had gone and it was a dreadful feeling.

When I arrived at the hospital to collect her personal effects, I discovered that some of the pills she was supposed to have been taking were hidden in her bed jacket pocket. It was obvious to me she felt she had suffered enough and wanted out.

I organized Mummy's funeral, although Len was very good and he helped me with it as much as he could. None of Mummy's family came.

Len and I decided to marry immediately. That involved tremendous pressure to finalize our wedding arrangements quickly but we married four days after Mummy's death, on 1 June. My wedding day was the day after her funeral. The somewhat subdued ceremony took place at Caxton Hall Register Office in St James's. As with her funeral, none of Mummy's family came. We held a reception for just a few friends at the St Ermin's Hotel.

Len moved into the B & B with me but I did not like him living there. Come to that, I just didn't like living with him at all, full stop. We weren't really in love with each other and our marriage was a farce because we were fundamentally different people. With the turmoil of everything that had transpired, coupled with the sadness and emotion I was feeling after Mummy died, it is no wonder our marriage was on the skids almost immediately.

Three weeks after the wedding I was asked to do another *Dad's Army* and although I still played Private Walker's girlfriend, I was mysteriously re-christened Shirley instead of Edith, for some unknown – but maybe prophetic – reason. The name may have changed but I still looked the same in the episode, called *The King Was In His Counting House*. Shirley had the same Betty Grable upswept hairstyle that Edith had worn but was a lot more chirpy.

Private Walker was a 'spiv' as they called them in those days, always on the lookout to make a bit of easy money on the side, however illicit those dealings in wartime rationed goods might be. The girlfriend character I portrayed liked a bit of fun and in this episode I had to accompany Joe Walker to a party at the Mainwaring house, where he and I were the only ones who seemed to have any fun – canoodling on the sofa. Not that there was anything overtly sexual written into the scripts – that would have been taboo in those days.

Meanwhile, back at home the situation with Len didn't improve as the weeks passed. Looking back I suppose our marriage didn't stand a chance in the circumstances. His friends were not my sort, they were considerably older than me and I didn't really like any of them. Unfortunately, even married to me, he still wanted his old lifestyle. Often he would go off for the day and not come home at night. He even tried to persuade me to sell the guest house and at one stage attempted to talk me into investing money in a building owned by some acquaintances of his. But Len was no businessman.

I tried to think of other things other than the problems with my marriage. Obviously, I kept thinking back to our pilot of *Are You Being Served?* wondering when it would get a showing. My prayers were soon answered – but in tragic circumstances. The massacre at the Munich Olympics in September 1972, when eleven Israeli athletes were killed by Palestinian terrorists, left the BBC with huge gaps in its programming schedules. The Games were cancelled and with no sport, one of the first programmes hastily pulled from the shelves of finished cans of film was our *Comedy Playhouse* pilot.

Are You Being Served? first appeared on BBC television at 9.30p.m. on Friday 8 September 1972. The pilot set the scene in Grace Brothers and introduced viewers to the new characters.

Ladieswear and Menswear departments were to join on the same floor, much to the annoyance of some of the older members of staff. Particularly Mr Grainger who, over-protective of his floor space, nearly had a fit when Miss Brahms asked him 'Can you take down your trousers to make way for Mrs Slocombe's strapless bras?' The pilot was well received, despite being unadvertised. I was sure that if it were to be made into a series, with David Croft's expertise, we would do well.

Whilst there looked like being a new beginning in my acting career, in my private life, my marriage to Len was coming to an end. The truth is we had rushed into our marriage and maybe his heart was elsewhere anyhow. One day I discovered a letter sent to him by a rich woman, who lived in the USA. In it she wrote that he must remember the promise they had made to each other: to spend at least three weeks together every year. Len disappeared soon after I confronted him with the letter. Throughout the brief time we'd been together, Len had never really bothered with me, or paid much attention to me. As even he said of our marriage: 'It seemed like a good idea at the time'.

I guess that was the bottom line for both of us. Our marriage had lasted only five months by the time we parted in October of 1972. I tried not to dwell on it. But it must have preyed on my mind because the break-up, coupled with missing Mummy, made the period following my split from Len one of the darkest times in my life. After Len left, deep depression set in and all I wanted to do was lie in bed all day. I could not be bothered to get up and do anything. My weight went down to seven stone. At my lowest ebb, I even tried to take my own life with an overdose of Aspirin and Mogadon sleeping tablets. All I wanted to do was sleep and sleep and forget about everything. Fortunately, the type of sleeping tablets my doctor had prescribed were not lethal and my suicide attempt failed. In the end, I somehow managed to pull

71

myself together. I realized how ridiculously I was behaving and that, in any case, I had the responsibility of a small dog and a cat to look after. They were dependent upon me, if no one else. One day I woke up from my drugged sleep – came to my senses I suppose – got out of bed and decided to accept the fact that I just had to get on with the rest of my life. After my split from Len I drifted in and out of a couple of affairs but nothing too serious. Work became my salvation, it was the one thing that kept me going, mentally, if not always financially.

Shortly after I had pulled myself together, I was asked to fly over to Belfast to entertain the troops at Aldergrove Army Air Base. I went with Frankie Howerd, June Whitfield, Elizabeth Larner, the Swinging Blue Jeans and Pan's People. Jimmy Moir and Bill Cotton Jr, who was BBC Head of Light Entertainment, came with us.

Elizabeth Larner (the actress/singer, whom I believe now lives in New York) had put me up for the job and I was to play an Egyptian hand maiden called Titty Fallar. Among the show's contributing writers were Johnny Speight, Ray Galton and Alan Simpson. While we were on the special charter plane flying us over, I commented to Elizabeth that it was strange Frankie had not come too.

She said 'Don't worry about that for now. I'll tell you when we arrive.'

Apparently, Frankie's manager had dreamt Frankie was in a plane crash on the way to Ireland and he wouldn't allow him to travel out on the plane. Although it was not safe for Frankie, apparently it was OK for the rest of us to risk it!

I was nervous about the prospect of working with Frankie again. He was a perfectionist and I knew he had already sacked two girls from the show. Anyway, it so happened that Frankie was very kind to me and took me to one side before we started work to say 'Come along darling, don't be frightened of me.' I thought that was lovely of him and during the time we were there I developed a great deal of respect for his professionalism.

We did the show in an aircraft hangar and I have to say Frankie Howerd was brilliant with those troops. He felt at home because it was being in the services that had originally inspired him to develop his own comedy act. After the War he appeared in troop shows and it was during one of them he was talent spotted by an agent who launched his professional career.

In Ulster several of the young soldiers were bandaged, some had been blown up in bomb attacks, it was terrible to see their injuries. Frankie went round and spoke to as many of the troops as he could, before we had to leave. Our plane was security checked prior to our flight, so Frankie was allowed to join us for the journey home. The soldiers who carried out the search had their faces blackened and wore packs on their back. Bill Cotton, Frankie Howerd and Jimmy Moir put bottles of champagne in their backpacks before we took off. The BBC recorded our performance in Belfast for a special compilation show of Frankie's concert tour of Ulster's military bases, which was shown a few months later.

I did various bits and pieces of work during the remainder of 1972. One was a part in the film *Bless This House*, starring Sidney James, Diana Coupland, Terry Scott and June Whitfield. It was a comedy, directed by Gerald Thomas, who'd directed the *Carry On* films. I played a waitress in a cafe.

Before I knew it Christmas was approaching, the first one without my mother and I knew I would be utterly desolate. But I knew Mummy would not have wanted me to be miserable. I would just have to make the best of Christmas, somehow. The more I thought about it, I realized there were quite a few people I knew who would be on their own too. So a crowd of us clubbed together

73

and spent Christmas Eve at a friend's flat in Soho, where we had a delicious Christmas dinner. Then, on Christmas Day, they came round to me and we did the whole thing all over again. There was quite a crowd: Mandy and Desmond, a chap called Brian the Burglar, Carol a costume designer, plus a friend of Brian's called Cosy Norman. (There was also a friend I'd made who worked down at Gerry's who everyone called Lavish McTavish. I never thought anything odd about this and only learned years later that her real name was Muriel. John Junkin had nicknamed her Lavish because of her curvaceous figure and McTavish thanks to her broad Scots accent. Muriel knew no fear and was not impressed by fame – I've seen Michael Parkinson visibly pale at the mention of her name!) From that year we spent a few great Christmases altogether, just keeping each other company.

The truth was though that I was still very lonely after mother's death. Len had not been the answer to that. I had been out with a couple of men but they had meant nothing to me. 1972 had indeed been a very bad year. I spent New Year's Eve wondering what on earth the New Year would bring . . .

As luck would have it, in early 1973 I received a telephone call that really changed my life – the BBC wanted to turn *Are You Being Served?* into a series! I think part of the appeal was it would be studio based and could be made on a low budget, without the need for any expensive location scenes. I was absolutely thrilled at the prospect of doing more *AYBS?* My immediate hope was – perhaps – this year would be much better than last, after all.

CHAPTER TEN

A New Start

We started rehearsing the first series of *Are You Being Served?* at the BBC Rehearsal Rooms in North Acton, or the Acton Hilton as we used to call it. It was simply marvellous working with everyone again and very quickly it began to feel like the extended family I'd never had. We all got on exceptionally well together and although we took our work seriously, we had so many laughs, right from the start.

The first episode in the new series was entitled *Dear Sexy Knickers* and in it Mr Lucas, who was infatuated with Miss Brahms, wrote her a note 'Dear Sexy Knickers, I don't 'alf fancy you. Meet me outside at 5.30 p.m. and we'll get together.'

His invitation went astray and ended up in the hands of Mrs Slocombe, who mistakenly thought that Captain Peacock had sent it to her. Well, you can imagine what mayhem ensued.

I had a scene where I had to speak on the phone. The sound boys made the phone live and what I was hearing down the line was a rude phone call. Well, being the giggler I am, I could barely speak. I can't say for certain, but I have my suspicions that Trevor Bannister set up that little prank.

John Inman and I shared the same sense of humour and he and I became especially great pals. He is one of the wittiest, funniest men I have ever met in my life; aside from being an extremely inventive actor. I'm pleased to say that the friendship that we built up in those days is still alive and kicking today.

Credit for the camaraderie we shared on *AYBS?* has to go to David Croft. He is a genius for casting and must have the most phenomenal brain when it comes to recalling the various skills of those he's used years before and I've always felt one of Crofty's repertory company.

Apart from working well together as a team on *AYBS?* because we enjoyed each other's company so much, we often socialized after work. Sometimes we would go for a drink, or occasionally dinner. John also started to come round to me for Sunday lunch, with his friend, Ron. Coincidentally, it was nice to meet up with Elizabeth Larner again, who'd suggested me for the job of entertaining the troops in Ulster with Frankie Howerd. Elizabeth played an indecisive customer in the episode *Diamonds Are A Girl's Best Friend*.

We made a total of five episodes for the first series, which were transmitted in March and April of 1973. David Croft produced them all but unfortunately they were greeted with mixed reviews. *The Times*, for instance, thought: 'There is some fine character acting,' but felt that the show 'was ruined by vulgar knockabout and silly jokes – silly old jokes.' The *Daily Telegraph* reviewer was optimistic: 'If the creation of credible, funny characters is the essence of television situation comedy, *Are You Being Served?* could prove a useful addition to the ranks . . .' The *Morning Star* was far less enthusiastic: 'Candidates for the most inept comedy series of the year so far should definitely include ATV's *It's Tarbuck* on Tuesdays . . . marginally worse is BBC1's *Are You Being Served?* on Wednesdays.'

The ambivalent reception did not dampen our spirits; the whole cast were right behind David and Jeremy. We were convinced that if we had the chance to make another series, Grace Brothers department store and its staff would, in time, win the hearts of British viewers.

In June 1973 a couple of months after the first series of *AYBS?* had been screened David Croft continued to show his faith in me and asked me to do another *Dad's Army*. We recorded the episode called *My British Buddy* in the studios that month and it was shown as part of Series Six which was broadcast in November. Again I played Private Walker's girlfriend, Shirley. The first contingent of American soldiers were due to arrive in Walmington-on-Sea and the platoon made preparations to greet them.

The majority of the actors in *Dad's Army* were no spring chickens. For example, Arnold Ridley was 72 at the start of the series, 81 at the end. Sadly though, it was Jimmy Beck, who played the spiv role of Private Walker and was one of the youngest cast members, who died during the run of the sixth series in 1973. *My British Buddy* was among the last TV appearances in *Dad's Army* that Jimmy ever made. He was taken ill on location and died shortly afterwards at the age of only 39, which was a great tragedy for his wife, Kay, his friends and all of us who had worked with him.

Supporting artistes are important on all shows and in *Dad's Army* the regular s.a.'s formed the main part of the platoon. One was Leslie Noyes, who'd been Arthur Haynes' side-kick in many of his sketches. Colin Bean, who plays Dame in pantos all over the country, was another. So too was Desmond Cullem-Jones.

I remember getting in the lift one day to rehearsals at *Dad's Army* and there was a chap already in there, wearing a sheepskin coat, Vyella shirt and cavalry twills, just like an off-duty officer. 'Oh hello,' he said. 'Are you with us again?'

'Us?' I thought, I'm sure I recognize him from somewhere.

'Yes, I'm doing an episode.'

'Oh lovely, I'm doing them all, as usual,' he remarked.

When we reached the rehearsal room, I realized who he was, Desmond Cullem-Jones. Talk about me being grand!

I made another film appearance in 1973: *Carry On Girls*, in which several of us played beauty queens. My character was called Ida Downes. I was pleased to be in it but the filming came during a really busy period for me. *Carry On*s were always hard work, although tremendous fun to be involved in. I had worked previously with the series producer, Peter Rogers on a couple of other projects and up to this point got on well with him. Unfortunately I was to blot my copy-book with Peter while filming *Carry On Girls*. One sequence of the film was the beauty contest, which was sabotaged by the Women's Rights brigade. We beauty queens were on stage when they struck – bags of flour came down, water, earth, the lot! It was mayhem. Instead of staying on stage with the other girls to get covered in muck, I fled the stage! It was most unprofessional of me and I bitterly regret what I did. I never worked with Peter again.

Ever since Mummy's death I'd struggled hard to keep the bed and breakfast hotel going but alongside my acting career it was just no good, I couldn't cope with it on my own. Also, I didn't think it was good for me to continue living there any longer, not with so many memories of Mummy all around me.

So in 1974 I decided it was time to sell the business. I moved into a beautiful flat at Chiltern Court in Baker Street, the first time in my entire life I'd had a front door I could call my own, which was not part of a business. Having my own home provided me with a wonderful sense of freedom. I also loved the village atmosphere around that area and I gradually got to know everyone who came into my newly adopted local in Marylebone.

During that period I met a Chinese lady called Cherry Black. You couldn't tell how old Cherry was, she could have been anything from 60–110 years of age but she was a lovely lady and we got on very well. She was an interesting conversationalist and we shared many a drink and meal together. She owned restaurants all over the world and her main home was in Beirut. She invited me to stay with her in Beirut for a break and I readily accepted the offer. I was physically and emotionally drained after everything that had occurred during the previous two years and happily, it turned out to be a most wonderful holiday. Beirut was a fantastic city, especially its architecture and natural beauty – the flowers and shrubs were particularly beautiful. The subsequent destruction of Beirut was devastating and however they rebuild, it will never be the same city. I was away for a month, mainly just lazing by the pool. It did me the world of good and to top it all, I had a fantastic tan when I returned home. Not that I ever tried Lebanese dishes while I was out there, with Cherry around it was always Chinese food that was the top choice!

Sometimes Cherry stayed at my flat when she visited London and we had some good times here too. Once I took her to Poons restaurant in Lyall Street and during the meal the owner, Mr Bill Poon walked in with a black cat on a pole! I nearly passed out but a very heated discussion ensued between him and his wife, Cecilia. Fainting was forgotten while I eavesdropped on the conversation – via Cherry – because they were talking in Chinese!

Fortunately, she understood it all and told me the cat was the Poons' pet. Apparently, Cecilia had earlier been telling Bill off for not treating the animal well. His way of making amends was carrying the cat home in a supposedly dignified manner – on the pole. With that reassurance, I could continue my meal in peace!

I was really thrilled when *Are You Being Served?* went into a second series in 1974 and I had a further chance to develop the character of Miss Brahms. David Croft remained as executive producer but Harold Snoad produced the series. We made five more programmes, which again were screened in March and April and were very successful.

I did other work that year too, including three more *Dad's Army* during May, this time for radio. The series had been adapted for radio by Harold Snoad (who'd been production manager on the TV series) and Michael Knowles (an actor who'd played a captain in several episodes). One of the shows, *War Dance*, was a new one for me and I played a new character, Violet Gibbons. The other two radio pieces were versions of episodes I'd appeared in on television – *Mum's Army* and *The King Was In His Counting House*.

All work was gratefully accepted and I even did an advert for the Milk Marketing Board, directed by Adrian Line, who later went on to direct *Fatal Attraction* (somewhat of a contrast!). He told me he'd always wanted to work with me ever since he'd seen me in *Gumshoe* and I thought that was indeed a lovely compliment.

Although I had become a regular cast member of *Are You Being Served?* the series did not run for long periods at any one time. Other acting work was irregular too. That, coupled with the cost of moving to Baker Street and the upkeep of the flat, meant I didn't always have a great deal of money.

So in between acting jobs I worked for a friend, Bill Burgess, who is an interior designer. My shorthand and typing lessons from Miss McColl came in handy because I did all his letters and typing, along with various other office jobs. I am not a person who can sit around all day doing nothing. So I was pleased to work for him not only for the money but to do something to keep busy. Bill was a wonderful employer: he brought me back a half bottle of champagne every lunchtime and if he was not due back, he'd ring me to join him. Just my kind of boss!

I also worked in The French House pub in Soho, which I enjoyed, having been brought up in the licensed trade. The landlord was a charming gentleman named Gaston Berlemont, who was like another father to me (sadly now he, too, has died). I used to make all the bar snacks for Gaston and cook the staff lunches. Gaston had accounts at all the best butchers and boulangeries in Soho, so it was lovely walking around and ordering exactly what I wanted. Every lunchtime while I was working, without fail, Gaston would send me up a half bottle of pink champagne. I told you he was a nice man!

I smile when I look back on those days because we always conjured up a laugh about some situation or another – often at the expense of Pepe, a Spanish barman who'd worked for Gaston for years. I hate frying food so I only ever made creamed or roast potatoes for lunch. Pepe continuously moaned that I would never cook chips for him but Gaston made a point of reminding us all: 'Don't worry, he can't have them anyway, he's on a diet.' So Pepe never got his chips from me but it was all part of the fun and camaraderie at the pub.

My career picked up and my face started to become better known among television audiences. However, the money I earned from acting had to last all year long. So when my income was insufficient and I couldn't obtain part time work elsewhere, I had to sign on as unemployed at the Labour Exchange and at times, even had to resort to selling some of my furniture or other belongings, in order to pay my way.

Meanwhile, the cast from *Are You Being Served?* were all keeping their fingers crossed to be called in for another series. The second series had been greeted with much higher critical acclaim and the viewing public had begun to relate to the characters in

Grace Brothers. So in 1975 we were all delighted when the BBC had the confidence to commission a third series and extend its run from five to eight programmes. They went out from February through to April with their usual run of banter, such as in the *Shoulder To Shoulder* episode when the shop floor is being redecorated. The decorators can only do one floor at a time so Mrs Slocombe takes down Mr Grainger's Y-fronts to make more space for ladieswear. Aggrieved, he asks her to take her underwear down as well . . . you can imagine the rest!

As *AYBS?* gained momentum, we were asked to do our first Christmas special, which was transmitted on 22 December 1975. The staff, including Miss Brahms in her curlers, were called in for an early morning meeting to discuss ideas for boosting Christmas sales figures. Much to our annoyance, on Young Mr Grace's orders, we ended up having to wear novelty Christmas costumes.

We got into the habit of doing a gag at every dress run, just for the cast and crew. One Christmas, we had an animated model of a talking Santa Claus that said 'HO HO HO little boy, have I got a surprise for you'. Then its arms would move in an opening gesture, the joke being that his robes would catch on the sleeves and the red coat would open. For the dress run I said to the designer, you have got to put something 'there' for a gag. She was new and a bit nervous but I told her I'd take full responsibility. Well, she did us proud. On the dress run the coat opened and there was a giant cracker and two Christmas balls! Everyone fell about. Mollie and I were stood at the end of the line-up and she asked, 'What are they laughing at? There was nothing there when I looked!'

You may have noticed that I was always a lot slower than Mollie coming down the stairs at the beginning of the show. It was because of my poor eyesight and those high heels! I was terrified of tumbling down them. Mollie, however, also in high heels, would come charging down like a bat out of hell. I enjoyed the musical numbers that were introduced to the show but, if you look carefully, you will notice that I'm always out of step – a bit like Jonesy in *Dad's Army*.

Doremy Vernon was a later addition to the cast; she played an extremely bad-tempered canteen manageress. All of Grace Brothers' staff were terrified of her. Actually, Doremy is a great girl and used to be one of the Tiller Girls. She wrote a very good book on the history of John Tiller's girls.

I did a spot of radio too and recorded another episode of *Dad's Army* – the *My British Buddy* episode – and I never seemed to be off the box each week in one thing or another. During 1975 I was also fortunate to be booked for a children's series for Southern TV called *Hogg's Back*. By coincidence, it was directed by David Croft's brother, Peter. In it I worked with a lovely actor called Derek Royle, who played a wacky and forgetful doctor with his own practice in the town of Belling-on-Sea. I was his housekeeper, Pearl.

We had really good fun doing *Hogg's Back*. One day we were filming by a river and for my part I was dressed in a nightie and had my hair in rags, as if I was ready for bed. During the lunch break I fancied a drink and one of the sound boys offered to drive me to the shops if I went in dressed as I was in the nightie. So off we went, with me in my nightie. Inside the off-licence he told the manager: 'We're on our honeymoon.' The guy behind the counter never batted an eyelid.

One scene we did necessitated Derek being in a coffin. The Co-op supplied one for us – we were told it was second-hand! Anyway, it had to be made so that it had a false bottom. When the studio chippie got to work on it, he discovered that the blue satin lining was stuffed with Co-op stamps, all shredded up. Talk about going to meet your maker and getting your 'divvy' as well!

Another occasion we were filming inside a tent. Dusk was falling, so they put the lights on and the tent immediately filled up with insects. I cannot stand insects and was really freaking out. It seemed to take forever but eventually they got the shots done and I raced off post haste, leaving the insects behind.

While we were in Hampshire making the series, Derek Royle and I stayed on a barge on the estuary at Southampton. It was owned by an old lady, who was a great animal lover and had a menagerie of rabbits, guinea pigs, cats and dogs. When Derek and I went in for breakfast there was always a bowl of bread on the table – not for us to eat – but for the swans and other wildlife on the estuary! Whenever the tide was out, the barge lurched to one side and we had to hold on to our breakfast plates firmly with one hand, while trying to eat with the other!

The series lasted for nineteen episodes during 1975 and 1976. Peter Croft was excellent to work for and was always open to suggestions. Such as the time that Pearl was supposed to cook lunch for the doctor. I suggested to Peter that I make a rhubarb pie – but two feet long – as if Pearl had forgotten to cut up the rhubarb! It was that sort of harmless humour we liked to introduce for the children. I was pleased to hear that the programme subsequently became cult viewing on an American cable station.

I also returned to London Weekend Television again during 1975 to play the part of Doris, a barmaid in the long-running comedy series *Not On Your Nellie*, starring Hylda Baker. Unfortunately, it was an absolute nightmare to work on.

Hylda may have been the top comedienne in the country but there were problems persuading her to rehearse and as a consequence – bless her heart – her lines were not coming easily. She claimed it was far too tiring for her to rehearse on studio day but as a result it meant the cameras could not line up correctly without her.

In order to circumvent the problems of the absent Miss Baker on studio day, what they did instead was employ someone to deputize for her. The difficulty was though that the stand-in was a young girl who was very tall. So they had to pin a photo of Hylda on the woman's chest at the exact height where Hylda's face should be and the poor cameramen had to line up on that!

It was in the course of 1975 that I met Andy Archer, an art and graphics agent and his French wife, Mireille. They lived opposite me in Baker Street and the three of us became close friends. Come Friday lunchtime, it was always a case of the weekend starts here! We piled into whatever car they had at the time and headed off for Soho.

We spent all lunchtime in The French House pub, followed by a meal at either Poons Chinese restaurant, or a wonderful fish and chip shop, called Neptune. Then we did our shopping and went back to our own local, Bill Bentley's in Baker Street. It was always quite a hairy day but great fun and relaxing for me after the rigours of learning lines and filming. We usually spent weekends together too, either at their place or mine. Sunday 'lunches' always continued through to midnight!

The crowd we mixed with at Bill Bentley's included some of the most important men in property development – Bill Wiggins, John Chalk, David Bulstrode and Peter Ellis (former chairman of QPR). We certainly sank a few bottles of bubbly in their company! Peter and I are still good friends. He once was kind enough to help me out financially during one of my bleak spells. In fact, I am going to be godmother to a yacht he is helping to raise funds for to enter the Gift of Life race in 2003. All the crew are recipients of either tissue or organ transplants. The skipper,

Simon Needs, had a kidney and liver transplant a few years ago. I feel very honoured to be asked to launch their yacht.

After some early disappointments workwise and a great deal of sadness in my private life, at long last, life was on the up again. My career was developing well. I was having a lot of fun in my social life and I'd met a guy with whom I knew I was falling in love . . .

CHAPTER ELEVEN

New Love . . . and a Summer Season in Blackpool

I'd first met Will Thorpe through friends around 1974. He was a very talented advertising art director who had won many awards for his work. Among the best-known adverts he directed were those he did for Martini. At first he was just one of the crowd but gradually we had become more than just good friends. I think it's fair to say that my feelings for Will were far greater than for any other man I'd met up until then. Although I'd been married to Len, I never felt that way about him. Will was the first true great love of my life.

He was handsome; nearly six feet tall, with light brown, curly hair and beard. The physical attraction was mutual, we clicked instantly. Unlike the huge age gap with Len, Will was only three years older than me, so we had a lot more in common and got on extremely well together. The downside was that he was married, with a wife and two children living in Suffolk. It is one of my big regrets in life that he left his wife for me and I still feel bad about it but I wasn't his first affair. Eventually, he moved into my flat in

Baker Street. We began to travel extensively together, as a result of his work.

I accompanied him to Australia on one occasion and while we were staying in Sydney, I visited Grace Brothers. It was totally different to the antiquated department store that we portrayed on television and was far more like Selfridges. I was also delighted to have the opportunity to meet the 'real' Mr Grace.

Unfortunately, while we were in Australia, Will was bitten by a poisonous spider. It was a very worrying time because he was extremely unwell and the doctor warned him that he would probably suffer from recurring bouts of the fever, which was rather like malaria. Another trip I made with Will was to southern Spain, where he was searching for suitable locations to shoot some new Martini adverts. I remember not being too impressed by the Marbella Club, despite its fame.

I also made a trip to the States with Will and that was a bit of an eye-opener. We flew to San Francisco where he was directing a Levis ad and I met Hell's Angels there for the first time in my life. The pair I remember were the head of the Californian chapter and his sidekick. By then they were well into their fifties and surprisingly, were charming. However, I could just picture them in their earlier days, haring up and down the freeways on their motorbikes, scaring the living daylights out of all and sundry!

Will helped relieve some of the sadness which had resulted from the traumas of my previous years and I was very happy with him in the beginning. At first there was no inkling of the way he would treat me later.

Acting work was not always plentiful and sometimes I found myself signing on again unemployed at the Labour Exchange in Lisson Grove, perhaps much to their surprise. Maybe people thought that if you were in a top TV series you earned fantastic money that kept you buoyant all year but the reality of the profession in the 1970s was far from that. So I was more than pleased when in 1976 the familiar introduction of: 'Ground Floor: perfumery, stationery and leather goods, wigs and haberdashery, kitchenware and food. Going up. First Floor: telephones, gents ready-made suits, shirts, socks, ties, hats, underwear and shoes.' rang out with a fourth series of *AYBS?*

The team was back together again for six episodes, which were televised in April and May. We also recorded another special – *The Father Christmas Affair* – for screening on Christmas Eve. In it Grace Brothers staff, including Miss Brahms, all ended up in Santa Claus outfits, complete with white beard.

We still used the 'Acton Hilton' for rehearsals during the week. The day of recording the episode in the studio was always extremely hard work and could last anything up to twelve hours. On studio day, which was usually a Friday, we had to be at the BBC Television Centre by 9a.m. to start rehearsing the complete run through of a whole thirty-minute episode.

In the afternoon we did the dress rehearsal. Everything had to be ship-shape and Bristol fashion by the time we went in front of a live audience at 8p.m. Recording in the studio took place on a Sunday. John, Trevor and I used to take in a lunch. Arthur Brough always joined us. We would look through the script at the read-through to see if there was a canteen scene and then we would have crockery, etc from props. If not, it was paper plates and plastic forks. John did starters and puddings and I did the main course. Trevor did cheese and wine. On Arthur Brough's birthday I poached a salmon and Mollie made a chocolate cake and we invited the others. Usually, though it was just us.

Although the end result of *AYBS?* always looked like light-hearted fun, I have always thought that comedy acting is much harder than straight acting. Yet, despite the seriousness of the job in hand, we always had a lot of laughs making *AYBS?* There was no jealousy among the cast, or big egos flying about because we were all established actors doing a job we enjoyed.

I loved playing the character of Shirley Brahms and somehow felt a strange sense of security behind that shop counter. It was a kind of shield for me.

Remember that long hot, humid summer of 1976? Well, that's when we were booked to do a summer season of *Are You Being Served?* in Blackpool. The success of the television series prompted a long list of requests from companies wanting us to do a live version of the show. It was Bernard Delfont who finally clinched a deal with David and Jeremy and they agreed to write a special stage adaptation.

As I would be out of London for months, I decided to let my flat in Baker Street. Will, my cat 'Pussy' and I moved from my enormous ten-room Baker Street flat into a tiny place in Knightsbridge. Shortly afterwards I was on the move again, to Blackpool, where I rented a small house.

It was good to have a break away from London. Very few people in my close circle knew but I was having problems with Will. He was a very talented person who could be extremely charming. However, he had a dark side to him. When he had been drinking, he became aggressive and was often violent towards me.

I'd done hardly any live theatre before, apart from two weeks in *No Sex, Please – We're British* up at Billingham in the North East. Billingham was certainly not the most brilliant of places to work and in that fortnight I think I bought every bottle of champagne they had on sale in the Co-Op, just to keep my spirits up! Derek Royle and Una Stubbs were in the production.

Although I hadn't kept in touch with most of Mummy's family, I did occasionally keep in telephone contact with my

Aunty Elsie, who lived in Ashington. As she wasn't far away, she travelled to Billingham to see me in *No Sex, Please – We're British*. She was absolutely horrified because I played a call-girl and wore a fur bikini which, when you pressed a button on the top, had revolving tassels and tails!

So the four-month summer season in Blackpool was really my first long theatre stint. John Inman was very good to me while I was there, he's a Blackpool boy and his mum still lives there. John kindly showed me around and recommended the best places to go. His brother Geoff was alive then, living there with his wife, Pat and their children. Aside from John and myself, Mollie, Frank and Nicholas from the original cast were in the summer show. Outside actors were brought in to play the remaining roles.

We put on two shows a day at the Winter Gardens Pavilion right through from June to October and although it was the hottest summer for years, we packed that theatre every night. Each morning there was a longer and longer queue at the box office. In fact we did such excellent business, with capacity audiences from beginning to end of the season, that we produced higher revenue for Delfont than any other show the organization staged that year. The Blackpool critic for *The Stage* (the well respected performing arts newspaper) who reviewed it, declared it 'the funniest show he'd seen in thirty years of summer seasons'.

After the show John and I took it in turns to cook a meal, one night we'd go back to his flat, the next to my house. There was a sweet elderly couple next door to me, so I gave them my keys and they popped in and turned the oven on before we arrived home.

The little house I rented in Blackpool had a tiny garden, so during the day I took advantage of the lovely weather and usually sunbathed out there. Sometimes John and a couple of the others came over to join me. On one particular day I was making a cheese salad for them, completely forgetting that John was allergic to cheese. I'd taken my cat up to Blackpool with me and had a good supply of her favourite pilchards in tomato sauce in the cupboard. So I opened a tin to put on John's salad instead of cheese. The only thing was John couldn't eat them for laughing because Pussy sat in front of him, staring at her pilchards. 'She knows I've pinched her tea!' John pointed out.

Another day when he came round we started making omelettes for lunch. I say 'we' but I'm not very good at making omelettes, so in the end I left the job to John. Unfortunately he had a fag in his mouth at the time and some of the ash dropped into the mixture. 'Now look what you've done,' I told him. 'Oh never mind,' he said, beating it into the mixture, 'We'll tell them it's ground pepper!' All the omelettes were eaten with no one any the wiser or harmed for it!

The next time he came round, I walked out of the back door . . . only to find John wearing my bikini top as a thong! 'Ere do you mind, I've got to put my tits in there!!' I exclaimed.

Aside from sunbathing and having fun in the garden, I had a wonderful time touring the town's antique and secondhand shops and it was in Blackpool that I first started collecting frogs – and that was John Inman's fault. All because he told me an hilarious joke about a wide-mouthed frog (I'd like to share it with you but you have to see it). Now, for years I'd been a collector of antique glass and I discovered several lovely examples up in Blackpool. During one of my shopping forays I noticed a frog in one shop and it reminded me of John's joke, so I bought it – a beautifully coloured porcelain frog cream jug. After that I realized there were some smashing frogs about, particularly those made in the Victorian era and that's when I became a confirmed frogophile.

I took another tram ride along the prom one day. The last time I'd travelled on one had been with my father when I was a young child – the day I was nearly sick from the ice cream.

Unfortunately, trams and I seem to have no affinity, on my latest trip it got stuck behind a traffic jam, so I had to get off and walk instead.

Throughout the summer we would often play jokes to each other on stage but never anything that would spoil the pleasure for the audience. In the opening scene Mollie had to make her entrance by backing out of the lift wearing Union Jack directoire knickers. That always got a good laugh and the knicks were an integral part of the plot. However, one night Frank and I were either side of the lift, Mollie made her entrance, bent down as she backed out – but no laugh from the audience. I looked at her bum, no knickers! . . .well not Union Jack ones anyway. Frank and I hissed to her 'You haven't got them on.' In the wings, Mollie's dresser, Dorothy was still clutching the missing knickers. Poor Mollie, her face was pinker than her wig! We spent most of the first act behind our counter, trying to work out how we could introduce the knickers into the plot to make the second half of the show work!

In the second act (set in Spain) we had to sit at a long dining table for a meal but the food was only melon balls and lettuce! To try and liven it up a little, I decided to introduce a bottle of salad cream from my bag and we each took it in turns, between lines, to add it to the food on our plates. One night we somehow got out of sync with using the bottle, Mollie used it before John and unfortunately she didn't screw the lid on properly. John picked it up and shook the bottle . . . the lid flew off and salad cream shot all down the front of his pink suit! That was more than enough to set us all off giggling – and the audience loved it too.

Another night I decided to play a little joke on Mollie. We both had a gap in our lines, as Frank was talking at the other end of the table. While he was doing so, I popped a green grape up one of my nostrils, so that it looked like a big bogey! Mollie had been busy pushing her melon balls about on her plate and had not noticed what I'd done until she turned to look at me. Unfortunately, I had underestimated the effect that the grape would have on her and she practically hit her head on the table because of laughing so much!

Mollie got her own back on me though. The following week I looked across at her eating her 'supper' and she had been to the joke shop and bought one of those nail through the finger jokes. That was me gone! It was no holds barred after that!

John had to run through our tents in one scene, when he was being pursued by a Spanish freedom fighter and on his way through he had to pick up a potty. Anyway one night I'd stuck a Mars Bar in the bottom! He barely paused in the action but then I said 'Oh sorry', picked it out and ate it! John ran off across the stage shrieking!

Nicholas Smith had recently done a commercial in which he was Frankenstein's monster, with a green zip across his forehead. It was too good a gag to miss. So during one performance, with my back to the audience, I had a green zip on my forehead. Poor John, he ran off laughing his head off that night too!

Overall, the summer season up North was excellent experience and huge fun for all of us. Although doing over four months of twice-nightly shows really took its toll physically, especially in that heat. Nevertheless, it probably did me a power of good as far as technique was concerned. If we had felt like an extended family before that summer, by the end of the run we were as close as any cast could be.

CHAPTER TWELVE

More Memories of Are You Being Served?

I have so many memories of *AYBS?* that it would be impossible for me to share them all but certainly one of the most colourful was during the Queen's Silver Jubilee in 1977 when Mollie's hair was sprayed red, white and blue. It certainly looked effective, I can tell you!

While we were doing the final run through in the studio during one of the 1977 episodes I began to feel unwell – as if my brain was boiling. Next thing I knew I had collapsed on the studio floor. Everyone was very concerned and I was taken to the medical bay and given antibiotics. Somehow, I managed to gather enough strength to do the show without a dress-run. The BBC were very good to me and next morning I was sent to see a specialist in Harley Street. It turned out I had a severe lung infection but at least I had got the show done.

I have to pay due credit to some of the best costume designers in the business who worked with us on *Are You Being Served?* Two I shall pick out for special mention are L. Rowland-Warne (whom we nicknamed Roll & Butter), who was in charge for Series Five, Six, Seven and Eight and Mary Husband, who took over for Series Nine. Rowland was formerly a dancer and there was nothing he liked better than spangles and feathers. When we introduced musical numbers into *AYBS?*, Rowland just had a field day and was totally in his element.

The same with Mary, she had such a good eye, especially when something special had to be done for a gag. In one episode we were doing a piece in the recreation room in the basement of Grace Brothers. I had to stand over an air vent, wearing a very light voile skirt. The idea was to recreate the Marilyn Monroe scene from *The Seven Year Itch* where she stood over a subway vent. Mary made a fantastic job of my costume which justly carried out the illusion.

On the days we rehearsed at North Acton we were fortunate in only having to work until lunchtime. John, Trevor and I often had a drink together after work before we went our separate ways home. On one occasion when Ray Butt was directing, John had a personal appearance booked to open a toy shop. During rehearsals Ray told everybody to come back after lunch, by which time John would have returned and we could carry on and do more work.

Well, that's the biggest mistake he could possibly have made. Everybody went down to the pub, including Arthur Brough, Trevor, Mollie and even Frank Thornton, who does not normally drink much. Anyway, we all got plastered while we were waiting around but eventually made our way back to the rehearsal room. I'm sorry to report that John and the director were the only two sober people there. We had the most hysterical run-throughs with everybody laughing so much that in the end Ray Butt told us all to bugger off and go home!

After we'd recorded the seven episodes of *Are You Being Served?* for Series Five in 1977 EMI approached David and Jeremy with the suggestion of making a film of *AYBS?* David considered they already had a good plot based on the previous year's summer show in Blackpool. The storyline being that Grace Brothers closed for redecoration and the staff, courtesy of Young Mr Grace, flew off on holiday together to the Costa Plonka. I thought the film script was far too similar to the summer show, which was a great shame because I considered we had a really good opportunity to do something different.

It was a pity too that the film's budget didn't stretch to a Mediterranean location. Instead we shot it at EMI's Elstree Studios. Everything had to be completed within six weeks, which was a pretty frantic schedule, I can assure you. You see we weren't used to working all day on the TV *AYBS?* because on those we rehearsed in the morning and cleared off home at lunchtime. The only full day's work was in the studio when the show went out.

Anyhow we found ourselves stuck out at Elstree filming all day long. One day though we noticed a row of pitched tents which were part of the setting for the film. 'Well, I could always bring in an R and R bag,' I suggested. 'Just to break up the monotony a bit.'

The suggestion was readily accepted by all and we started taking in a bottle of champagne, a bottle of Plymouth gin, a bottle of vodka, some tonics, Angostura bitters and an ice bucket. We hid the goodies in a different tent each day! Fortunately the props guys were very good and organized the ice for us, tipping us the wink as to which tent it was secreted in. I am not insinuating we were a load of piss artists – we weren't – but if you are used to having a 'heart-starter' at 11a.m. like Arthur Brough, or a drink at lunchtime, then so be it.

Eventually we did get one day's location shooting – at Gatwick Airport, on a Dan Air training plane. When time came for our lunchtime drink and refreshments, no facilities had been laid on for us. Instead we had to go into the main airport bar. Well, as you can imagine, that turned out to be a nightmare because it was full of holidaymakers, many of whom instantly recognized us. John was wearing a pink suit, with a white scarf and a white Fedora sun-hat.

The barman rushed up to serve him, asking: 'Going far, Mr Inman?'

Gesturing to his costume, John answered: 'I think I've gone far enough, don't you?'

The poor barman really believed he was travelling off on holiday dressed like that!

I didn't really enjoy making the film that much because of the script similarity and lack of location scenes. After it was released I heard a lot of complaints from the public who said that they'd seen the summer show in Blackpool, paid to see the movie and felt – as we did when we saw the script – a distinct feeling of *déja vu*.

Arthur English had joined us by the time we made the film, playing Mr Harman the maintenance man. What a valued addition Arthur was to our team. Even if he only had a couple of lines to deliver, he'd turn them into a complete speech and have us all in hysterics. Arthur was a lovely person, a real gentleman. He was still low following the death of his wife and so John tried to coax him into doing pantomime with him. After a while Arthur agreed to take the part of the Squire in *Mother Goose* at Wimbledon and it was there he met the lady who was later to become his second wife: dancer Teresa Mann, who was thirty-five years his junior.

In 1978 all those connected with *Are You Being Served?* suffered a great sense of loss when we heard the sad news of the death of Arthur Brough. Arthur, who played Mr Grainger, the senior salesman in gentlemen's ready-to-wear, had been a major name in repertory theatre for forty years and had worked extensively on stage with his wife, Elizabeth. She died in the early part of 1978, after which he felt he no longer wanted to continue with acting.

David and Jeremy tried to persuade him otherwise and wrote him into the new series but before Arthur could take on the role again he passed away at his home in Folkestone, only six weeks after Elizabeth.

I thought Arthur was a wonderful man, a highly lovable character. He was very amusing and on the set of *AYBS?* always referred to me jokingly as: 'that horrid child'. I didn't notice first of all but on the dot of 11a.m. he disappeared out of the rehearsal room and apparently rushed across the car park into The Castle pub next door for a large pink Plymouth gin. It proves how well John and Trevor worked together because they would find something to do to delay the director, so that Arthur was back before he was missed.

Except on one day, when David Croft was in charge. Something happened and they realized Arthur wasn't there. We all rushed over to the window and there he was, scurrying back across the car park. Unfortunately for him, it had started to rain heavily and by the time poor Arthur returned to the rehearsal room, he was looking rather wet.

David Croft asked him: 'Where have you been?'

'Only for a pee,' Arthur replied.

'Well, you must have been aiming rather high then because your head is wet!' David retorted.

We vowed that one day we would quickly disappear into the lift, arrive in the pub before Arthur and all be leaning on the bar by the time he walked in. Sadly we never managed it. Everyone on *AYBS?* felt awful about Arthur's death and we missed him badly when we came to make the sixth series. I remember David Croft commenting about Arthur that it was always extremely hard to edit his scenes. 'His mouth starts moving three seconds before any sound comes out, almost as if he's trying to rev himself up!'

Anyone who has ever worked for the BBC knows that trying

to park at the Television Centre in Shepherds Bush is an absolute nightmare. We had been doing one episode of *Are You Being Served?* based in the toy department at Grace Brothers and after rehearsals at North Acton, Trevor Bannister arranged to drive the director, Ray Butt, John Inman and myself back to Television Centre with the toys. We thought we'd have a drink at the club there before we all went home. I was in the back of the car with John plus all the toys and Ray was up front with Trevor. Now *Are You Being Served?* was the BBC's top comedy show at the time but despite that the security guard stopped us to enquire who we were. Trevor piped up: '*Play School*!'

'OK, you can park right there at the front,' came the immediate response.

Well, that certainly put us in our place. It was obvious *Play School* had priority over the Corporation's No 1 comedy programme.

We encountered parking problems on another occasion when we wanted to go the club at the Centre for a drink. Once again Trevor was driving and I was in the back of the car with John. Once more the security guard stopped us at the entrance: 'What do you want?' he demanded.

'This is the MP Bernadette Devlin. I'm delivering her for an interview,' was Trevor's invention that time.

'Yes, right fine. Park up there, young man.'

When we were with Trevor was the only time we ever got a good parking space!

I always made a point of telephoning my Aunty Elsie each week after *Are You Being Served?* had been televized to hear her reaction to the programme. 'Well, Aunty Elsie, what did you think this week?' I asked of the episode based in the toy department, in which there were two clockwork dogs on the counter and one of them mounted the other.

'It was quite funny,' she conceded 'but I don't think that bit with the dogs was necessary. I just do not know what the vicar will say.'

Normally we worked on a new series of *Are You Being Served?* around the time of John Inman's birthday in June. Mollie, who is the most wonderful cook, always made him a birthday cake and I organized the champagne. On his special day after rehearsals were completed we presented John with his cake and champagne and had a little celebration. However, in 1979 we did the series later in the summer during July, when it was my birthday on the 20th and Mollie's on the 21st. In the rehearsal room Mollie and I were leaning on the ladieswear' counter when she asked me: 'We have a little problem this year. Should we still do the cake and champagne bit or not? It's embarrassing, as we are the ones who are supposed to be celebrating.'

'I'll go and ask,' I offered.

I trotted off to the menswear counter but before I could even open my mouth, John Inman said: 'It's all under control, now bugger off!'

That's the sort of mental rapport we shared, along with the same wicked sense of humour. Trevor Bannister arranged the champagne and John organized the cake, which had a diagonal line across it, with a tiny cat decoration on one side for Mollie . . . and a frog on the other, for me.

The seventh series, comprising seven episodes was televised in October and November, plus a Christmas special *The Punch and Judy Affair* which went out on Boxing Day. In the special Miss Brahms had to wear a false chin and nose and there were some hilarious moments when Mr Lucas, also wearing a false chin and nose, attempted to kiss her.

During its time, overseas sales of *Are You Being Served?* were fantastic, in countries as far afield as Australia, Zimbabwe, the United States, Slovenia, Israel and New Zealand. It was particularly big in Holland and we frequently went over there on personal appearances to open shops or sign autographs.

We were fêted as big celebrities there and on one visit to Holland we had police motorcycle outriders accompanying our vehicle convoy. On another we were in a horse-drawn tram and Dutch crowds were lining the streets to see us pass by. That particular trip had its frightening moments too. We were in one building signing autographs and a right panic ensued. People were pushing against the counter, so much so, that we were practically crushed against the wall. Ah well, all in a day's work, I suppose but it was lovely to think that we were so much appreciated by the Dutch people.

On one of my last trips to Amsterdam with the *AYBS?* team, we went to film on a Sunday in a very smart department store. It must be every shopaholic's dream, to be let loose in a department store, with a credit card, and no other shoppers to get in the way! I was up and down the stairs like greased lightning. We were there to film a sketch which was actually the prize in a Dutch television channel's competition – the two winners got to act in a sketch with us! As Mollie wasn't with us, Trevor had to dress up as Mrs Slocombe. The rest of us were our usual characters. An older man had won the prize to be Young Mr Grace and a young girl to be his secretary. The young girl was very excited to be with us. 'I can't believe I'm here with you – it's just wonderful!' she said, adding 'And you all look so old!' 'That's because we are darling,' drawled Trevor.

CHAPTER THIRTEEN

Mrs Thorpe

In July 1980 I married Will Thorpe. We had been together for six years before our marriage but it had been a tempestuous time and we'd split up six times. Each time we split we'd both gone out with other people but neither of us were happy and we always drifted back together again. As many women who have been beaten up would admit, if you really love a man, there's a compulsion to return, even though you suspect it's not good for you. It was the same with Will and I. He kept promising he would change and that everything would be all right for us. I had severe pre-wedding nerves, wondering whether to believe him but we were both determined to make a real go of things.

We married at Marylebone Town Hall Register Office. Gaston from the French House gave me away and we held our reception at his pub. Afterwards we went on a luxurious honeymoon around the champagne districts of France visiting Épernay, Rheims, Beaune and Bordeaux. The honeymoon was wonderful but while travelling back to Boulogne for our return ferry crossing we had an argument. In Boulogne Will went one way and I, the other. I made my way to the beach and must have fallen asleep in the sun because next thing I remember I was awakening with a start, only to see our ferry leaving the harbour. The problem was Will had both sets of travel tickets and passports!

A right fiasco ensued as I attempted to sort out the problem of lack of documentation with port officials. Meanwhile, Will thought I was on the boat, hiding away from him in the ladies' toilets. Somebody actually reported him to the purser for loitering around the toilet door! He was taken before the purser in order to explain his behaviour.

After much ado I was allowed to catch the next ferry leaving port. I met a very polite American gentleman on the crossing, who bought me dinner and several glasses of wine. As it turned out I had quite a pleasant trip back while Will, after his humiliating episode with the purser, was left waiting for me on the other side.

'I can't let you out of my sight for one moment,' he complained as soon as we met up again. I tell you, I just could not stop laughing. Neither, could any of our friends, when I told all of them the story!

'Fancy leaving your new wife behind in France on your honeymoon,' was all Will heard for weeks afterwards.

A month after our wedding I had to leave London for a provincial tour of Portman Theatrical Productions version of Noel Coward's play *Blithe Spirit* in which I played Edith the maid. I was very unhappy in the production because I thought two of the cast were up to all sort of tricks to put me off, which made my life a misery. When I was performing Edith's main scene, where she's in a trance, they'd be laughing and giggling on the other side of the stage, which was very unfair. One of my friends even suggested that while I was supposed to be in the trance, I should wander across the stage as if I was sleep walking and slap them in the face. I nearly did but somehow resisted the temptation.

I desperately wanted to leave the tour and told my agent to

have me released from my contract because I couldn't stand it any longer. Then the stage manager pointed out to me: 'If it helps, you are earning more money than they are.' So I stayed on just out of spite!

Anna Quayle was Madame Arcati and she and I were terrible gigglers. The production was sponsored by the Tomkinsons Carpets company, so to stop myself giggling when I sang 'I'll Be Loving You Always', I stared at the carpet. Then one night I realized if you looked at the carpet in a certain way you could see Daffy Duck in the pattern. Suddenly, I heard Anna's voice: 'That's enough singing, Edith.'

At which point I realized I hadn't been singing at all, instead I'd almost hypnotised myself staring at the carpet.

Another night when we were in Lincoln we were running slightly late towards the end of the play. In one scene I had a bandage on my head and had to come rushing through a door which had garlic garlands surrounding it. Suddenly, the bells of Lincoln cathedral rang out and the crescendo caused a piece of garlic to fall off and hit me on the head. Well, I thought Anna was going to wet herself, she was laughing so much. How we got through to the end of the scene I don't know, it was absolute hysteria!

So it wasn't all bad but I did discover during this tour that I wasn't really cut out for this sort of acting. I love pantos and it's great working to a live audience – I've given my best to them all – but I realized that I couldn't possibly do a long run in a stage play. I would feel far too restricted having to turn up at a theatre six evenings a week and possibly for a couple of matinees as well. It'd be much too repetitive for me doing the same thing night after night. I'm the first to admit that I've a short attention span and I'd just get bored with the same old lines time and time again. No, I much prefer the type of acting that I have mainly stuck to throughout my career – series with ever-changing lines – I like the variety that goes with it and for me, it seems much more challenging.

Richmond was one more stop on our tour and another venue was the Devonshire Park Theatre in Eastbourne. Aunty Betty lived in Eastbourne and her son, Norman was in the police force there. I hadn't seen her for years, so we took the opportunity of meeting up. I was pleased to see her again after so long but I was very worried about her because she seemed very depressed. I never saw her again because shortly afterwards, Aunty Betty died.

In 1981 the BBC commissioned an eighth series of *Are You Being Served?* Unfortunately, Trevor Bannister was unable to continue in the role of Mr Lucas because he had already accepted another part in a tour of *Middle Age Spread*. John and I especially missed Trevor's banter. His place as junior salesman in menswear was taken by Mr Spooner, played admirably by Mike Berry, who had been a successful pop singer in the 1960s with hits like 'Tribute to Buddy Holly'. He'd also made a big comeback record 'The Sunshine of Your Smile' in 1980 the year before he joined us.

Again there were seven episodes and we also did another Christmas special, *Roots* which was transmitted on Christmas Eve. *Roots* was Harold Bennett's last appearance as Young Mr Grace, the lecherous department store co-owner. Harold had made a wonderful job of the role, along with his stock phrase of 'You've all done very well!' He died that year of a heart attack, aged 82 and was a sad loss to the show. That episode will likely never be repeated on TV since all the cast but Shirley were blacked up for the finale, which wouldn't go down too well these days!

In between series of *Are You Being Served?* when I was having a lean time workwise, my friend Richard Price, who during the

1970s had put me in various sitcoms at London Weekend Television, was again very good to me. He booked me as a panellist for many of the game shows the company did at the time and I was jolly grateful for the £50 or £75 that they paid. It fed me and the cat!

One game show contestant I had to partner on the *Pyramid Game* sat down opposite me on the set just before the programme was due to commence recording. 'I've got to win a lot of money because I'm overdrawn at the bank,' she whispered into my ear. Well, that certainly put the onus on me! I did do my best for her but unfortunately she was none too quick about catching on to the clues I was giving her. So I doubt our joint efforts made much of a dent in her overdraft!

By 1982 my relationship with Will had deteriorated very badly, despite our best intentions. On several occasions, when Will started to become violent, I escaped from my flat in Baker Street and slept overnight across the road at Andy and Mireille Archer's house. Other times I'd walk the streets and, on occasions, shelter in an underground station for warmth.

The physical violence was hell enough but his verbal abuse was wearing me down beyond measure. In the end, I had to call a halt to our marriage. I had an idea someone was going to end up dead and I was damn certain it wasn't going to be me. We decided to split up permanently and certainly not in the happiest of circumstances.

Looking back I don't know why I put up with all the aggro and violence. I must have been crazy but I suppose I kept on hoping he would change and that I could help him. It wasn't only our relationship that suffered as a result of his drinking, it was his career too – such a waste. Although we had a highly volatile marriage, if it hadn't been for his bouts of heavy boozing, I'm certain we would have stayed together. What a pity, Will and I could have been a very formidable team and if we had remained a couple, through our respective careers, would have made a lot of money together.

I shall say nothing further about Will. I feel through the years he has had more than enough dragged up in the Press about his behaviour towards me. Not always from my lips, I hasten to add . . .

Yet again I found myself at a low ebb. My second marriage had ended in ruins and once more I felt very alone.

Working again with the lovely cast of *Are You Being Served?* provided a respite from that loneliness, when we were asked to do a ninth series of six episodes in 1983 but this time the BBC didn't want a Christmas special.

Later that year I was booked to do a summer season with Dora Bryan at The Pavilion Theatre in Weymouth. *Let's Go Camping* turned out to be a disaster. We were doing very little business in the Dorset resort and then, half-way through the run, I put my back out and was unable to continue. I spent the remainder of the summer nursing a bad back, while an understudy took over my role.

One saving grace from the disastrous Weymouth summer season was that I became friends with David and Lizzie Wiggins. Even though they have just recently moved to Spain, we are very much in touch and Lizzie has been invaluable in the writing of this book. When I appeared in pantomime they would travel up from Weymouth to attend the last night. We've had some good parties over the years!

John Inman was doing a summer season in St Helier, Jersey at the time, a play called *Pyjama Tops*. He had rented a lovely house on the island and invited me over for the weekend. As I'd had such a miserable time in my Weymouth summer show, I jumped at the chance of spending a couple of days in the Channel Islands with my friend, knowing I would be guaranteed a good laugh.

John introduced me to one of the local businessmen, a restaurant owner named Herbie Buchholz (his brother's the famous German film actor, Horst). He and his delightful wife, Barbie ran Banks wine bar/restaurant in King's Street, St Helier and were very active in the local branch of the children's charity, the Variety Club of Great Britain.

Together with comedian Pat Mooney, Herbie had started up the Monday Club on the island, a fundraising luncheon which was attended by business people and the various artistes who were appearing in the many shows staged in Jersey. A lot of money was raised at the Monday Club luncheons but needless to say, an awful lot of wine was consumed into the bargain. Fortunately Monday was a free day for most shows. Everyone had such a good time and Herbie was a very kind and generous man. I left with even more happy memories of Jersey, the few days with John Inman had done me the world of good.

One of the many aspects of his career in which John excels is pantomime. I, too, was to discover how great a pleasure pantomime is for any actor or actress, when I was invited to do my first over the Christmas/New Year period of 1983–84.

It was *Cinderella* with Dickie Henderson and Jack Douglas, at The Orchard Theatre in Dartford. I was Dandini, Jane Fyffe was Prince Charming and Sandi Toksvig was the Fairy Godmother. I thought I was in for an easy time. Then I heard Dickie Henderson saying, 'This is where I'll do such and such a routine – she'll do it with me. Then I'll do so and so and she'll do it with me.' I was never off! He was such a generous actor that I ended up being in the whole thing.

Dickie, who was an old-hander at it, taught me a vast amount about acting in a panto. One of the main things I learned from him was that on-stage jokes might be funny to those on stage but they usually mean nothing to the people sat in the audience. I agreed with that principle because as punters have paid good money for their tickets to come and see you, they must be treated with respect.

We made up for it by having a lot of fun backstage. Dickie nicknamed me 'Tonto'. Why I never knew, until someone told me that Tonto is apparently Spanish slang for 'stupid'.

''ere, Dickie, why are you calling me stupid? I've just found out what Tonto really means!' I asked.

'My dear, Tonto, would I ever call you "stupid",' he replied, burst out laughing and walked away. I took no offence and still have his autographed photo – 'To Tonto, thanking you for a lot of laughs, love Dickie' – framed on the wall of my office today.

As the years progressed, I would eventually find myself participating in a further three pantomimes but as I look back, my first *Cinderella* with dear Dickie – for whom I had tremendous respect – beat the lot and was the happiest I was involved in.

CHAPTER FOURTEEN

East 8

On a personal level, life had improved. I'd started a relationship with a younger chap – OK a toy boy, I suppose you would say. He was twelve years younger than me and was an artists' agent, working at Andy Archer's.

On the career side, things looked like they might improve too when a few months later I bumped into astrologer Russell Grant at the BBC. Russell told me I was approaching a time when important decisions would have to be made but that everything would work out fine for me. I cannot tell you what a boost that was to my ego. I've been interested in astrology since a teenager. Since the 1970s I had regularly visited the clairvoyant and medium called Don Galloway, whom Derek Keller introduced me to. I still use clairvoyance today, for guidance on professional and personal matters. I also find it very comforting to be told by mediums about those you've lost who were close to you and to be assured that they are happy in their new spirit life. I am absolutely certain that I will see my parents again one day and that is a great consolation to me.

In 1984 we made the final seven episodes of *Are You Being Served?* and they were shown during 1984 with a re-run in the spring of 1985. We'd enjoyed a successful run for thirteen years since the pilot in 1972 and had produced a total of sixty-nine episodes. I was devastated when we had to shut up shop, as it were, for the last time. However, as David Croft stressed: 'I would like to take the show off while it is at the top.' Which it was, regularly having attracted viewing figures in excess of twenty million.

The BBC had liked *AYBS?* because it could all be filmed inside without expensive location shots but that had limited our storylines somewhat. In reality, we knew it would finish sooner rather than later but it was very sad for us all when the team split up. We had become such a tight-knit family community after all those years together.

My career at the time was being looked after by a lovely man called John Mahoney. After *Are You Being Served?* finished I did a couple of one-off comedy shows. Then one day my agent had a telephone call from Julia Smith. I'd worked with her before when she was a young director on *The Newcomers*. In more recent years she had become a very powerful lady in the drama department at the BBC, having directed *Z Cars*, *Doctor Who* and *Doctor Finlay's Casebook* and produced *Angels* along the way. Apparently Julia asked John 'What's Wendy like these days? Is she still the same, or has she become grand?'

'Oh yes, she's still the same Wendy all right; she hasn't changed much,' he told her.

'Well, I'm ringing because I've got an idea which I'm putting together for a new soap on BBC that will rival *Coronation Street* for its top slot in the TV ratings. Wendy might be interested. It is not a glamorous role at all but I want her to do it.'

The project, which was all very hush-hush, was codenamed East 8.

I went to see Julia and the co-creator Tony Holland. Tony was an actor who had turned scriptwriter and editor for the BBC. He

112

and Julia had worked closely together on *Angels* and they outlined their new story idea to me. Tony told me the programme would not duck social issues but would be a hard-hitting drama including teenage pregnancy, drugs, racial conflict, prostitution, rape, mental illness, homosexuality, alcoholism and muggings among its subjects. In order to carry such strong subject matter, they'd invented some pretty powerful characters to whom things just naturally happened.

According to Tony Holland, two families – the Fowlers and the Beales, who were to form the core of the storylines in Albert Square – were based on real people, who were part of his own East End family. If I accepted, my character was to be Pauline Fowler. A middle-aged mother of two teenagers, with a late baby on the way, Pauline worked part-time in a launderette, voted Labour and supported Arsenal. She was married to Arthur, who was out of work and was really a bit of a failure, not much good at anything in life.

Pauline was a stark contrast to buxom bombshell Miss Brahms but it certainly sounded like a strong and challenging role. Although it would be such a huge transformation of my screen image, it was after all my twenty-fifth year in show business and I'd already realized that I couldn't carry on playing dolly birds forever.

By the time the programme was televized it would be exactly twenty years since I had last starred in a new BBC soap – *The Newcomers*. By coincidence, that too had been intended as a rival to *Coronation Street* but then I'd played a teenage daughter. Now the roles would be reversed and I'd be playing a mother of a teenage daughter. I knew right away I would be mad to turn down the part of Pauline. However, there was one drawback.

Julia said to me: 'I'm afraid you will have to change your appearance – including your hair. It must be cut!' I was very

113

proud of my long hair, which had taken me years to grow. I hadn't had it cut short for nineteen years but reluctantly, I agreed. Perhaps that was one of Russell's 'important decisions'! It certainly was for me, I cried my eyes out for the rest of the day after that traumatic hair cut.

In the autumn I was called to Threshold House at Shepherd's Bush, where I was introduced to Bill Treacher, who was to play my husband Arthur. I also met Anna Wing, who was to be my mother Lou Beale; Susan Tully, my daughter Michelle and a very quiet young man called David Scarboro, who was to play my oldest son, Mark. Sue Tully was a familiar face to younger viewers, having played Suzanne Ross in *Grange Hill*, the BBC children's drama set in a London comprehensive school.

At a later meeting I was introduced to Peter Dean, who was to play my twin brother, Peter Beale, who ran a stall in the market. Peter was ideal for the role because he was a former market trader himself, who'd been spotted by actress, Prunella Scales (Sybil in *Fawlty Towers*) and it was she who suggested he go to drama school. I also met Gillian Taylforth, who was to be my sister-in-law, Kathy and Adam Woodyatt my nephew, Ian Beale. That, in a nutshell, was our little family unit. The casting of *EastEnders* was masterminded by Jonathan McLeish: it was he who brought Anita Dobson into the cast and, years later, James Alexandrou.

The plan was for the action to revolve around Albert Square, in Walford E20, a decaying Victorian area of private and council houses, complete with a pub called the Queen Victoria, a street market, shop and a café. In time I was introduced to Leslie Grantham who was to be pub landlord, Dennis Watts. Also I met Jean Fennell, the first girl whom they had cast as his wife, Angie Watts.

From September 1984 I was involved in a whole series of pre-production meetings covering every angle, from hair to costume design and make-up. All aspects were discussed in the minutest detail, the BBC wanted to ensure absolutely everything was just right for their new flagship soap.

The Corporation had recently bought the old ATV Elstree Studios at Borehamwood in Hertfordshire. It was on an old back lot there that the outdoor action for *EastEnders* would take place. All the indoor scenes would be shot inside the studios there. Full marks were particularly due to Keith Harris – or Bomber Harris, as he was known – for his superb design of the outside lot. Keith had been painstaking in his research around the East End, in order make sure that Albert Square looked realistic. Credit must also be paid to the chaps who built it because years later when we had that major gale – the one that Michael Fish never saw coming – I wondered what state Albert Square would be in when we returned to work next morning. Not a slate was missing, the whole construction was still standing, completely intact.

In October 1984, even before anything had been recorded, we had a massive Press call attended by most of the national newspapers and major magazines. I remember walking on to the lot and looking around Albert Square where there were hundreds of photographers, standing on scaffolding, waiting to get a shot. The exterior set had taken six months to build and was so realistic, it was fantastic. I knew immediately: 'This is it. This series is not going to be just a five-minute job, it will run and run and run.' I had that feeling in my bones. I knew the programme was going to be *SPECIAL*.

When we started filming in November 1984, Tony and Julia already had 102 scripts in the bag. As Jonathan Powell, head of BBC drama commented at the time: 'There is nothing tentative about our commitment to *EastEnders*. We begin as we mean to go on – absolutely confidently.'

The characters had been built in as minute detail as the scripts, with full biographical details on each from the time of their birth. It was vital we should get to know our own characters intimately and so the cast initially sat together in family groups to learn our lines and bond with our 'relations'. You couldn't go on to the screen being cold with each other, it was essential to develop the rapport that families, who'd been together for years, would naturally have. Anna Wing and myself even helped organize the interiors of our own 'homes' on the set, placing the furniture, crockery etc. where we felt it should go – after all we were supposed to have lived in the house for years.

Every detail of production was comprehensively discussed, inside out. A great deal of care was also taken over script content. Bill Lyons, whom I mentioned earlier as one of my fellow drama school students, was one of our early scriptwriters and that was very nice for me because it made me feel more at home.

The next stage was for us to complete several screen tests but it was very frustrating for the cast because it felt as if we were working in a vacuum. Nothing had been transmitted thus far and we didn't know what we looked like in our parts on screen, or how we interacted with each other and our new surroundings.

I very well remember my first ever scene on the lot – I had to work in the middle of a snow blizzard! So too did Gretchen Franklin, who was playing Ethel, a long-standing close friend of my mother Lou Beale. Gretchen had started her showbiz career as a chorus girl in a Bournemouth panto and had risen to become a well-respected veteran actress. She was the darling of the West End stage during the War in such big hits as *Sweet and Low* and *Sweetest and Lowest*. As *EastEnders* progressed we were to witness that Gretchen had lost none of her former sparkle, in some of the party scenes on the set it was always Gretchen who was doing the high kicks!

But on our first ever outside scene together in those wintry

Meeting Diana, 1991.

Potato planting for *Grace & Favour*, 1992. (BBC)

The *AYBS?* team down on the farm with Billy Burden and 'that cow'. (BBC)

Me and Billy Burden. (BBC)

With dearest love to Wendy, Paul and Shirley xxx

My favourite picture of Mollie and Shirley on lunch break while filming *Grace & Favour*, taken by John Inman. (Author's Collection)

Me and John on location for *Grace & Favour*. (Author's Collection)

Miss Brahms gives
you her Portia.
(Author's Collection)

Blithe Spirit, 1980, where
I discovered that long
runs weren't my cup of
tea.

Me as Dandini in
Cinderella, Hayes,
Middlesex.

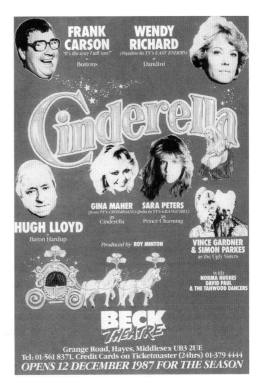

Fairy godmother, 1989, Bromley.
(Author's Collection)

Me and one of my fans, Sharon Kielty, on my wedding day to Paul – this is the only picture of the day that I've kept. (Author's Collection)

Here I am leaving the Princess Grace after my cancer operation, 1996. (Picture by Arthur Edwards, *Sun*)

John meeting HRH Princess Royal – unusually lost for words... (Doug McKenzie)

Chatting with John Major – another committed Archers fan.

My number one son, Todd Carty and me. (Author's Collection)

Me and my second son, James Alexandrou. James is lovely and sends me a
Mother's Day card every year. (Author's Collection)

conditions, it wasn't poor old Ethel but her dog, Willy, the pug, who was much better wrapped up than either Gretchen or myself! It was so cold, even the cameras were wrapped for protection. My face was frozen, so much so that I even considered right there and then just jacking the whole thing in. I cannot stand the cold. If I have to suffer I'd rather be starving hungry than cold.

That was my ordeal by snow, with Gretchen on the lot but anyway, despite the conditions we finished the first ever day-shoot on time.

The following morning we were sitting in the green room at Neptune House out at the Borehamwood studios when the floor manager, Robert Gabriel came rushing in. He told us 'Right you can all go home, everybody just go!'

Feeling rather confused, we all left.

In the early days of shooting *EastEnders* I used to try and do the return journey by train and so did Leslie Grantham. We walked to the station together, wondering what on earth was happening back at the studios.

Next day when we returned to work we discovered that Jean Fennell, the girl who'd originally been cast as Angie Watts had had her contract withdrawn. According to Julia, she somehow hadn't come to grips with the 'Angie', that she and Tony Holland had originally visualized. As it turned out Jean was not to be in *EastEnders* at all and Angie's role was to be recast, which must have been the most horrendous thing to happen to any actress. It made everyone feel a little apprehensive, fearing if one of us had been fired so soon, who else could be for the chop?

Anyway, Julia started searching for a new Angie and the role was given to Anita Dobson. One of the television critics subsequently wrote that Anita had enough energy to light up all the lights in Albert Square and it was true. The way Anita and

Leslie worked together was fantastic, they were pure dynamite.

By the same token, Bill Treacher and I worked extremely well together too. On occasions they would give us a scene to do at the very last minute. We had to learn our lines and perform it literally within hours. This happened to regulars like Anita and Leslie as well. I guess they realized that whenever they were under-running, or something had gone wrong, they could rely on us to do a scene and get it in the can in time.

The research department at *EastEnders* has always taken fantastic care over the work they do on storylines. Apart from entertaining, at times we also have to put across a public message. So it is important that we have the full facts. For example, at the beginning when Pauline was expecting a late baby, we included scenes about her having amniocentesis tests.

Pauline is a grafter and while she was pregnant she took on cleaning work, helped part-time in the launderette and had a third job as well, in order to bring money into the home while Arthur was out of work. In one scene she collapsed, was rushed to hospital and ordered to rest before the baby was born.

The pregnancy situation did have its amusing side though. During the very first episode there was a scene in which Pauline and Arthur had to break the news to the matriarchal Lou Beale about the baby. Lou ranted and raved, telling Pauline: 'Why can't you be like your brother, Peter and Kathy? They only had one child, so they can have lovely things. They have a television and a video and all sorts of other nice belongings.'

With that she stormed off upstairs and I was supposed to call after her 'I'd rather have a baby than nice things, any day.'

Unfortunately, I got my lines round the wrong way and shouted upstairs 'I'd rather have all those nice things than a baby, any day!'

In due course because of the longer schedules and frequent

unsociable hours, it became too difficult for me to travel to work by train. So I started to take a cab over to Bill Treacher's flat. He lived nearby in Paddington and he gave me a lift into work. Later I found a cab company, set up an account and travelled backwards and forwards alone, sometimes picking up Anna Wing on the way to work.

There was a tremendous amount of hanging about on set in the early days before the show went out. The system became much more streamlined as the programme developed but it was so fast-moving and chaotic in the beginning that people wondered what they had let themselves in for. The initial situation was also made worse because nothing had yet been televized and we were working on episodes that even we weren't allowed to see because everything was being kept very hush-hush. It was an extremely difficult and frustrating time for the cast.

Despondency crept in and one afternoon everybody became particularly pissed off with the whole state of affairs. I tried to lift their spirits by pointing out, 'One day you are going to be really famous and you will have a good career in this. Come on, you mustn't take this attitude. Be positive.' I did my best to buck them up and some rallied. Eventually though, to alleviate the tension, it was decided to show the first two episodes to the cast. They took us all off to a large empty rehearsal room, where they had set up screens and laid on refreshments for us. We watched the episodes and that did the trick in alleviating the tension – they were really good, something to be proud of!

That's what we all felt too when *EastEnders* eventually hit the screens for the first time at 7p.m. on Tuesday 19 February 1985 – and had 17 million viewers watching it. The programme grabbed headlines and that is exactly what the BBC wanted. *EastEnders* led the way, right from its infancy. Initially, some newspaper TV critics claimed it was too fast moving but if you look at soaps today, they seem to have taken their lead from us. I believe scenes should never be too long anyhow; they should move at a pace to keep the viewers' interest.

It is what Julia Smith and Tony Holland had intended all along. As Julia said at the time, 'Neither of us believed in the kind of slow start where people say, "Let's see what develops." Instead, we wanted to create the feeling, here we are folks, we've arrived.

'We started with a bang because there doesn't seem any point in pussyfooting around. We weren't concerned about being nice, we wanted to show we meant business.'

In the beginning it was programme policy not to cast well known actors and actress as characters in *EastEnders*. As I was one of the few known faces in the cast, initially I was used heavily to promote the programme in newspapers and magazines, on radio and television. In fact launch week was very busy for me and not just to do with *EastEnders*.

My face was never off the box, on Monday 18 February I was a guest on the first ever *Wogan* show. Tuesday night was the launch of *EastEnders*, Wednesday evening I appeared in a repeat episode of *Dad's Army*. On Thursday it was the second episode of *EastEnders*, on Friday I was in a re-run of *Are You being Served?*, on Saturday? – well, nothing unfortunately – but on Sunday it was the omnibus edition of *EastEnders*!

For many in the cast, this was their first brush with television fame and dealing with this was sometimes difficult. You have to remember what an incredibly intense spotlight *Eastenders* was under at the beginning. It was a tense time but usually there was something to lighten the mood. I remember one day when we were all slumped about our sixth floor green room. Gilly Taylforth suddenly appeared at the windows, pretending to clean them. I nearly passed out with fright. There were some workmen outside and Gilly thought it would be a good idea to go up in the cherry-picker they were using. That was typical of Gilly – always joking and laughing. You don't really realize how much you miss her until she comes back for a short spell and cheers you all up again. She always remembered everyone's birthdays as well.

As soon as the programme became popular the BBC asked us to do a sing-along album of old Cockney songs, such as 'Knees Up Mother Brown' and the like. It was to be recorded on a Sunday but I was determined I didn't want to give up my only free day of the week. We were already working twelve hours a day, six days a week and Sunday was my one day of rest, when I could potter at home and do essentials like washing and ironing. I can't sing anyway, so there didn't seem much point in my taking part. Although I didn't participate many of the others did. Like Bill, for instance, who commented to me soon afterwards: 'Julia is thrilled with the album and says she's humming some of the songs already.' I thought it a strange comment to make, taking into account that most of the songs were old traditional favourites which would have already been well known from years previously.

As a result of the strenuous schedule I was too shattered for much of a social life. John and I seemed happy enough though. Besides being a very intelligent young man, he was witty and always clowning around, which relieved some of the stresses and strains from work. He had moved in with me in my flat in Baker Street but shortly after *EastEnders* got off the ground, my Aunty Elsie died. According to her brother, she left no will. So the proceeds from the sale of her property, furniture and other belongings were divided among her surviving relatives. Being her sister's daughter, I received what would have been Mummy's share. It came at a fortuitous time for me because Richard Price, head of casting at LWT, had recently told me of a lovely flat up for sale in his block in W1 which was very close to Baker Street.

With the *EastEnders* contract then in the bag, I was able to secure a mortgage and buy the flat. John and I decided to go 50/50 on the mortgage.

Most viewers would know one of the main features in Pauline's home is the fruit bowl on the table. There was a bit of a carry-on one day and so someone wrote the word 'Bollocks' on a banana in the bowl. Fortunately it was noticed before recording but we never knew who the culprit was because obviously no one would own up. That bowl became quite a joke between me and some of the cameramen because often when we were shooting a scene sat at the table, they would try and move it in order to obtain a better camera angle.

'Keep your hands off my fruit bowl!' I always warned them because I'm very protective of the possessions in my television house.

Although it was a bit of a laugh, on the more serious side, I'm certain viewers don't like change and if they are accustomed to seeing the fruit bowl, it should remain in the room. Over the years people have become used to seeing Pauline's home a certain way, though it has, in fact, been redecorated twice since the show began.

The whole idea of *EastEnders* when it first started was that it was intended to be a fly-on-the-wall in people's homes. I firmly believe that was the main reason for the popularity of the programme from its early days. We're all basically nosey and by watching the programme viewers can have a nose into someone's house: what do you have for breakfast, who's gossiping about whom, how do you cook your Sunday lunch? All the strange and ordinary events of people's daily lives appeal to viewers' curiosity.

Each time we had a new director, I would ask them: 'Now, have they warned you about me? I'm no good with props. I can't walk and talk at the same time. I'm not very good at opening and closing doors . . . but I am all right doing sitting down scenes, or making a cup of tea.'

When Bill Gilmore, a Scottish director, joined us we were due to film a scene between Bill Treacher and myself outside the launderette. Bill Gilmore stood there, holding a broom: 'I think I might have you sweeping the pavement,' he suggested to me.

'What?' I demanded.

I could see all the crew beginning to laugh but he repeated his suggestion. I narrowed my eyes and stared at him silently. Then, Brian, one of the props boys came forward, walked between the two of us and whisked the broom away, telling poor Bill Gilmore 'See, I told you she wouldn't fucking do it!'

In one of the early episodes the Beales and the Fowlers visited a churchyard to look at Pauline's dad's grave. The programme's designers had obviously gone to a great deal of trouble to find a suitable location. There was a grave in the churchyard which hadn't been touched for many years, so they cleaned it to pretend that was Albert Beale's and do you know . . . as they pulled the creepers away from the stone, the name of the family buried there emerged – Beale! What a spooky coincidence that was.

Right from the beginning of the series someone was always starting up a rumour about *EastEnders*. All types of stories began circulating in the papers and tongues started wagging as to who was leaking information. On principle, I would never dream of leaking a story about anybody. Yet, at times, the finger of suspicion was pointed in my direction, which I was very cross about. Especially as I thought that the person probably responsible for the leaks was trying to detract from their own misdeeds with the Press. The situation escalated when it was revealed that as a young man and while in the army in Germany, Leslie Grantham had served a long spell in prison for murdering a taxi driver.

We all suffered in one way or another and it was never very pleasant. In the early days, no one, not even the BBC, was prepared for the insatiable and high level press interest. So it felt like we were on our own. We've all learned though and these days on *EastEnders* now there are strict guidelines about our contact with the Press in an effort to protect actors and the show. All we could do was rally around and support each other but it was horrible to see one of your mates sat in a corner crying their eyes out because some nasty piece had appeared about them in a paper.

Despite always being willing to offer mutual support, we do respect each other's private lives as private. When the Leslie Grantham story hit the headlines I was one of the first to see him on the set that morning. I simply enquired him if he was OK. 'Yes, thanks, mate' was all he said and it was all that needed to be said.

One of the main people to suffer at the hands of the Press, was David Scarboro, who first played my son, Mark. David was finding it difficult to cope with being in *EastEnders* because of the sudden-found fame and stress of a heavy workload.

So Julia and Tony decided to write his character out of the series for a while, which meant a hectic round of script re-writes in early 1985. It transpired that Mark Fowler left home and naturally, Pauline and Arthur were frantically worried about his whereabouts. In real life David had a breakdown and spent some time in hospital.

After a while the producers agreed to give David another chance, to see how he would cope. They created a good storyline and in one episode Pauline, Arthur and Michelle travelled to Southend searching for Mark. When Pauline and Arthur finally tracked Mark down, they discovered that he was living with a Swedish girl and her two small children, who referred to Mark as Daddy! I remember David and I had a lovely scene on Southend

Beach – the first time that *EastEnders* had done outside location work.

It was a bitterly cold day and snowing, and I said to him: 'When we walk along talking, David, put your arm around me.'

'Why?' he asked.

I told him: 'Because that is what the public wants to see.'

I forgot I was miked up at the time but Julia and Tony who were in the control box must have heard me. We did the scene, which was very touching and afterwards Julia was kind enough to comment to me: 'Well done, Wendy, you know what it's all about.'

However, life in the limelight with all its inherent pressures was still too much for David. Over the following three years, he did return to the series but only for short periods. We were very saddened three years later in 1988 when we received the most terrible news – David had thrown himself off Beachy Head and taken his own life. It may seem harsh but I firmly believe the Press literally hounded that lad to his death. Some months later they did a television documentary on David and as the lawyer representing his parents commented: 'Corpses cannot sue for libel.' David's treatment at the hands of the Press was so unfair. If he had lived, he would have been a teenage idol. David had the looks and the girls loved him. He had everything going for him.

Unfortunately, money caused several disagreements early on. The original format which had been agreed was we should do two episodes a week and an omnibus version on Sundays for which, they suggested, we would be paid an extra ten per cent of our fee – if we were all agreeable.

I certainly felt it was worth more than any ten per cent. We had a company meeting with a representative from the actors' union, Equity, in attendance. Some people were prepared to settle for ten per cent but the majority of us wanted to bump up the figure. In the end, it was decided we should receive eighty per cent of our fee – quite a big difference to the initial suggestion.

In the very early days of *EastEnders* Pauline used to talk a lot about Dot Cotton, Nick Cotton's Mum, who helped her in the launderette. Although she was spoken of often, she did not actually appear on screen until episode 40 in July 1985. So it was quite exciting waiting to see who was to play Dot Cotton. Of course that turned out to be the wonderful actress, June Brown and no one could have portrayed the role better than her. June is Dot Cotton. She put such a mark on the character right from the beginning. I admire June tremendously, she is a true professional and pays great attention to every detail about Dot.

I also have to say that from day one, Nick Cotton – played superbly by John Altman – has always been the best villain in *EastEnders*. A case of local boy made bad – and everyone loves to hate him! It is always a joy when he makes a return appearance and indeed, it's also wonderful now having June permanently back in the series.

What a year 1985 had turned out to be for me, as Pauline. There had not been a let up in her storylines. Right from episode one with the murder of Reg Cox and Pauline's teenage son, Mark (a mate of the dastardly Nick Cotton) implicated in the murder. As if Pauline didn't have enough on her plate, with Arthur out of work and a new baby on the way, which her mother, Lou Beale wanted her to abort.

As the early episodes developed, Mark became involved with a racist organization called The New Movement, Nick was tempting him on to heroin and to escape everything, he ran away from Walford, much to Pauline and Arthur's great anguish.

No sooner had Pauline's new baby arrived on the scene in July than she was aghast to discover that her schoolgirl daughter,

Michelle was pregnant. Michelle refused to have an abortion, or tell anyone the identity of the father of her baby.

The icing on the cake of the first year of success of *EastEnders* was when the cast was asked to participate in the Royal Command Performance on 24 November. It was held at the Theatre Royal in Drury Lane in front of Her Majesty Queen Elizabeth, the Queen Mother. Fergie was also present that evening, as were the Ogilvys. I cannot tell you how excited I was because it is always a credit for any performer to say that you have at least one Royal Variety under your belt.

The show is definitely a marathon. Ours seemed to go on forever and I began to feel sorry for the audience having to sit through it for such a long time. The *EastEnders* crowd were housed at the nearby Waldorf Hotel, where rooms had been made available for us to use as dressing rooms.

When we were backstage before the show, the area was completely crowded out with hundreds of artistes, including Paul McCartney who was appearing with his group Wings. Despite the hubbub, Paul made a point of coming over to speak to me.

'Hi Wendy! It's been a long time since we did *Help!* but I have followed your career since and I am so pleased that you are doing well,' he told me.

You can imagine how thrilled I was that he had come over. We started chatting and reminiscing about the early days and that film, when his wife, Linda, walked up and Paul introduced her to me. It was a lovely moment and I felt extremely flattered that Paul had remembered me and been so utterly charming.

It was only topped by the biggest thrill of the evening for me – being introduced to the Queen Mother in the Royal line-up after the show.

It had been a year of hard slog on *EastEnders* but careerwise, I was riding on the crest of a wave following the huge success of the show since it was first televised in February. As the end of the year approached, I began to look forward to a well-earned break over Christmas.

CHAPTER FIFTEEN

Pauline and The Press

Just when it looked as if I had everything going for me, my relationship with John Holmes disintegrated, right before Christmas, of all times. It was the pressures of my work that drove us apart. The schedules were so punishing, with me often working well into the evening, that it all started to get him down.

Then, as so often happens when a woman is involved with a man much younger than herself, he had met a younger girl. John decided he wanted to be with her and so we separated. I paid him £8,000 – his share of the deposit that he'd paid out on our new flat – and thought that was the end of that.

It seemed after two failed marriages and now, a broken romance, I was destined to spend the rest of my life alone.

I was indeed on my own for several months but work continued to take up so much of my time and there wasn't much chance to think of the loneliness.

Nineteen eighty-six wasn't much of an easy year for Pauline either, she didn't know if she was coming or going with all her family's carryings-on. The weak but well-meaning Lofty proposed to Michelle, she turned him down, then changed her mind. Pauline's first grandchild, Vicki was born in May but Michelle had to return to school immediately afterwards to take her exams.

By that time in my own personal life I had met Paul Glorney. Paul, a tall, good looking Irishman – who worked as a carpet fitter – was eight years younger than me. I knew his brother, Sean, who worked as a porter in a block of flats nearby. One night I saw the two brothers together in my local and cracked a joke about them which made Paul smile. He had a lovely smile, which was the first thing that attracted me to him – along with his devilish sense of humour. Paul was charming and polite, not at all pushy. He mentioned that he had a wife, two daughters and a son who lived on the Isle of Wight but he had left the previous summer, following the break-up of his marriage. Anyway, after a while he started to walk me home from the pub each evening. Then he began to woo me with flowers and gradually our romance blossomed.

The early days of a new romance should have been an idyllic time but they were spoiled when John discovered I'd found someone else. Although he was in a relationship with another girl, for some reason or other, he did not like the idea of me going out with another man.

By that time the cheque book journalism concerning *EastEnders* was in full flow and the Press would pay *anyone* for a story to slag off a member of the cast. I would never have believed that John could have done such a thing but he did. He went to the Press with a series of stories about me. One installment appeared in the *News of the World* but through my solicitor I managed to obtain an injunction against the paper to stop any further material being published.

That is what life was like: my own ex-boyfriend sold me down the river, apparently for a fee of around £8,000. I have no idea whether he actually received his fee in the end, after the injunction was issued.

After the *News of the World* stories were suppressed, John

started to ring and leave messages on my answer machine. During one he alleged that he'd taken photographs of me while I was asleep and he intended to sell them to the newspapers. Fortunately, I was very friendly with two smashing girls in the CID, called Jackie Moulten and Sue Weston. I went to them to ask for help and they were absolutely brilliant. They advised me to arrange a meeting with John. A venue was arranged in Chingford, where I was taken to the local police station and miked up to record any conversation which might take place between us.

Eventually John turned up as arranged and we walked around and around for what seemed like an eternity. I kept asking him: 'Why are you doing this to me?'

He would not answer.

I told him: 'I have never done you any harm. I've paid you back any money that I owed you from the flat.'

He still didn't say a word but continued acting strangely.

Suddenly the police pounced. John blurted out repeatedly, 'Did you do this? Did you do this?'

I broke down in tears. It was a very nerve-wracking experience.

The police took him away for questioning and Sue Weston drove me home.

After questioning John at length, the police were convinced there really were no photographs. It had just been a blackmail threat. I decided not to press charges against John but I'm glad I made him realize that he couldn't attempt to blackmail me, or anyone else for that matter.

The end of my relationship with John and all that followed was but a foretaste of things to come. Exactly the same sort of situation happened to so many members of the cast. All sorts of ex-boyfriends and ex-girlfriends came out of the woodwork.

Anybody sold anything, simply to make money. It was all so tacky and totally unfair. I suppose it was just one of the things that as high profile personalities on television we had to put up with and unfortunately, it still goes on, even to this day.

Not all blasts from the past were unwelcome. For over twenty years people had continued to refer to that eternal record of 'Come Outside'. Ever since Mike Berry and I had started working together on *Are You Being Served?* in 1981 we'd joked that with Mike's previous experience in the pop business, it would be fun to do a follow-up version of the original disc.

Finally in 1986, thinking that my increased public profile in the role of Pauline might give a song an added push, we got around to doing so and teamed up with a mate of Mike's who had a recording studio. The new record was quite amusing and I did a bit of 'singing' on it, although I'm the first to admit I've no singing voice. What Mike and I did was to reverse roles: instead of the boy asking the girl to come outside, it was the other way around. Mike wrote the flip side himself, a song entitled 'Give it A Try'. We released the record in 1986 and the new 'Come Outside' made it into the Top 100 but that was about all it did. So, it was back to the day job!

Which involved a wedding for Pauline with Michelle and Lofty finally tying the knot in September. The Fowlers made plans, only for Pauline to find out – to her horror – that Arthur had withdrawn all the money from the Christmas club he organized, in order to pay for the reception. He needn't have bothered, as it turned out, Michelle called off the wedding at the last minute!

Realizing that he'd have to account for the missing funds, in November Arthur made a big point of withdrawing the savings for the pre-Christmas pay out, staged a fake robbery and claimed all the dosh had been stolen. That same month Michelle changed her mind – yet again – and did marry Lofty.

Under questioning, poor Arthur confessed to the police it was really him who'd pinched the money and went into a steep decline, finally smashing up the Fowlers' living room on Christmas Day – some Christmas present for Pauline!

As we record an episode five or six weeks in advance, at least all that heavy stuff was forgotten by the time I celebrated Christmas Day in my own home, with my new love.

But that was my only day off during the festive season because I was playing Dandini in panto in Brighton for most of December and January 1987. The production was *Cinderella* again, starring ex *Dr Who*, Colin Baker, in the role of Buttons and Hugh Lloyd as Baron Hardup. We all got on like a house on fire and had a terrific time together.

It was during the panto run that Prince Edward resigned from the Royal Marines and that same night we had a crowd of leather-clad chaps in the audience, who were regulars at the Vauxhall Tavern in London, and who had travelled down to Brighton for the panto. Miss Brahms had developed quite a big gay following. Colin and I were on stage and he had to ask me 'Are you sure you are a boy?'

To which I replied, 'Yes, of course I am a boy.'

Then Colin, just to be topical, added, 'Well, the Marines certainly wouldn't have you.'

With that, all the Vauxhall Tavern boys stood up as one and shouted out 'Yes but we would!'

Well, Colin and I, our faces just hit the floor, we could not believe our ears, it was so funny.

The Trollettes (David Raven and James Court), a drag act, were also in the production, playing the Ugly Sisters. Aside from being an absolutely fantastic act, David and James were fabulous fun to be with. Carol Kaye – who had been one of the famous singing Kaye Sisters – was also part of the company, playing the Fairy Godmother. As a take-off, she, Colin and Hugh did a special version of the Chaos Sisters. Never mind the sound, what a sight they were! Colin is a big chap and to see him dressed up in a tight frock, well it boggles the imagination!

He even confided to me one evening 'Do you know, I actually enjoyed dressing up in drag!' Typical of Colin's sense of humour.

He would make additions to his performance for the sake of humour, even down to drawing a tattoo on his arm one night. It was the funniest thing ever to watch those three doing the same routines that Carol had once done as part of the original singing trio.

CHAPTER SIXTEEN

Princess Di and My Thermal Undies

Nineteen eighty-seven started on a low note for Pauline. Not only was Arthur in hospital having treatment after his nervous breakdown but she'd begun to harbour suspicions that it was the dastardly Den Watts who'd put her Michelle in the family way.

Arthur eventually came out of hospital but before he and Pauline could start to rebuild their lives, Arthur had to stand trial for the theft of the Christmas Club money and was sent to prison for twenty-eight days. The judge told Arthur he had betrayed people's trust and Pauline didn't know how to show her face in Albert Square for the shame of it.

Her only moment of light relief that year was a little flirtation with Derek Taylor, the knight in shining armour who helped the Queen Vic Ladies Darts team, when their coach broke down on a day trip to Greenwich and the Isle of Dogs.

The Press continued to love any story from *EastEnders*, whether it was true or not. A rumour began to circulate that I was jealous of Anita Dobson. Why? I don't know. I have never been jealous of anyone in my life. I've not had any reason to be. Apart from anything else I've always maintained Pauline Fowler was the best part in *EastEnders*. She is the salt of the earth. Look, for example, at how well she coped with the shock news of Michelle's pregnancy.

When the cheque book journalism stories started flying around after John had sold his story about me to the *News of the World*, I remember Paul remarking: 'I think what he did was dreadful. I would never do that to you.' Well, Paul didn't do it first but his older brother, Sean, was to go to the *News of the World* soon after Paul and I got together to sell a story about me.

Sometime after Paul moved in with me, I met his mother when she was over visiting Sean, staying at his porter's flat with him nearby. She seemed friendly enough and I liked her. That Christmas I sent her a hamper from Harrods, thinking she would really like a little something luxurious. However, I was dumbfounded when one of the sisters rang to tell me, 'Don't send my mother expensive presents. Send her money instead,' she suggested.

I was so angry. How I wish that when my own mother was alive, I'd been able to afford to buy her a hamper from Harrods. I only intended to make a thoughtful gesture to Paul's mother and that was the thanks I got in return. I should have clocked the signals then by the way things were developing.

Another example of the terribly treacherous betrayals was from a woman where Paul worked. He was very friendly with her but the next thing we knew, she had gone to the Press as well. She alleged that I'd travelled over to the Isle of Wight with Paul and pleaded with his wife to speed up the divorce. The story was a total lie because the weekend I was supposedly on the Isle of Wight, I was actually working in London. It was correct that Paul had been over there to see his children that weekend but the rest of the story was a load of bunkum.

However, as a result of those lies, reporters started to pursue Paul's children by following them to and from school and doorstepped his estranged wife, Annette. The arrangement Annette and Paul had already made between them was that they would separate for two years and then obtain a quiet divorce, in order to protect the children. Obviously, in the light of events both Paul and I were extremely concerned about his daughters and son being upset by pursuing journalists. It was not a happy time for any of us, especially when we decided to sue the *News of the World* for libel over Sean's stories.

Shortly afterwards, we heard from Paul's sisters that Sean had swanned over to Spain. He threw money about and seemed very pleased with himself. Apparently the sisters gave him a good ticking off and he returned home.

In the summer of 1987 Paul wanted to take me on holiday to Middleton in Ireland. It was where his mother, brother Bert and sister-in-law Eileen lived. Paul had only recently bought a new car and wished to travel over to Ireland by ferry, to show it off to his brother.

We spent some time with them in Middleton and then moved on to other places in Ireland. We stayed at a lovely hotel at Sneam, which was not cheap by anybody's standards. There we were joined by Bert and Eileen. For some reason, Paul's sister-in-law, Eileen changed from being charming and friendly towards me, to ignoring me totally. She began to be extremely rude and blanked me completely. I was like the invisible woman, as far as she was concerned. I warned Paul I would not be treated in such a fashion. To my knowledge I'd done nothing wrong to upset the woman; it was all so unnecessary. Anyway, I never did find out exactly what I was supposed to have done. Paul's mother, who I thought was lovely, was embarrassed about Eileen's behaviour and couldn't understand it either.

That, then, was my introduction to Paul's family. I have never been so pleased to catch a ferry back to England in my life.

My fellow launderette worker, Dot Cotton continued to be developed brilliantly by June Brown. She really cared about the part and when later it was decided that Dot's husband, Charlie (played by Christopher Hancock) should be killed in a lorry crash, June fought tremendously hard to keep the role of Charlie Cotton. He was a good character, he looked like a spiv and was just the sort of person Dot Cotton would be taken in by. Anyway, June failed in her attempts and Charlie ended up in his coffin. We were due to go round to see Dot, the grieving widow. The scene involved Nick, Dot, Pauline, Arthur and the Reverend, who were all in the house. Tea was poured and without thinking, Bill inadvertently put his tea cup down on the coffin, which looked so bizarre! They decided to keep the tea cup in its place for the final scene. All of us were perched on the edge of our seats, just staring at the coffin. We had to control our laughter for the recording tape but I can assure you the rehearsals were absolutely hysterical.

When it comes to strong male roles, Nick Cotton has to take the biscuit! In one episode we were filming Arthur had to go over to Dot Cotton's because she had not been seen in the square for ages. Nick Cotton answered the door and Bill said he didn't know how he controlled himself from laughing because he had to say 'Is Dot there?'

To which Nick replied: 'There's just the three of us: me, her and . . . God!'

Nick was still taking drugs and doing all the rotten things he always did but was pretending he'd changed his ways, found religion and was a born-again Christian . . . but the way John delivered that line, it was so funny!

Viewers will have noticed that Pauline always has a tea cosy on the teapot in her house. They are made for me by an elderly lady called Dolly, who lives in the East End. She has been making them and sending them to me since *EastEnders* started. Dolly once wrote me a lovely letter saying all her friends at bingo are extremely envious when they see her tea cosies on my pot. Therefore, I treasure them dearly and when they become stained and grubby, I even take them home and wash them myself.

Lots of viewers also showed the same sort of kindness when Pauline was expecting baby Martin and I received loads of baby clothes. In those days, such was the need to maintain secrecy that the baby's name had been kept a total secret, even from the cast. It was only revealed on a need-to-know basis. Kathy, who was to be the baby's godmother, was the first one to be told. The name was whispered into Gillian's ear as the scene was being shot.

I admit I do get very upset by Press criticism of Pauline's character. They have never criticized me for my acting but I hate it when they hit out at her. Pauline has had a lot to put up with in her life and, of course, when they find out an actress is a good crier, they inevitably write a lot of teary scenes for the character.

We used to have an excellent writer called Charlie Humphreys, who has now sadly passed away and he used to write lovely stuff for me, real tear-jerkers. In one scene of his I did in which Pauline broke down and cried her heart out, I even ended up receiving fan letters from producers of other programmes. Nearly everybody involved in the scene on the studio floor congratulated me when we finished the recordings.

I've always done my best to help towards keeping a happy atmosphere in the studio. It is very important because we are working under tremendous pressure on *EastEnders* and if we did not work as a team, there's no way we could get all the shows out. Especially in the early days when we worked from nine in the morning until ten at night and we had six to eight scripts on the go each week. It was like being on a treadmill.

In those conditions you have to make an effort to lighten the working atmosphere. I don't mean mess about and waste time but just try and lift things. I know the technicians appreciate it. There is more than one camera supervisor who has said to me: 'I always look forward to working on your set.'

Well, we certainly had a bit of a fillip one working day when we were forewarned that a very important visitor would be coming on to the lot next morning. I had a gut feeling it would be Royalty and sure enough, I was right. A black car pulled up early and out stepped Princess Diana!

Apparently Julia had met Diana at a Woman of the Year luncheon and the Princess had talked about her interest in the series. So on the spot, Julia invited her to come and see Albert Square and the interior sets in the studios. When Diana arrived Sue Tully had Vicki in her arms and the baby started crying. Diana went straight up to them and started fussing over the baby, telling Sue, 'It's a pity you don't have any brandy. I find if you dip your finger in brandy and then rub it on their gums, it works wonders.'

Diana was fantastic. She and I had a discussion about thermal underwear, of all subjects! I explained we definitely needed it when we were working out on the lot in winter and she told us that she often had to wear it too, on some of her outdoor official visits, particularly to cold and windy parade grounds.

She chatted with all the props boys and had a good look around the lot. Inside the studio she was fascinated by all the sets and couldn't get over how small they were in reality, nor how they were in such close proximity to one another.

Diana revealed that Den and Angie were her favourite characters and so she especially enjoyed chatting to Leslie and Anita and looking around the Queen Vic. She came and sat down for a chat in the Fowlers' house, too.

Her enthusiasm for the programme was refreshing and it was lovely to see her at such close quarters. She stayed for several hours, which showed how much she was enjoying herself and with the help of security to keep the Press at bay, her visit was kept entirely private.

Diana may have been a great fan of *EastEnders* but it appears that the Queen Mother is not! I had the great delight of meeting the Queen Mother once again, at a charity event for the Greater London Fund for the Blind, which was held at St James Palace. The Queen Mother does not really like formal line-ups, so we were stood in groups in small semi-circles. A young lady introduced me to her: 'Wendy is in *EastEnders*, Ma'am.'

'I don't think I know that programme,' she replied.

'Possibly not, Ma'am but I have appeared in a programme which is a favourite of yours.'

'Oh and what is that?'

'*Dad's Army.*'

'Yes, of course I know that very well. Do you know when you have had a bad day, you come home, put your feet up and pop in a video of *Dad's Army* – and there you are, laughing again,' she remarked.

What wonderful praise – I thought it was so sweet of her, I really could have hugged her! I am sure that both David Croft and Jimmy Perry – who, deservedly are now both OBEs – are very proud that their work is held in such high esteem.

CHAPTER SEVENTEEN

Going, Going . . .

Bill, Sue Tully and I worked very well together as a team and it was rare for us to go beyond three takes. Many were even done in one. Sometimes, however, such good relationships can work against you. As happened in the early days with Leslie, Anita, Bill and myself, the Fowler foursome would suddenly find ourselves in the last few scenes of the day because they were running short of time. We were on last because they knew we could work under pressure. They realized we'd get the job done on time and thus avoid costly overruns.

Several times Bill and I went to see the producer to make the point: 'Last again every time, it's not fair.'

Things would be better for a while and we would be first in. Then we would be middle of the day but eventually it slipped back to end of the day yet again!

Although Bill and I worked very well together I have to admit that we would occasionally have a pretty tetchy relationship off screen. I pride myself, however, on never letting that interfere with our working relationship – though I did secretly wonder whether, in an episode where Arthur had to slap Pauline across the face, whether Bill got more pleasure out of it than he should have done!

At the end of 1987 and beginning of 1988 I had some lighter

relief, when I went back to playing Dandini again in panto with Frank Carson and Hugh Lloyd at Hayes in Middlesex. Although that *Cinderella* was good fun, as all pantos are, it was also a bit of a nightmare working with Frank because he never came to rehearsals.

Frank was playing Buttons and as was normal practice during the performance we threw out little packets of Cadbury's chocolate Buttons to the kids in the audience. The packets were kept in Frank's dressing room but the problem was he kept eating them all. Sometimes I'd wander in there and be ankle-deep in chocolate Buttons wrappers! Eventually they had to be moved into my dressing room for safe keeping.

For a change 1988 started on a high note for Pauline: Michelle and Lofty were expecting a baby and she was to become a grandmother again. It was all too good to be true because for Michelle having another baby was the last thing she felt she could cope with. So before January was out, she had an abortion – much to Lofty's distress. To Pauline's as well because as a result of the abortion row, Michelle and Lofty's marriage started to fall apart.

In the spring Pauline was happy to see her elder brother, Kenny again when he arrived in Walford from New Zealand, accompanied by his daughter, Elizabeth. But the visit caused great consternation. Like *Bill and Ben The Flowerpot Men*, was it Pete or was it Ken who had fathered Simon Wicks? Only Pat Wicks (brother Pete's first wife) probably knew and she wasn't saying . . . that's because she wasn't entirely sure, it could have been either!

Her brother's problems brushed off onto Pauline, who already had enough on her plate with mother Lou ill throughout the early part of the year. Pete drove Lou to Leigh-on-Sea for a spot of convalescence but while he was away, Pauline's sister-in-law, Kathy was raped by Willmott-Brown. Lou returned to Walford in July but died shortly afterwards. As if Pauline's grief was not enough, Lofty then walked out on Michelle.

The storylines were good but it was a taxing year, aside from a lot of dialogue to learn, you just cannot walk away from the set after emotionally-charged scenes without it affecting you for sometime afterwards. With Lou Beale's death, we'd lost one of the original members of cast in Anna Wing.

In my private life I still seemed to be taken advantage of by Paul's family. It annoyed me greatly when Paul's sister, Helen came over to London from Spain. She was on a stop-over before travelling on to Ireland. I was at the hairdressers having my hair washed when Paul came in to say Helen wanted her hair done. One of the stylists stayed behind to wash and blow-dry her hair but when it was finished, Helen announced: 'I haven't any money, put it on her bill.' I thought it was somewhat of a liberty, to say the least but like a fool I ended up paying for her.

The next big mistake I made with Paul was in standing guarantor for a Ford Escort Cabriolet which he wanted to buy. But he didn't keep up the payments which made me very cross and, because I'm not used to having final demands and bailiffs, I paid off the balance owing on the car. That gesture cost me several thousands of pounds.

I was just so damn daft, I really should have seen the writing on the wall.

The start of 1989 was yet another low one for Pauline, with brother Pete in court on a drink-driving charge. He'd hit the bottle because of worries over the state of his marriage. No wonder he was worried, before the end of January Kathy had left him and Walford. Pete's solution? The bottle again but this time he stole a car, crashed it and injured a passenger – while banned already from the first charge.

During the year my agent, John Mahoney rang me to say that

the marketing department of Cambridge Diet wanted me to endorse their products. Their first offer was for £6,000 but John was a brilliant negotiator and after a series of meetings, the fee was increased to £20,000. My accountant advised me to invest the sum as a down payment on another property. I'd enjoyed a very happy pantomime season down in Brighton and Paul suggested maybe I should look for a flat in that area.

Eventually I found a suitable apartment in Hove. I furnished it tastefully, installed a dishwasher and various other items, until it felt like home from home. We regularly spent our weekends there and sometimes Andy and Mireille came with us too. We always had such a good time down in Brighton because there are some wonderful restaurants there and we also found ourselves a very nice local pub.

One day we were travelling down to Brighton in Paul's van with some more furniture for the flat. He was car mad and on the journey he saw a Porsche. He became so intent on looking at the Porsche, rather than where he was driving, that he drove into the back of another car. Instead of being up-front with the guy, he refused to pay for the damage done. The dispute dragged on for weeks until in the end I paid out £800 on his behalf.

It was a little while later that Paul suggested to me we should marry, as soon as his divorce was finalized. In retrospect, I really don't know why but I agreed and he immediately telephoned his mother and his sisters in Spain to break the news. Apart from them, we kept it quiet. Paul bought me a sapphire and diamond engagement ring and don't ask me how but soon afterwards the papers got wind of our engagement and so eventually we agreed to let them take a few photos.

I knew in my heart of hearts, there was no way I could marry Paul. Nothing felt right any more. I thought I'd let the relationship run its course and hopefully, we would just drift apart. With hindsight, I should have just got rid of him myself but as crazy as it sounds, I really didn't know how to. It would have been much easier said than done at the time.

Meanwhile, Paul was trying to push ahead with his divorce. In due course their divorce agreement was drawn up. Paul was supposed to pay her maintenance of £175 per month but he was forever falling behind with his payments. Often he'd ask me to send her a cheque, on the promise he would repay me the cash shortly afterwards. I thought if that was to be a regular occurrence, I might as well put it on a standing order because I was far too busy concentrating on work to keep remembering to send cheques on his behalf. Also, I wanted to ensure he paid it on time. So I began making the regular monthly maintenance payments myself. But unfortunately after a while, he stopped reimbursing me for them. At the beginning of our relationship Paul had been very good and contributed towards food and housekeeping bills but eventually he stopped doing that too.

Annette rang me one day to say she'd been offered a large sum of money by a newspaper to speak out about her relationship with Paul. I quickly reminded her that part of the divorce agreement she had signed included a clause that she would not speak to the Press. 'Yes, I know but it is a lot of money,' she claimed.

'Fine,' I told her. 'I'm contacting my solicitor immediately.'

My firmness must have done the trick and warned her off because the story never appeared.

Here's another little example of what life was like with Paul . . . one weekend Andy and Mireille, Paul and I were staying at the flat in Hove. We'd gone down there to see Peter O'Toole at the Theatre Royal and afterwards we had a meal in an excellent Chinese restaurant. All in all, it had been a lovely evening and everyone was thoroughly relaxed.

Now opposite our apartment was a flat that had been occupied by a young couple until the girl moved out, leaving her partner Jamie by himself. Unfortunately Jamie had started to hold the most dreadfully noisy parties, which began to ruin our stay in our own apartment. It wasn't just the horrendous noise that disturbed us but incidents like people being sick over the railings outside our bedroom window, which was very unpleasant, as you can imagine.

Anyway, we returned home from the theatre and Chinese meal only to find Jamie and his friends in the street and they were all roaring drunk. Andy, Mireille and I went into our flat but Paul stayed outside. I don't know what was said between them but next moment Paul hit Jamie. The police arrived and Paul was carted off to the police station. I contacted my solicitor who arranged for a barrister to bail out Paul. Eventually the case went to court. Again, it was muggins who had to stump up all the fees. Paul's indiscretion cost me over £1,000.

On the day of the hearing, Paul attended court with a friend of his, Paul Devine. On their way back to London Paul spotted a blue Range Rover on a secondhand car lot. Apparently, he said to Devine: 'That's what I want. Let's go and have a look at it.'

Devine asked him how he thought he could afford it.

'Don't worry. *She* will pay for it,' he insisted.

Yes, I did because somehow he managed to talk me round to it and within a short space of time, off he went and traded in the Cabriolet against the Range Rover. Like a fool, I paid off the balance owing on the Cabriolet and ended up paying for the Range Rover, as well. Why? Don't ask me, when I look back now it seems absurd.

The first weekend he had his new toy he drove off to the Isle of Wight. Ostensibly, to see the children but in reality, to show the Range Rover off to his mates.

There were occasions when I also had to help Paul with debts he owed to the Inland Revenue. It may have seemed stupid of me to keep dishing out good money after bad but the reason I did it was to protect Paul's children from adverse stories in the Press. Paul had become high profile because of his relationship with me and I felt I owed it to his children not to allow any bad publicity about their father which might affect them. They were lovely kids, all very intelligent and due to stay on for higher education. I didn't see why their lives should be disrupted through no fault of their own.

On the work side, Pauline was suffering ill health in the summer – little wonder with all the surrounding family problems – but she refused to see Dr Legg. Instead she resorted to homoeopathic remedies for her 'woman's problem.'

It was at this stage of the storyline in 1989 that an attempt was made to write me out of *EastEnders* altogether. A few people on the set seemed to know about it but not me and when I discovered the truth, I was pretty pissed off about it, I can tell you. Rumours circulated that some of us were to be replaced and I never really felt secure in the job until Michael Ferguson took over. Michael Ferguson was a smashing bloke and turned out to be a real tonic for the show.

Pauline made a miraculous recovery! Ricky knocked her over in his car, she was subsequently medically examined and went from having suspected cancer to fibroids. Pauline spent Christmas in hospital but was back at work in no time at all.

As I looked back on Pauline's illness, which in the script had been building since the previous summer, I recalled that on my birthday in July, I had taken champagne into the studios and invited people into my dressing room for a drink. Even Bill pitched up and bought me a plant.

While Pauline was in her hospital bed, I was with Lionel Blair and Stephanie Lawrence at the Churchill Theatre in Bromley. I left *EastEnders* for a few weeks to appear in the pantomime *Cinderella*. It was good to work with the pair of them, along with the rest of the cast, which included Ross Davidson, who played the male nurse, Andy O'Brien at the start of *EastEnders*. I was also delighted to meet up again with another cast member, Michael Medwin, who had produced *Gumshoe*, the film I'd done with Albert Finney.

Again the production was *Cinderella* but on that occasion I was given the part of the Fairy Godmother, instead of my usual role as Dandini. Although it was enjoyable, I much preferred playing principal boy. I love all that thigh slapping, it's a great deal more fun. Some gay friends of mine travelled up to Bromley from Brighton to see me in the show and afterwards, while we were having a drink in the bar, they asked me how I was liking the panto run.

I admitted to them, 'I am not sure I like being a fairy.'

To which, one of them ever so quickly replied, 'Well, at least you've got the choice!'

During Christmas/New Year of 1989–90 when I was doing the pantomime with Lionel Blair, I was also asked to deputize for Ken Bruce on his BBC Radio 2 programme. That involved doing two pantomime shows a day, getting home late but having to get up at 6.30a.m. next day to do the radio programme. After the show at Broadcasting House, I had to rush home, pick up my bags and race off to the theatre again. Sometimes I tried to snatch a little sleep between shows but it was a very tiring schedule. I didn't have a cleaner at the time and annoyingly, Paul never lifted a finger to help me.

On New Year's Eve I attended Midnight Service to take Communion and returned from church to find the pub still open. Paul was inside, so I popped in to tell him how much I had enjoyed my visit to church. 'I was moved to tears,' I added.

'So was I moved to tears, when I saw the state of the flat,' was all he could say to me.

Just a cotton-picking minute, I thought to myself, all the hours I'm working and he cannot be bothered to turn round and lend a helping hand – but that's what he was like.

Towards the end of the panto run I received scripts for 32 scenes, which were scheduled for my return, so despite the threat of my demise earlier that year, Pauline was well and truly up and running again! At least I could sink myself back into *EastEnders* and try to forget about some of my own personal problems.

My on-screen family blossomed again during 1990 when it was decided to revive the character of Mark Fowler and the producers brought in Todd Carty to take on the role. I must say I could not have asked for a nicer 'son'. Todd is a lovely young man, who was born in Ireland in 1963 and had started appearing in commercials at the age of four.

His face became known to television viewers from the part he played in *Grange Hill* – Tucker Jenkins and the title role in the spin-off series, *Tucker's Luck*. Apart from being a lovely person, Todd is a very professional actor and he and I built up a marvellous working rapport from the first day he became a Fowler. Todd and I both work instinctively – it's no good saying to us what our motivations are, we know what we are doing and how to do it. Whenever we get a new director I usually sound them out and probably make them a bit nervous. On one occasion, Todd and I were about to do a scene together when this new to us director started 'Your motivation for this scene is so and so, your thoughts will be . . .' 'Don't tell me what to think please,' I said. 'Just let me and Todd do it and then you tell us if we were wrong. I don't have a thought in my head at present, and if you tell me to start thinking, you'll blow my cover!' The director just stood there. Todd looked at me and said 'Oh Mummy, I just love it when you talk dirty to them.' The crew fell about, the director let us get on with it, the scene was completed and everyone was happy.

The crew liked nothing better than a good laugh. Once, when we were filming the discovery of Dirty Den's skeleton in the canal, Letitia, Susan and I were driven to the location, somewhere near Watford. Bruce Abraham, who was then a third assistant director and responsible for props, called out to me, 'Hey Wendy, I've got your favourite actor in the car!' When I turned and looked I saw that he'd driven all the way with the skeleton sat in the passenger seat, complete with seat belt. That must have shaken up a few motorists along the way.

Pauline was delighted when son Mark returned to Albert Square. Bridge Street Market rocked under the council's threat to revoke its licence for a street market and Peter Beale's stall was bulldozed. But good old Michelle – who was working in Walford Council offices at the time – uncovered information there which revealed corruption that ultimately saved the market.

As time wore on and with everything that had occurred, I became even more unhappy about the dreadful situation I had got myself into with Paul. My hope still was that our relationship would come to a natural conclusion and I would then be rid of him. However, at the beginning of 1990 Paul rang me at work and caught me on the hop when I was very busy between scenes, which was a bit of luck for him.

'Shall we get married?' he asked. 'There is a space left at the Register Office for 17 March.'

God knows what possessed me to say: 'Yes, all right, book it,' but that is what happened, and book it he did.

The wedding and reception cost me £8,000. The only items Paul paid for were my engagement ring and the marriage licence. He didn't even pay for my wedding ring.

At one stage he had it in his head that he'd wear a kilt for the wedding but fortunately I managed to talk him out of that. Instead, I persuaded him to go to Austin Reed's where he bought a Hugo Boss suit for which – yes, you've guessed it – yet again, I paid.

He'd caught me on the rebound but at the beginning of our relationship, I was very much in love with Paul. By the time I married Paul, I was certainly no longer in love with him. I really don't know why I married him – and I certainly wish I hadn't.

Despite my misgivings, I must admit the wedding – on St Patrick's Day – was fantastic. Even though it was the middle of March the weather was beautiful with lots of unseasonably hot sunshine and everyone enjoyed themselves thoroughly.

Following the civil ceremony at Marylebone Register Office (where ten years previously I'd married Will), we had a lovely service at St Marylebone Parish Church. Peter Dean, who played my brother, Pete, was one of the witnesses at the Register Office, Andy Archer was the other. Several other members of the cast from *EastEnders* attended including Anna Wing, Sue Tully, Letitia Dean and Michael Cashman, who read the lesson. Apart from Paul's three children – Emily, Natalie and Liam – not one member of his family came to the wedding.

One of our hymns was *Lord of all Hopefulness* which had special significance to me because during the reception at the nearby Windsor Castle pub, I remember being hopeful myself that perhaps his family and the Press would leave us alone, now we were married. I thought maybe we would be able to get on with our lives from that point in time and settle down peacefully together. Possibly things might get better between Paul and I.

Yet even on my wedding night Paul went off and left me on my own – he went out with friends for a Chinese meal! It seemed that all Paul was ever concerned about was having plenty to eat and a nice car to drive. They were always his main priorities.

In spite of my hopes, our relationship deteriorated rapidly after the wedding. I very quickly realized what a terrible mistake I had made in marrying Paul. It seemed as if the only reason he wanted to be with me was for me to write out cheques for him. The contrast in Paul, from the beginning of our relationship to what he turned into, was truly staggering. When he'd first moved in with me he'd brought all his clothes and possessions in two black bin liners. I have only myself to blame but I went out and bought him good shoes, an Armani suit, Hugo Boss clothes and many other items.

Once, the Guild of British Tie Makers invited us to a luncheon at The Savoy for the annual Tie Wearers of the Year Awards. As part of their promotion they also gave the spouses of several celebrities a complete head to toe outfit free of charge. Paul was bought a new suit, shirt, tie, shoes, hat – they all cost him nothing.

He adored his newly acquired expensive lifestyle and loved dressing the part. I bought him two dinner suits and a selection of bow-ties for when we attended official functions because he couldn't afford to buy them for himself. He revelled in the places we went to and the people we met. Apart from many top London hotels, we were also once invited to the 'Not Forgotten' Association garden party at Buckingham Palace. On two occasions Paul was with me when I was introduced to Princess Anne, once at the Hampton Court Flower Show and again at a Save The Children reception at Buckingham Palace.

After we were married my friends, particularly Andy and Mireille, remarked 'Once you married him, he altered his personality – immediately after the wedding.'

The same year of my wedding, 1990, I met Princess Diana

again, at a charity event held in aid of Children with Spinal Injuries. It was a star-studded night, with performers such as Shirley Bassey and I was there to announce one of the acts.

After the show in the Royal line-up Diana asked me, 'How are you enjoying married life?'

'It's all right,' I answered ruefully and looked at her thinking, 'Well, we're both in the same boat aren't we?'

Just over a year after Paul and I married we moved from my flat into a four-storey Georgian house nearby in Marylebone. The house cost me £280,000 and most of my earnings have subsequently been poured into it. No man has ever put a roof over my head – and it was no different with Paul.

Although I bought the house I kept my London flat on too thinking, God forbid but if anything went wrong and I should lose the house, I could always move back into the apartment. At least I knew I could afford the mortgage on that and it's only in the past couple of years that I have actually sold that flat.

In 1991 I won the libel action against the *News of the World* over the story that Paul's brother, Sean had sold. I attended High Court to hear that the *NoW* had wrongly branded me as a 'spoilt and domineering woman'. The publishers agreed the story had been without foundation and paid damages to Paul and I, plus all legal costs.

On the strength of the money we received we decided to book an around-the-world trip with Peter Dean, who played my brother in *EastEnders* and his wife, Jean. It was a marvellous holiday. We visited Singapore, Sydney, the Great Barrier Reef and Hawaii, travelling first class all the way. We should have had a super time but, unfortunately, my relationship with Paul had deteriorated so badly that for me the trip was ruined.

After we returned to London our relationship slid even further downhill. There were many nights when I returned home from a hard day's work to find Paul sitting in an armchair in front of the television. He'd just sit and watch while I did all the household jobs, including carrying out heavy bags of rubbish for the refuse collection next morning.

As I don't drive, if we went anywhere in the car, it was always Paul who drove us. However, when I had to get up early for work, he'd usually stay in bed – with the car I paid for parked in the street – while I had to fork out for a taxi to take me to the studios.

On the odd occasion he would collect me from work and one of those days was shortly after I'd appeared at a garage opening for a friend of a friend. On the journey home Paul started: 'Why don't you get in contact with that bloke from the garage and suggest that if he'll let you have a car for nothing, you'll do garage openings for him up and down the country?'

'Just a minute, I can't do that,' I protested. 'I am working flat out as it is. When am I supposed to have time to do all this? I'm definitely not phoning him.'

With that Paul went into another of his sulks.

On my birthday I started the celebrations early, with some of my friends in our local pub. We were having a glass or two of bubbly when Paul drove up outside. He was in an old Jag which my hairdresser, Maurice, had up for sale.

'What are you doing in that?' I asked Paul.

'I want you to buy it for me.'

'I am not buying that car,' I insisted.

Yet again, he went off in an angry mood, ruining my birthday celebrations. I stayed to have a few more drinks with my mates but I was so upset. I wondered how on earth he could do that to me, on my birthday? It would have been bad enough any other day of the week, blatantly expecting me to write out a cheque to buy him yet another damned car – but spoiling my very special day of the year? It was quite obvious he didn't really care about me.

Pauline wasn't having a much better 1991 either, the family were still giving her problems. Mark's old girlfriend, Gill had visited Walford and shortly after her departure he'd proposed to Diane Butcher but she turned him down and popped off to France. Mark had also kept popping off for 'appointments' and Pauline kept wondering why.

She was soon to find out, when Mark exploded a bombshell by revealing to his parents that he was HIV positive – and chose Boxing Day to divulge his secret. To say she was shell-shocked was an understatement and not knowing enough about HIV, she and Arthur were worrying that their eldest son might die of Aids at any moment.

Pauline has always been one for her family but sometimes there are limits and she was far from pleased with Michelle, when she took Vicki and ran away with Clyde Tavernier who, at the time was a prime suspect in the murder of Eddie Royle. In fairness, in the end it turned out Clyde was not the killer but if it wasn't one thing it was another.

The one high spot of 1991 for me was that six years after the staff from Grace Brothers last appeared on the screens, I received a telephone call to say the BBC intended to make a follow-up series to *Are You Being Served?* The offshoot series, was to be called *Grace and Favour* and the old team would be back together again – I couldn't wait!

CHAPTER EIGHTEEN

Grace and Favour... And Shirley Brahms II

Again written by David Croft and Jeremy Lloyd, *Grace and Favour* was to be produced and directed by Mike Stephens. The storyline was that after Young Mr Grace's death, the department store had to close down and we staff gathered for the reading of the will. Only to find out, to our horror, that he had bequeathed all his money to a charity for fallen women and raided our pension fund to buy the dilapidated Millstone Manor House. The storyline was that the manor was being run as a hotel and managed by Mr Rumbold! As the rest of us had only been left with a small income for a pension, we decided to step in, roll up our sleeves and help Mr Rumbold, in order to look after our investment.

The first series of six episodes revolved around Mrs Slocombe, Captain Peacock and Messrs Humphries and Rumbold's attempts to convert the decaying mansion into a hotel. Once more I was back in my familiar and favourite role, as Miss Brahms, ably assisting the quartet with the conversion. Of course, it was wonderful to be working with the old team again – John, Mollie, Frank and Nicholas and I quickly rekindled our friendship.

There were also three new people who became members of the

regular cast: Billy Burden, a wonderful West Country comic who played a neighbouring farmer called Maurice Moulterd; Fleur Bennett who played his daughter, Mavis; plus Joanne Heywood who played Miss Jessica Lovelock, Mr Grace's former nurse and companion, who also came to help out at the hotel.

Coincidentally, one of the actresses brought in for Episode One of the first series was Shirley Cheriton. Shirley had been one of the original cast members of *EastEnders* and had played the yuppie character Debbie Wilkins. I hadn't seen her since she left in the spring of 1987 and so it was nice to meet up again and reminisce about the early days of *EastEnders*.

After we did the pilot of *Grace and Favour*, arrangements were made for Pauline to be temporarily written out of *EastEnders* so I could film the rest of the series during 1991 and 1992. It was great to be doing some location work on the new show, instead of being stuck in the studio as we always had been with *AYBS?* I think it added a new dimension. For each of the series we filmed for about nine days at Chavenge House, an Elizabethan stately home near Tetbury in Gloucestershire, then went back to London to do all the studio work.

The daughter of the people who owned Chavenge House had a Cairn terrier, who had recently given birth to puppies. Paul was there to watch the filming and during a break he suddenly appeared with one of the pups in his arms. I am very shortsighted and without my glasses, at first sight, I thought it was a fox cub. I walked over to take a closer look and found a lovely, little furry bundle. 'What is it?' I asked him.

'It is a pedigree Cairn,' Paul told me. 'Are you interested, I think you could do a deal for cash?'

'Is it a bitch?'

'Yes.'

'Well, she will be Shirley Brahms II, then!'

Looking back, buying Shirley was the only sensible thing Paul ever persuaded me to do After I finished filming in Gloucestershire we took her back to London with us.

We also took Billy Burden, whom I got on with very well since first working with him during the summer season at Weymouth in 1983. I'd invited Billy to come and stay with us for a few days but warned him beforehand: 'Bear in mind we only moved in a couple of weeks ago. You can hardly move in the house, it is still total chaos.'

What a situation I let myself in for. A new home, where I still hadn't got the hang of everything yet; a six-week old puppy, who required house-training and Billy. I don't mean this unkindly but Billy was a law – and a liability – unto himself. I had to look after him all the time he was with me.

Born and bred in Wimborne, Dorset, Billy was a total eccentric. I remember once being with him inside Wimborne Minster when he lit up a cigarette.

'Billy! Billy! Put that out, you are in a Holy Place.'

'No, I'm not,' he retorted.

'Yes, you are. You're in the house of God,' I insisted.

Billy stood his ground: 'Look, I've already had a word with Patrick Moore and asked his opinion. Do you know what he told me? He said he'd looked really thoroughly through his telescope but there's no bugger up there.'

There wasn't much more I could say to Billy that day on the subject of religion!

Anyway, when he arrived at my house I suggested to him, 'If you get caught short during the night, to save you coming all the way down to our bedroom where the bathroom is, just pee out of the window. You'll be all right, nobody will see you, there's only a small roof terrace out there where we keep our pots of roses and other flowers.'

A couple of mornings later, about 9.30am I was sat by the lounge window overlooking the terrace, waiting for Billy to come downstairs so we could take a taxi to work. It was a brilliant morning, with lovely sunshine. Suddenly, a load of water gushed past the window on to the roof terrace. Paul leapt up: 'Jesus, Christ what was that?' I thought Oh no, Billy has taken me at my word but I didn't mean in broad daylight! I kept thinking, Please, God, don't let any of the neighbours see him.

Dear old Billy, if it wasn't one thing it was another with him. He was the cause of most of the hilarity when we were filming *Grace and Favour*, usually when he forgot his lines, although that was understandable – he was getting on a bit in years.

However, it wasn't Billy who caused one of the biggest fiascos of the series – that dubious honour went to a flock of sheep. The flock were supposed to be ushered from the main farmyard into another yard. The problem was somebody left the door open to the costume store and during the round up some of the sheep strayed into the store, saw their own reflections in the mirrors and promptly shit on the floor – all over the costume notes carefully prepared by our designer, Mary Husband.

Mary happened to be watching the playback on the monitor but she didn't realize they had got into her store. 'Mary, the sheep, the sheep,' I kept warning her. Suddenly it dawned on her what had occurred and she ran off crying 'Shit! Shit!' There certainly was plenty of that, all right. The props boys had a helluva mess trying to clear up the costume store. The first series of *Grace and Favour* comprising six episodes was transmitted in January and February of 1992 and the reviews were generally favourable. For instance, critic Jeanette Kupfermann in her column in the *Daily Mail* considered that the characters had survived the move from department store to countryside intact. 'The contrast between their genteel snobbery and the earthy, straw-in-the-ear country life, gives the series a new lease of life.

'Miss Brahms (Wendy Richard) is still her cheeky Cockney self and remains miraculously girlish in spite of the ballroom dancer's chignon, *Dynasty* suits and the fact that we know her as a grandmother in *EastEnders*.'

Even Shirley Brahms II was a star in one episode of *Grace and Favour* with the end credits acknowledging her name. She played a farm dog and stole a scene from John Inman!

Shooting *Grace and Favour* was a bundle of laughs, compared to the tremendous pressures Pauline was under once again. Nineteen ninety-two had started as a downer for her with Arthur refusing to accept the fact that Mark was HIV positive, no matter how much Pauline argued the matter over with him. They even came to blows about it but he would not budge in his prejudice.

Finally he did come around and father and son worked briefly together in Arthur's gardening business. One of their first customers was a woman, named Christine Hewitt. Mark found he really couldn't work with his dad because they argued too much. Arthur advertised his vacancy, which was initially filled by Jonathan Hewitt. The lazy and unreliable youngster was not up to the job, so his mother filled in for him. The last person to realize where all this was leading was Pauline. Always putting family first, she travelled over to New Zealand to be with brother Kenny, who'd been involved in a bad car accident. While the cat's away the mice will play and that situation left Mrs Hewitt a chance to get her mitts into Arthur. Pauline is no fool and when she returned she guessed there was something wrong. Well, she could hardly miss it, with gossipy old Dot only too willing to point the finger of suspicion.

Pauline had it out with Arthur and believed his tale of a platonic friendship until she discovered a letter and photo from Christine Hewitt. Bracing herself for a battle, Pauline marched round to Christine's house and instead of verbally attacking her, found herself strangely sorry for the pathetic lonely figure, who obviously drank too much.

Arthur's affair was one of the really excellent storylines in *EastEnders*. Mrs Hewitt was played by Elizabeth Power, Michael Aspel's wife. It was while I was away from *EastEnders* filming *Grace and Favour* (the storyline about Pauline's extended visit to New Zealand) that Arthur's friendship with Christine Hewitt turned to romance.

By Christmas I had returned to the set and the Arthur affair had developed further. Something awful always seems to happen to Pauline at Christmas and it did again in 1992. On Christmas night, Arthur sneaked out of the house and ended up in bed with Mrs Hewitt.

As much as Pauline was having problems in her marriage, mine was going was from bad to worse too. During 1992 my relationship with Paul had deteriorated even further, so much so that if I went into our local with friends, he would acknowledge them but blank me completely. However, when I was at work one day I saw a story in the papers claiming I had allegedly received a £25,000 a year pay rise. I remarked to Letitia Dean (who played Den and Angie's daughter, Sharon): 'I bet when I get home that bastard will be talking to me tonight.' Lettia drove me home that evening, we called in at the pub and sure enough, I was right. Paul was all over me.

'Hello, Letitia, lovely to see you. Are you all right Wendy? I'll get you a glass of champagne.'

The false pleasantness didn't last long though and soon he started nagging me again, this time about my smoking. What annoyed me about that was that he knew I smoked, long before he even went out with me. One day at home as soon as I started to light a cigarette, he commented: 'Must you do that in here?'

I had to go into the garden to have my cigarette but I remember thinking: 'What the hell is going on? This is my own fucking house! He has never paid a penny towards anything. His only contribution to the place has been some off-cuts of carpet.'

We drifted even further apart. One Saturday night I had been out with some girlfriends of mine and I'd had too much to drink. Paul was out elsewhere with his cronies. When I returned home I went to bed and instead of sitting down to take off my jeans, I stood up to do so, stumbled backwards and caught the bedroom door, which slammed shut on my finger. The skin was broken down the complete length of the finger and there was blood everywhere. I immediately phoned Paul on his mobile and he came back to the house but with no words of sympathy for my predicament.

'It's your own fault,' he kept telling me.

I went outside to try and hail a taxi to take me to the casualty department at St Mary's Hospital in Paddington. Paul left me standing there alone, even though he knew I was crying and in terrible pain. Eventually, I caught a cab to St Mary's where I was seen by a consultant. A member of the casualty staff telephoned Paul and insisted he should come to the hospital because I was, by then, in shock. I heard someone ask Paul whether he had caused the injury but in fairness, no he hadn't, it was an accident. Eventually Paul arrived and stayed with me while they stitched my finger. Then they had to pierce the nail to allow the blood pressure to disperse. I was in a terrible state. I left hospital with an enormous bandage on my finger. When the anaesthetic wore off the pain was intolerable and I felt completely on my own.

On the day I was due to have the stitches removed, I arrived home late from work and was in a bit of a panic about arriving at hospital on time for my appointment. Paul was not there so I rang around to see if anyone else could help. One friend, Joan, offered to take me to St Mary's. We had been sat waiting at the hospital for quite a while when Paul turned up.

'You don't have to wait here, I've found a private doctor to attend to you,' he informed me and dismissively told Joan: 'You can go'.

He drove me to the block of flats where his brother had been head porter. One of the occupants was a retired doctor. Paul took me up to see the old man, who must have been 90 if he was a day. He had a very old set of surgical instruments laid out but it appeared to me that nothing had been sterilized. He attempted to take the dressing off my finger but I immediately protested, making it quite clear I would not allow him to touch my hand.

'Please yourself,' he replied curtly. 'But leave me some money before you go.'

I left him £5 – all the change I had on me.

'Now what do you want to do?' Paul moaned grumpily.

'Take me to the pharmacy in Edgware Road, I can have my finger re-dressed there. I don't know how you could even contemplate me risking infection by allowing someone like that to touch my hand.'

Paul just didn't seem to care. Frustrated by the incident, I went home to bed and next day returned to casualty at St Mary's. The young nurse on duty was very kind and took me aside: 'I've organized for you to see the consultant on duty.'

When I'd dressed that morning I'd put on the first thing that came to hand. It happened to be a sweatshirt I'd bought in Le Touquet. Anyway, into my cubicle came the consultant, a charming dark-haired gentleman. He recognized me and stopped in his tracks. 'Well hello, Wendy, I am your consultant Mr Touquet.'

'Isn't that a coincidence,' was my quick reply, 'because here is your sweatshirt!'

He sat down and laughed. 'Good heavens, Wendy, God must have been talking to you this morning.'

'Yes but unfortunately he wasn't saying much to me the night I did this,' I replied wistfully, holding up my injured finger.

Then we both had a chuckle before he checked my finger carefully and said it had healed well. I lost the nail and my manicurist feared it would never regrow properly but it did and today you can hardly see a mark where the stitches were. So I am extremely grateful to all the staff who looked after me at St Mary's but the whole episode made me realize how little Paul really cared for me.

The second series of *Grace and Favour*, again six episodes, was televised in January and February of 1993. David and Jeremy believed both sets of programmes were very good and I'm sure viewers felt equally enthusiastic.

Unfortunately, the BBC didn't agree and declined to commission a third series. I don't really know why for sure but it was probably something to do with viewing figures. Jeremy felt that it would have helped if the BBC had run repeats, which initially had assisted in building up the audience for *Are You Being Served?*

Anyway it was a great pity it had to finish so soon. We'd all enjoyed slipping back into our former roles and it was disappointing to have to go our separate ways again.

I would be extremely interested to see the audience reaction if *Grace and Favour* is ever repeated again. Maybe the re-runs would be as popular as *AYBS?* turned out to be.

CHAPTER NINETEEN

Paying Off Paul

It had been terrific fun doing *Grace and Favour* and we had some wonderful times filming on location in Gloucestershire. I have particularly fond memories of Billy, who always had everybody in hysterics with his broad West Country accent.

He was such a dear man. Attending his funeral in Wimborne Minster a few years later was an extremely sad day for me.

At least *Grace and Favour* had produced one beautiful spin-off and that was Shirley. It was lovely having a dog again after so many years and I derived a great deal of pleasure from Shirley. Although like any other young puppy, she could be very mischievous at times and managed to destroy numerous fuchsias, hydrangeas and shrubs as she dug around in the patio garden at the back of my house.

She quickly learned to twist me around her little paw and the only way I could get her to do anything was mention the word 'food'. Shirley certainly loves her tummy and once I caught her stealing a roast beef sandwich, complete with horseradish, from John Inman's shopping bag!

When Paul and I took her to the pub with us, her favourite trick was to wait for a bowl of ice cubes and then crunch some of them up in her teeth, while playing with the other pieces on the floor. (I don't know who she learned it from!) but Shirley certainly knew – and still does – how to play to an audience.

Apart from her mischievousness, Shirley was a fantastic little puppy. I was very upset though on some days when we were house-training her because on occasions Paul would hit her hard if she didn't pee on the newspaper he'd put down for her. I witnessed it more than once, such as during the summer that Paul invited his oldest daughter to stay. One day I heard Shirley whimpering and asked Emily what was wrong with the dog? 'Dad hit her because she peed on the floor.'

'Well, why didn't you tell me? I would have cleared it up and then he wouldn't have hit her,' I retorted.

I didn't mind Emily staying with us but she turned out to be rather lazy and often stayed in bed for most of the day, usually watching videos. Eventually she got a temporary job and I told her she would have to pay something towards her keep. It's not that I am a mean person but as Paul was only working spasmodically at the time – and I was already sending the maintenance home to the ex-wife and children – I wasn't prepared to finance one of those children in two places simultaneously. That seemed to be held against me.

Trauma and tragedy were on the cards for Pauline in 1993. Trauma when Pauline's grand-daughter, Vicki, was abducted. A full-scale search was launched and eventually the little girl was found safe and well but not before the kidnap had produced more than a few heart-stopping moments for Michelle, Pauline and the rest of the family.

The biggest storyline of the year though was when Arthur finally admitted to Pauline that he was having an affair with Mrs Hewitt. Angry and stunned, she hit Arthur over the head with a frying pan, threw the television at him and kicked him out of the house.

The day we filmed the scenes in which Pauline found out about Arthur's affair with Mrs Hewitt was one of the heaviest days I've ever had at work. There were twenty scenes of just Bill and I together and of course, such scenes are very emotional.

Well, the props boys – the unsung heroes of *EastEnders* in my opinion – kept us going throughout the day with cups of tea and when I went into Pauline's kitchen to do the frying pan scene they'd left a stack of six frying pans with a little note – 'Take your pick!'

I thought that was really sweet of them, especially as the tension had been building up and it certainly lightened it for me. When the scenes were eventually transmitted, it turned out to be a bloody good episode, even if I say so myself. Some viewers who'd seen Pauline hit Arthur with that frying pan afterwards approached me with comments, including one who said 'You could stand for Parliament and get voted in, after what you did last night!' I also had loads of fan mail about the incident, which was very gratifying.

Miserable and lonely, Pauline's situation worsened with the tragic death of her twin brother, Pete. He was killed in a car accident that had obviously been arranged by the family of a local gangster because Pete had been having an affair with his wife.

While all this drama was spicing up Pauline's life, I returned home from work to find two men on the doorstep. 'Can I help you?' I asked.

'We are looking for Paul Glorney.'

'That is my husband.'

'Well, do you know anything about his business affairs?'

'No, I am afraid I don't.'

They left but I soon found out they were bailiffs and I became increasingly worried about Paul's financial state of affairs. Especially as it was always me who had to prop him up in the end.

Paul then wanted to go into partnership with a guy called Peter but I warned him against it. 'There is something about him I do not trust. Don't do it.'

'He has promised to get me work. You don't know what you are talking about,' Paul protested.

Anyway just before Christmas Paul and his mate Steve did a whole series of jobs for Peter but he pushed off without paying them. As a result, I found Paul in a most terrible mood, slumped in the armchair. It was Christmas and I had to do something to raise his spirits. As well as being concerned about Paul, I felt very sorry for Steve too because he had a wife and children and I knew he would be depending on his wages. So I went up the road to our local and cashed a cheque to cover the amount that Peter should have been paid for them both.

Paul and I were really on the skids by then and I became increasingly infuriated by the fact that I was expected to keep paying out for everything. The time had come to call a halt!

My first step was to cancel the standing order for his maintenance. I was still continuing to pay it on his behalf and I wasn't prepared to do so for one moment longer.

By now, Paul had started sleeping in the spare bedroom, which suited me just fine because he was such a heavy snorer after he had been drinking. Some nights he didn't even bother to come home at all.

The pressure was mounting on all sides both at home and work. Fortunately for Pauline at least the scriptwriters finished the Arthur affair storyline by reuniting Arthur and Pauline. He returned home to console and help her after Pete's death.

Later in 1993 I flew over to New York to do a telethon for *Are You Being Served?* The TV company arranged for me to fly out First Class on Virgin but I decided to treat myself, pay the extra and come back on Concorde. I didn't offer to take Paul with me, which incensed him. When I returned on the Sunday night he was in the pub, so I rang him on his mobile to let him know I'd arrived home safely. 'If you'd come back and carry my case upstairs for me, you will find some clothes in it which I bought for you in the States. It's Dallas Cowboys gear, your favourite US football team.' He came home but barely spoke to me. His behaviour that night was one of the final nails in the coffin, as far as I was concerned.

All I wanted was to concentrate on my work. In November 1993 a new family – the Jacksons – started to move into Albert Square. That's when Patsy Palmer first joined us as Bianca, the oldest daughter of Carol (Lindsey Coulson). Carol's youngest daughter was called Sonia.

Sonia was only a girl then, played by a fine young actress called Natalie Cassidy, who was 10 years old when she first joined *EastEnders*. I think we have been incredibly lucky with the youngsters on *EastEnders*. It is difficult not to have favourites but I've watched Natalie grow up, both on and off set, through her teenage years and she has become a lovely young lady.

In my view she is also an astounding young actress who, I would say, is certainly destined for the top. She has the capacity for strong drama through to comedy and her timing is wonderful, as is her sense of humour. Providing Natalie keeps a level head – which I've no doubt she will – my guess is she'll turn into one of the best actresses that Britain has developed.

I have to say I have always had a soft spot for Daniella Westbrook. She reminded me of myself when I was playing Miss Brahms in *AYBS?* I know she had a problem with her private life and indulged in 'exotic substances', but I have to say whenever I had to work with her, she was always spot on with her lines and never kept me hanging about. Unfortunately, she did get unreliable at times, but the last occasion she was in

EastEnders she seemed fine. Both June Brown and I hoped that she had got her act together, she had a little boy to consider and she seemed in a stable relationship. Hopefully it is not too late for her to get her life back on track again; she is such a pretty girl, well mannered and a good little actress when given the opportunity.

My relaxation on Sunday mornings was (and still is) to listen to *The Archers* omnibus edition on Radio 4. After the programme I used to go and meet a friend of mine, Charlie, to play cribbage, which I really do enjoy. Just to be awkward Paul then decided he would play squash on Sundays mornings with his mate, Alan. He'd rush out early and not even think of taking Shirley for a walk before he went; so frequently it meant I couldn't have my own precious hour of peace and quiet. As Alan was head porter at the block of flats where the squash courts were located, I know they didn't have to be on court at any particular time. Paul just did it to annoy me. I continued to cook Sunday lunch for both of us but Paul insisted on sitting upstairs in the lounge to eat his meal, leaving me alone in the kitchen, with the dog. It was absolutely no existence at all and I felt terribly alone, yet again.

My life was in the doldrums and I realized it would be for the best if Paul and I split up. Eventually I decided to confide in Letitia about my situation. Letitia and I frequently swam together and had a Turkish bath at a nearby health club. It was there I revealed to her 'All the personal side of my relationship is finished completely. I cannot even stand the sight of Paul any longer,' I admitted.

'You cannot go on like this. You will make yourself ill,' Letitia warned me.

'Do you think I should offer him some money to leave, then?' I suggested.

'Yes, straightaway,' she insisted.

The next day I contacted my solicitor and told him what I wanted done. 'Tell Paul I will pay him £3,000 to leave,' I instructed.

Later that day, Paul was in the pub on one side of the street by our house. I was in another with Letitia, on the other side. My solicitor went backwards and forwards between the two of us, negotiating terms.

'Paul says he wants £5,000 before he will agree to leave,' he informed me.

'He must be joking,' was my immediate reaction.

'Wendy, give him the money – and tell him to fuck off!' Letitia urged me.

'OK, I'll give him £3,000 in cash and send £2,000 to his ex-wife because he hasn't sent her any money for ages and I've stopped paying the maintenance on his behalf.' The deal was struck.

I wasn't certain exactly when Paul would leave so, like a fool, I still continued to cook him an evening meal. I left it in the microwave ready for him to reheat when he returned home. I must say it amused me in one sense but on the day he actually left for good, I'd cooked him pork chops in white wine sauce. Although he was leaving, he still made sure he had his dinner before he departed! Whatever the circumstances, it seemed all he could ever think about was his stomach.

Paul had asked me if he could store some of his belongings in my flat, which is only five minutes walk from my house. Perhaps it was stupid but I agreed. Sometime shortly afterwards I was sat outside a local cafe, having coffee with a friend, when I saw Paul go past towards the flat. Later he walked back again. Something aroused my suspicions, so I checked the flat, only to discover Paul must have had a spare set of keys cut and had taken up residence.

His clothes were in the washing machine and it was obvious he was living there without my permission. I was furious.

A few nights later I was home in bed when Paul rang. It was nearly midnight and he was in a very agitated state. 'I want your solicitor's home telephone number,' he demanded.

I'd been fast asleep for ages. I usually go to bed early and it's very rare for me to be up after 10p.m. Anyway, I found the number and gave it to him. Next day, Letitia drove me home from work and during the journey my mobile telephone rang. It was Stuart Higgins, then editor of the *Sun*.

He informed me Paul had been carrying on with another woman. A woman reporter had followed them and caught them canoodling in a pub at the end of the street where I live. The reporter approached them but Paul went ballistic and lashed out, hitting the journalist. A right carry-on apparently then ensued and, as a result, there had been a big spread in the *Sun*. That's what he wanted my solicitor's telephone number for.

Afterwards he moved in with Lee, the woman he had been seeing but the relationship didn't last long. He frequented several local pubs and on one of his sorties when he was selling raffle tickets he met another woman, Sue, whom he struck up a relationship with (eventually the pair of them were to marry).

Pauline's marriage was faring a little better by 1994, as she and Arthur worked at rebuilding their own domestic situation. Marriage was on the cards that year too for their son Mark, who had met Ruth, a Scottish nursery teacher. She agreed to marry him, despite his HIV status.

After that storyline, there were several episodes revolving around the Queen Vic, including one in which Michelle was held hostage at gunpoint in the pub and shot by an ex-Army pal of Grant Mitchell. Corrine Hollingworth came back as producer. Corrine had been Julia Smith's assistant when we first started.

She is married to Robert Gabriel, who is now one of our directors. Since then Corrine has left to become head of Channel 5 and is one of the most powerful ladies in television today. Corrine is a smashing woman and it was marvellous having her at the helm of *EastEnders* again.

During the year Michelle then fell in love with her course tutor, Geoff Barnes – much to Arthur's disgust because Geoff was about the same age as himself. Happier times also followed when Michelle obtained her degree.

In the middle of August 1994 I had four days off work and went down to Torquay to see John Inman in his summer show. When I returned to London my mobile phone rang and I received devastating news. The call was a tip-off from a reporter – Paul had done a story on me for the *News of the World*.

I was dumbstruck. I just couldn't believe he would do that to me, not after all his comments about what his brother, Sean and my ex-boyfriend had done in selling tales. The very thought of Paul disclosing details of our married life was despicable and disgusting. What price does loyalty have? I alerted a bodyguard friend of mine, called PJ, just in case there should be any trouble and I might need his help.

Next I tried to contact my solicitor, only to discover he was away on holiday. I then telephoned the firm's duty solicitor but when I rang he denied he even worked for them. In desperation, I telephoned another solicitor I knew, who was a customer at my local pub. He put me in contact with a barrister. By the time I'd made all the calls, the rest of the Press had obviously got wind of the story that was about to appear because reporters started to congregate in the street outside my house. It was an awful situation.

In the middle of all the turmoil, my mobile phone rang again.

This time it was Paul. He was causing me so much anguish, yet what he called about was that he wanted to take the rest of his belongings from my house. All of his that remained anyway were two Chinese rugs and a few clothes but what a time to make such a call. I asked him: 'Why have you done this to me, Paul? Haven't you told them about how I helped you financially?'

'They didn't ask me,' was all he could reply.

'Why haven't you told them about all the clothes I bought you and the other things?'

'They didn't ask,' he kept repeating, over and over again.

PJ came to the house and folded up the Chinese rugs. His wife, Gabriel helped me sort out Paul's remaining belongings, which I packed up for him – even though I'd paid for them. We bundled everything into PJ's car and he drove round to the Windsor Castle pub, where we knew Paul was having a drink. PJ threw the whole lot out on to the pavement!

Apparently, Paul raced out of the pub. He was ashen and protested: 'You just don't understand; you haven't heard my side of the story.'

PJ and his wife moved me out of my house to a secret location where the Press could not find me. I went for a drink in a small pub called The Beehive, where the landlady, Sheila Ord, her assistant, Trish and Sheila's daughter-in-law, Sharon were absolutely marvellous to me and very supportive.

Once I'd recovered from the initial shock of Paul's betrayal, I next checked with the police about my rights to the car. They confirmed I would be legally entitled to reclaim Paul's Range Rover because I'd paid for it and the vehicle was registered in my name.

PJ toured the streets and spotted the vehicle still parked outside the Windsor Castle pub. He broke the steering lock and drove the car away for me. Two of my neighbours happened to see Paul when he returned to collect the Range Rover later. They told me his face was a picture and I'm sure it was!

Anyway, there was nothing the barrister or solicitor could do to stop the horrendous story appearing next morning in the *News of the World*. There it was, on the front page, under the headline 'Wendy's Boozing Sank Our Marriage.' In it, he virtually labelled me an alcoholic and said that I preferred the pub to him. I found his comments hurtful.

After all, if I had been an alcoholic – as Paul alleged – how would I have been able to hold down my job? I certainly don't have the face of an alcoholic, as anyone can see. Yes, I do enjoy a couple of drinks after work to help me relax but I also like to go to bed early. During the week I even take my scripts to bed with me, so I can learn my lines for the following day. Could I do that if I was drunk every night, as he insinuated?

I also consider that whatever item of clothing I want to wear in bed is entirely my own business. However, in the *News of the World* article Paul even criticised me for that, saying 'I just wasn't turned on by a drunk in a Daffy Duck nightie'. It's true that I had bought two nightshirts: one Daffy Duck and one Bugs Bunny – and I did wear one in bed but guess who sometimes wore the Bugs Bunny nightie around the house? It was Paul!

I was expecting all sorts of snide comments as a result of the story but in actual fact after the article appeared, nobody said one unkind word to me. I was not due into the studios that week but someone even telephoned me from *EastEnders* to assure me the tacky story was not being discussed there behind my back.

Sometime previously Paul had revealed that his brother Sean had told him it was his ambition to destroy me, although God only knows why. When Paul's *News of the World* story appeared, it seemed to me that he'd taken on his brother's mantle. When I thought back to the times that Paul had protested about other people's behaviour in approaching the Press, swearing that he'd never do the same, I realized what a total hypocrite he'd turned out to be.

Maybe I was naive but I was convinced by 'friends' that if I spoke to the papers about the real reasons for my split with Paul the press might leave me alone. My soliciter arranged for me to talk to the *Sun*. In the article, I talked about how hurt I was about the break-up and how my work may have come between us. Admittedly, I do tend to have tunnel-vision when I am working and, so, I said I had neglected Paul because of *EastEnders*.

Hindsight is wonderful. However, I must have been incredibly stupid at the time. Supposedly, Paul was paid £15,000 for his 'revelations' to the *News of the World*. He bought himself the most dreadful old Rolls Royce with the money. It was what he always wanted.

One year I'd bought Paul personalised number plates with his initials for his birthday. He put them on the Cabriolet, then the Range Rover and finally, apparently, they ended up on the Rolls Royce. I heard that people were laughing about it and not surprising really. After all, would you expect a carpet fitter to turn up at your house in a Rolls Royce, with personalized number plates to boot?

Not long afterwards I was walking near home, laden down with shopping when I heard a car being driven slowly behind me. It was Paul, with a friend, in his Rolls Royce. He drove round the block once and then again. Maybe in his own way he was trying to make me jealous but it meant nothing to me. I am not materialistic in any way and certainly not of his Rolls. I thought it was all rather sad.

When all the fuss over the *News of the World* front page piece

Filming in Jersey – what a team! Lucy Cain, Cathy Kirby and Nicola Matthews. (Author's Collection)

Two of my favourite prop boys, Lionel and Graham. (Author's Collection)

Shirley aged one, pretty as a picture. (Author's Collection)

Wendy and Shirley at work. (Author's Collection)

What do you do when you're bored at work? Dress the dog up! (Author's Collection)

John and I with the royal corgis at Buckingham Palace. (Author's Collection)

California here we come –
John and I first class all the
way to LA.
(Author's Collection)

Keeping John under control at a Lady Ratlings Ball. (Doug McKenzie)

Filming *Eastenders* at Gorey Castle in Jersey. (Author's Collection)

Me, Mr & Mrs Howard Keel, Betty Boothroyd and my dear friend David. I miss him a lot. (Doug McKenzie)

Me and heart-throb Tony Curtis – what a star! (Author's Collection)

Doing my bit for the Variety Club.

At a Water Rats Ball – Jean Ratcliffe, Lorraine Chase and the wonderful Frankie Vaughn. (Doug McKenzie)

Me and John with Debbie and Roy Hudd at a Lady Ratlings Ball. (Doug McKenzie)

Being made a dame chevalier at a marvellous banquet in the vineyards of Beaune.

A letter I received from a fellow passenger after my MBE was announced as I was travelling on the QE2.

ARCADIA

Cabin A 167
16 June 2000.

Dear Wendy,

I'm the fellow who joined you taking some photos of the ship this afternoon on the launch coming back from the island and it was absolutely brilliant to hear the news of your so well-deserved MBE from the Captain's announcement a few minutes ago.

It was a pleasure to spend a few minutes speaking to someone who so obviously cares about other people and your award is obviously a reflection of this.

Away back in 1990 I had the fantastic experience of receiving my MBE from the Queen at Holyrood Palace in Edinburgh; yours will be no doubt at Buckingham Palace and I'm sure you'll find it an exhilarating experience I'll be watching out for the news coverage when that happens and it will bring back pleasant memories of our brief, simple chat today.

May you keep on bringing pleasure to so many people for many years in the future.

All the very best, and again — Congratulations.

DAVID M. BRODIE, MBE.

died down, friends who came to the house remarked on how different and more relaxed the atmosphere at home had become. It was true, it was so much better once Paul had gone. All he left me was his mobile phone bill, which again I ended up paying. I changed the locks on the front door because by my own past experience, Paul was not to be trusted. He had proved that already by having keys cut to my flat and daring to stay there, without my knowledge. He'd obviously felt no guilt about using my electricity, washing machine or anything else in there.

After the *News of the World* episode, I took out an injunction against Paul which forbade him supplying further stories about me to any newspaper. However, various tabloids continued to write stories about us, some of them referring to Paul and his 'stunning new girlfriend'.

My divorce from Paul – on the grounds of mutual separation – came through in 1994. I was absolutely relieved to finally get rid of him for good. Without Paul around, I could really concentrate on my work. Yes, I was lonely but I was very fortunate; friends stood by me and of course, Shirley was my mainstay.

One of those good friends was a lovely young man called David Jeffrey, who was gay. We'd only recently met but had become great mates because he was wonderful company to go out with. He attended a number of charity black-tie affairs with me, at venues such as The Dorchester, Grosvenor House and The Savoy. David was fantastic fun and we had some fabulous evenings together. (Sadly he passed away in 1996 and I still miss him dreadfully).

Good old Shirley, unless I was at work, or having a quick drink in my local, she was my sole companion. When I went home unless someone telephoned, I didn't speak to another person until I went back to work next day. I took Shirley everywhere with me that I possibly could and if she couldn't come, then her rapturous greetings when I returned home were marvellous. I knew I had to keep going because of the responsibility of looking after Shirley. Plus, of course, it was necessary to continue working, in order to maintain a roof over my head.

CHAPTER TWENTY

Desert Island Discs *and* *10 Years of* EastEnders

In 1995 when I reached my 1,000th episode of *EastEnders* Des McCarthy, the floor manager, called the cast on to the studio floor. He announced that Jane Harris, the executive producer wanted to say a few words to us. I thought here we go, another lecture about something but as I turned around to face her, she started talking about me in glowing terms and of the length of time I had been on the show. Then she presented me with a magnum of champagne and a bouquet of flowers. Plus a beautiful cake which had a miniature china Cairn terrier, a tiny fruit bowl and a washing machine on the top of it! I was really thrilled to bits.

That same year I was selected as a castaway for Radio 4's *Desert Island Discs* programme. I considered it an honour and a privilege and was really looking forward to recording the programme.

I picked out what I considered a good selection of music, such as 'Land Of Hope and Glory' and 'Rule Britannia'. Thinking that, if I was to be on an island on my own, at least I could sing along to those at the top of my voice because there would be nobody else there to disturb! I'm not a singer at the best of times but I do enjoy a rousing sing-song.

I was geared up for an enjoyable time but unfortunately, as it turned out, I found Sue Lawley's attitude towards me left something to be desired. She didn't appear to comprehend my choice of music and I had to point out to her: 'It's all about memories.' Our interview didn't proceed smoothly and I had to stop the recording four times because the conversation didn't follow along the lines of what I had previously discussed with the programme's researchers.

After it was broadcast a number of people commented to me about how much they had enjoyed the programme and my choice of music. At least they appreciated my selections, which was more than I thought Sue Lawley seemed to do.

Out of interest, if you didn't hear the programme, my selection was:

1. 'Land of Hope and Glory' by The Last Night Of The Proms Audience with the BBC Symphony Chorus and Orchestra, conducted by Sir Charles Groves.

I am tone-deaf but alone on a desert island I could sing my heart out to this. It's one of the best pieces I can think of that makes me want to truly sing at the top of my voice.

2. 'In the Mood' by Glenn Miller.

I loved the film *The Glenn Miller Story*. The Christmas scene was so sad when you realized his plane had crashed and that he wouldn't be coming home ever again. I attend a number of evening charity functions and the band usually plays this – it always puts me in the mood to get up and dance.

3. 'Jerusalem' by The Choir of Winchester Cathedral accompanied by The Bournemouth Symphony Orchestra, conducted by David Hill.

We often sang this marvellous hymn at school and I always become emotional whenever I hear it.

4. 'Who Do You Think You Are Kidding Mr Hitler?' by Bud Flanagan – the theme tune from *Dad's Army*, written by Jimmy Perry OBE.

This brings back so many happy memories of working with the *Dad's Army* team. It was a privilege to work alongside such wonderful actors.

5. 'Flower Duet' from *Lakmé* by Delibes sung by Joan Sutherland and Jane Berbier with The National Orchestra of Monte Carlo, conducted by Richard Bonning.

I had one simple reason for selecting this – it is a beautiful piece of music to listen to quietly.

6. Ravel's 'Boléro' by The London Philharmonic, conducted by Andrew Litten.

I was 12 at the time I first saw the old film *Bolero* on TV and thought George Raft was one of the most handsome men I'd ever seen in my life. This is wonderful music, which I could sit and listen to on an island and conjure up all sorts of fantastic images in my mind.

7. 'Barwick Green' – the theme tune from *The Archers*.

I am a life member of *The Archers* Fan Club and it's my one hour of peace and quiet on a Sunday morning to sit and listen to the omnibus of the week's episodes. If I was on a desert island, I would have to arrange to have the omnibus edition sent out to me in a bottle each week. The music also reminds me of Sunday mornings when I was a child and used to listen to *The Archers* at home.

8. 'Rule Britannia' with Anne Collins and the Royal Liverpool Philharmonic Orchestra and Choir conducted by Sir Charles

Groves. This is one of the most rousing pieces of music I've ever heard and kindles a huge amount of national pride in me.

If I had to take only one piece of music with me to the island, my top choice would be 'Land Of Hope And Glory'.

Despite prior negotiation with the programme's researchers, Miss Lawley wouldn't allow me to take Shirley, my Cairn terrier, to the Desert Island as my one luxury. I was furious because on a previous programme, Princess Michael had been allowed to take her cat to the island. 'Anyway, why is the dog such a life-and-death business?' she asked.

I told her the truth. 'Because she is my best friend.'

'What do you mean by that?' she wanted to know. 'Is life on your own otherwise manageable? Don't you find it depressing that you have been married three times and still not found happiness? Are you looking for husband Number Four? Do you find life fulfilling, as it is?'

I wondered exactly what was she trying to prove?

Nor would she allow me a compendium of the works of Tom Sharpe, as my chosen piece of literature. Instead, I had to settle for just one of his books and chose my favourite Tom Sharpe novel, *Wilt*. I love that book because it makes me laugh so much.

Finally, having to accept life on the desert island without Shirley, I was torn in my choice of one luxury item. Should I take a manicure set, packets of cigarettes with my filters and holder, or my unfinished tapestries?

'Perhaps I could take a few packets of cigarettes, rolled up in the tapestries?' I suggested tentatively.

'You can only take one,' she stressed.

There was no point in trying to bargain any further with her. 'I'll take the tapestries.'

With that she thanked me and we bid each other a cool goodbye and the theme tune played us out.

Afterwards, I emerged from Broadcasting House feeling wretched, as if I had done five rounds with a tabloid journalist. I was exhausted by her verbal battering and felt a deep sense of disappointment. I don't feel the same way about the programme anymore though I used to enjoy it enormously.

The 10th anniversary year of *EastEnders* in 1995 was greeted with a host of publicity. For Pauline it was the year that her daughter was due to marry again and she was delighted that at last Michelle would become a respectable married woman again. Despite Arthur's objections to Geoff, at least Michelle was happy with him.

With the departure of actress Sue Tully, I had lost a daughter and *EastEnders* had lost yet another of its original cast members.

Having lost the companionship of her only daughter, the next loss for Pauline was Arthur! Poor old Arfur was sent to prison – on this occasion for a crime he had not committed. He had been framed for stealing money from Flowering Wilderness, a local campaign he had launched to brighten up Walford. He was framed by his friend (or so he thought!) and fellow allotment holder, Willy Roper.

Life in the Fowler household became lonely with both Arthur in prison and Michelle gone to America and in my own personal life, after my separation from Paul, I was living entirely on my own in the house. I had only Shirley for company.

CHAPTER TWENTY-ONE

I Discover I Have Breast Cancer

Early in 1996 I noticed that I was starting to lose weight. At first, I didn't take too much notice attributing it to stress, from the break-up of my marriage. However, on the morning of Saturday 10 February 1996 – how well I remember that fateful date – I discovered the true reason behind my rapid weight loss. I was feeling particularly cold that February morning and decided to warm myself up by popping along to my hairdressers, where they have a sun tanning salon. After a warming sun cabinet I returned home to shower but while I showering, I suddenly felt a large lump in my left breast. I was poleaxed and went icy cold again, this time with fear. I dashed to the mirror to take a closer look. The lump was clearly visible – the image of it will stay in my memory forever.

The best person I could think to ring was my friend Carole, whom we all nickname 'Nursie' because she works at St Mary's Hospital in Paddington. I told her she had to meet me straightaway. We met up and went for a walk. I found it hard to form the words but eventually, I told her: 'I've found a lump.'

'Where?'

'In my breast here', I said, pointing out the spot.

'It is probably nothing,' she tried to reassure me.

But I had a gut feeling that it was far from 'nothing'. Next day I went to play cards at The Beehive and another friend, Joy Barry was at the bar. 'Good heavens, what is the matter with you?' she enquired. 'You look absolutely dreadful.'

I confided in her too that I'd discovered a lump but that it seemed to have disappeared again.

'It can't be cancer then can it?' I asked tentatively. 'I've always understood that cancer attaches itself to something and my lump has gone. So I must be OK . . . mustn't I?'

'Well, it is probably OK, just fatty tissue,' Joy suggested.

It didn't matter what reassurance people tried to give me, I was so worried I couldn't eat all weekend. First thing Monday morning I telephoned my doctor who made an appointment for me to have a mammogram at The Princess Grace Hospital. They could not fit me in until the Wednesday – 14 February.

On St Valentine's Day morning I made an early appearance on GMTV to promote the Gold Heart Campaign for The Variety Club of Great Britain. From the studios I was driven over to The Princess Grace Hospital for my appointment and afterwards I was due to go over to The Bonnington Hotel for a Lady Rattlings' charity lodge meeting.

When I'd had the mammogram done, I could tell by the radiographer's face that there was a real problem. I'd known all along anyway, in my heart of hearts. 'Some Valentine's Day present this has turned out to be,' was all I could keep thinking.

'I think there are a couple more tests you should have done while you are here,' she informed me. I resigned myself to the inevitable: 'Yes, OK.'

Next, they did a biopsy and took cells from my breast through a needle.

After the biopsy I telephoned Carole and asked her to meet me at the pub. I was shaking so much I don't even know how I dialled her number. Next I rang The Bonnington and asked them to pass on my apologies for absence at the lodge meeting, although obviously I didn't disclose the real reason why. Carole came over from work to pick me up and we went into my local, where I downed about four glasses of champagne in quick succession. I remember standing at the bar, just staring at the wall. I couldn't believe what was happening to me.

A short while after I returned home, my doctor rang and confirmed the worst . . . but I already knew, by instinct. By that time I had become very angry. Angry that I had cancer. I shouted and screamed at the wall: 'Why me? Why me?'

I felt desolate but after a little while I had to pull myself together because Shirley was whimpering by the door, she desperately wanted to go out for a walk. Life had to go on, I realized. After walking Shirley I rang Corrine Hollingworth, our executive producer on *EastEnders*.

'Corrine, I have something to tell you which is strictly confidential.'

'What is it, Wendy?'

'I am afraid to say that this morning I was told I have cancer.'

Corrine was stunned into silence and it was obvious she was terribly distressed by my news.

'I can't come into work but I don't want anybody to know the reason why.'

'Of course not,' Corrine replied and promised to cover things for me.

My private doctor, Adrian Whiteson OBE was absolutely brilliant to me and a terrific support. He told me I would have to see a consultant, Mr Gerry Gilmore. 'He is the best surgeon for you,' he assured me.

Thankfully, Joy Barry came with me to see Mr Gilmore at the London Breast Clinic in Harley Street. As soon as we entered his consulting room, I warned him: 'I am telling you right now, I don't want anything cut off. I have enough trouble as it is trying to pull a fella and I certainly don't need an added handicap.'

'Don't be ridiculous,' Mr Gilmore retorted. 'I am not going to cut anything off.' With that he pointed to my X-rays hanging on the light-box.

'Here you are. This is your cancer. You are not very well but I am going to make you better.'

As simple as that. He made everything seem so straight-forward. Mr Gilmore is the sort of man in whom you can have the utmost faith and I believed what he said.

When we left his consulting rooms Joy said to me: 'I don't suppose you noticed all the photographs of those beautiful children?'

'No,'

'Well, it is understandable considering the state you were in.'

However, when I returned to see Mr Gilmore once more with Joy, she could not contain herself. 'Are all these wonderful children yours?'

'Yes, I have eight,' he told her.

Joy and I just looked at each other and when we looked back, Mr Gilmore was staring at us, knowing exactly what reaction his remark had provoked in our minds! Even in the darkest of moments, thank God there is usually something to smile about.

I saw Mr Gilmore again the following week, on the day before my operation. By then I'd already had more tests done, including gamma ray X-rays. They revealed that my heart, lungs and liver were all OK and that, apart from the cancer, my body was clear of any other illnesses. Mr Gilmore and I discussed the final arrangements and I had complete confidence that he would do his very best for me. That evening I telephoned Tom, a taxi driver friend of mine and asked him to pick me up at the house early next morning. I tossed and turned all night. Eventually, Tuesday 20 February dawned but I'd been fully awake before first light. At 8a.m. Tom arrived to drive me to The Princess Grace.

'Are you all right, Wendy?' he enquired on the journey.

'Yes, I'm going to be fine,' I assured him.

When I arrived in my room I felt so alone. Shirley had gone to her 'Auntie Isobel's' (my Spanish friend). I just sat there waiting for proceedings to commence. The administrator came in to take my details. When she asked for my next of kin, I was stumped. I could hardly put down Shirley Brahms, Cairn terrier, so I gave details of my friend Joy Barry. I then had to phone Joy and ask if she minded what I'd done. Of course she didn't but she said, 'What if, not that it will, anything goes wrong, who do I contact?' Stumped again! In the end I put down my agent.

Next I met Brian, the anaesthetist. I warned him: 'The problem is I do tend to use shall we say 'colourful' language and I'm worried that when I'm under anaesthetic I might start shouting my head off.'

'Don't worry, you will be fine, I'm sure,'

I had the pre-med and was supposed to be drifting off to sleep but the telephone never stopped ringing. So when they wheeled me on the trolley to theatre just in case they thought to the contrary I alerted Brian that I was still not asleep yet.

'Yes, we know!'

Within seconds I must have nodded off because the next thing I remember was coming to and seeing Brian and Mr Gilmore sat by my bedside.

'Good news!' Mr Gilmore informed me. 'We have taken away the cancerous lump, plus part of your lymph glands. They've been checked by biopsy and you're all clear.'

I could not begin to describe my feelings of relief. 'Thank you, thank you,' I kept on repeating to them and then – as a last-minute thought – I gave Brian a questioning look.

'Oh, never heard a word,' he murmured but I could tell by his face he was lying!

That evening as I was lying in bed with a drip attached to my left breast, Nursie arrived accompanied by another girlfriend of mine, called Lynn. The three of us sat and watched television together. There were already some lovely flowers in the room and two bottles of 'my favourite medicine' sent in by Corrine Hollingsworth. The nurse gave permission for me to have a drink, so the three of us each enjoyed a couple of glasses of champagne to speed my recovery.

Next day, Wednesday 21 February I rang Corrine to tell her that everything had gone well. However, somebody must have leaked information to the Press that I was in hospital because by that time a number of journalists had started to gather around my house. They knew something was up because I had been written out of the script without a word of explanation. It must have taken a lot of re-jigging at short notice. Apparently it was initially passed off as a 'family problem' until someone remarked 'But Wendy hasn't got any family'. So I don't know what excuse Corrine made next to tide things over.

Peter Holsten, our costume designer on *EastEnders*, sent a fax to my house, which was brought in for me. It was a drawing of everyone in the costume department with the message: 'We don't know what's wrong but whatever it is, we hope everything will be all right soon.'

Poor Carole and Lynn ended up having to play hide and seek with all the journalists. One of them even went into the pub at the end of my street and started questioning Angie, the barmaid.

'No comment,' was all she would say.

'She's got you well trained,' was the terse reply.

I thought that was really good of her because the Press can be very persistent and a tremendous nuisance but she firmly stood her ground. When they could not find the answers they wanted from Angie, some of them started ringing neighbours' doorbells, which annoyed me greatly because I hate thinking of my neighbours being disturbed and upset on my account.

I thought the best solution would be for me to telephone my solicitor and let him know what was going on. He advised me to make an official announcement to the Press. So I rang Neil Wallace, who was then deputy editor of the *Sun*.

'Neil, I'll ring you back in ten minutes, by which time I want you to have a tape recorder set up by the telephone. I just want you to let me speak and then I'll answer your questions afterwards.'

Which is what I did – I provided the *Sun* with a really good exclusive for which, I hasten to add, I received no fee at all. Neil asked if one of their photographers could take a picture.

'No, I do not want you coming to this hospital taking my photo.'

He fully understood my position and next day the *Sun* sent a most beautiful bouquet of flowers to me in hospital, together with some balloons and champagne to cheer me up.

Of course other newspapers saw the *Sun*'s first edition, picked up their scoop and ran with the story in later editions. My solicitor suggested we should call a Press conference at the hospital on the following day, Friday 23 February.

The press were there in force. There were TV cameras present too which, ironically, turned out to be very unfortunate for Nursie and Lynn. Earlier they had telephoned their respective employers and reported in sick, so that they could accompany me out of hospital. Unluckily for them, they were both filmed by the

TV cameras with me!

I spent half an hour talking to the journalists inside and told them I was determined not to be downbeat or miserable by what had happened. Then I had to face all the photographers outside.

'Gentlemen, I will pose for all your photos now but afterwards please do me a favour and leave me alone, so I can recover in peace.'

As it turned out they were true to their word bar three of them.

After the photo session I was driven home and Isobel, my friend who'd been looking after Shirley while I was in hospital, brought my wonderful little dog back home. I had kept Shirley's photo beside my bed in hospital and I cannot tell you how absolutely thrilled I was to be reunited with her at long last. Then I had a lovely surprise because my friend James Gamez who lives in San Francisco, turned up unexpectedly at the house. It was marvellous to be home once more, surrounded by people I loved and as for the flowers, well, the bouquets just kept on arriving, until there were no vases left to put them in. The gang had to go out and beg, borrow, or buy more vases and glass jars. I have never seen so many flowers in one place in all my life. Of all the many flowers that I received after it was announced I had cancer, it was Todd Carty's (Mark Fowler's) bouquet which touched me most. His message read:

'Dear Mumsy, I can't manage this family all on my own. Please, hurry up and come back. Your loving son.'

The words reduced me to tears.

Comments such as those gave me a tremendous uplift during the period of my recovery. Occasionally it has seemed that the radiotherapy would never finish but I hadn't given in. I am the same as Pauline – a fighter.

Support from members of the public was overwhelming too. Taxi drivers leaned out of their cabs to yell good wishes to me from across the street, bus drivers held up traffic to enquire about my progress, lorry drivers honked their horns and gave me the thumbs up. Spontaneous good wishes such as those helped sustain me so much.

Over the following few days a flood of cards and letters started arriving from well-wishers, all sorts of people were so kind to me. For instance, one evening I went into my local and was greeted by Kerry Newlands, a local hotelier, who is a very big but charming chap with a heart of gold. He came over and asked me how I was doing. Next minute he picked me up into his arms and gently hugged me. He had tears in his eyes – and I certainly had them in mine too because his reaction surprised me. There were other similar touching moments from a variety of well-wishers and collectively they proved to be a great source of comfort to me.

While I'd been in hospital I'd received *EastEnders* scripts for the following week. Although I'd only been discharged from hospital on the Friday, I decided that I ought to return to work on the Monday. That decision nearly proved to be the most costly mistake I have ever made in my life. In the beginning I was relieved to discover that I did not have to have chemotherapy after my operation. But what I didn't realize was that I would have to take radiotherapy treatment instead over a period of weeks. Nor did I realize that radiotherapy would turn out to be tiring in the extreme and nearly worse than the illness itself.

The only reason I returned to *EastEnders* so quickly was because I knew that in the work schedule I was due to travel to the Channel Islands to film some scenes. They were the ones in which Arthur's fellow allotment holder, Willy Roper had persuaded Pauline to join him on a trip to Jersey. Being lonely, Pauline was flattered by his attentions but eventually recognized Willy for the rogue he truly was, when she noticed a host of credit cards in his wallet – all under different names.

Mark, who was very loyal to his dad, even in prison had been

197

suspicious of Willy all along. He tried to warn Pauline off but she wouldn't listen, so he'd hired a private detective to follow them around Jersey. The sleuth photographed Willy buying and selling a series of cars. Mark's action vindicated, it eventually led to the re-opening of Arthur's case.

We did some filming at Gorey Castle, which was pretty drafty so Lionel and Graham made a cosy little hideaway for us in one of the castle turrets. They even found a heater for us!

Whilst filming at the castle, the sound boy, Kevin, was getting a buzzing sound over the sound track. The two sparks (electricians) traced it to a junction box in one of the towers and, thinking there would be nothing of any great importance electrical in a ruined castle, they turned it off. A couple of hours later a car drew up at the castle gates and two men got out, looking a bit cross. Well, it turned out that they had turned off the transmitter for the mobile phones on the island. I suppose it gave some respite for mobile phone haters in restaurants!

I realized that logistically it would have been a very expensive exercise to set up the filming in Jersey. So I told the producers that I would be prepared to travel across to the Channel Islands, as long as they provided somewhere for me to rest during the lunch break and while they were setting up scenes. They were true to their word and organized a caravan for me. The caterers were marvellous too and ensured I had an early meal so that I could have an hour's sleep before we started the afternoon's filming. The crew were brilliant also; almost everyone seemed to appreciate what I had been through.

CHAPTER TWENTY-TWO

Silver Linings

They say every cloud has a silver lining. Some people believe that even in your darkest hour and at times of real trouble, somehow, someone is sent along to help you – just when you need help the most. That happened to me too. In the midst of me agonizing over my cancer, a newly-formed acquaintanceship turned into a relationship full of support, understanding and ultimately love.

A month before I discovered the lump I'd been to see a clairvoyant, called Linda Dawkins, for a reading. She told me that there were two young men, who were known to me, who would like to get close to me. 'One of them is really keen, you must know him?' she insisted, 'I get the name John.' It meant nothing to me and I thought no more about her prediction.

However, one night soon afterwards I was having a drink with Lynn, a girlfriend of mine and another friend, Peter Lawford. Peter was joined by a young man whom I had seen in the pub many times before. He was a painter and decorator, who came from Belfast but had lived in London for several years. He was so funny that he soon had us all laughing our heads off – and his name was John!

After that it seemed I was always bumping into him. Eventually we got chatting on our own, without other people around and he told me that he had been separated from his wife for some time and that he had two little girls. Afterwards we often met up – by chance – until eventually he started to come to the house. I'll always remember our first 'date', when we went out together, away from our 'patch'. It was to the greyhound stadium at Walthamstow. We were in a private lounge, as guests of Mrs Chandler, who owns the track. We were greeted by old friend Peter Dean, who asked John what he would like to drink. I didn't hear John order a pint of lager but it was rather a shock for me to see his pint perched in the middle of the tray, surrounded by six glasses of champagne and two G & Ts – not quite in keeping with the private lounge!

Worse still, as the evening wore on John got talking to one gentleman who runs the betting Tote. I thought they were discussing form and the guy asked John, 'Are you a doggie man?' To which he immediately replied 'No, missionary!'

Well, I didn't clock on at first and was looking down my race card for a dog called Missionary. Suddenly, I realized what John had said. OH! did we get some funny looks for the rest of the night! Anyway, it was a splendid evening and John thoroughly enjoyed himself.

In the beginning, apart from Nursie, Joy, Lynn and my executive producer, I had told no one about my cancer. But John had a kind and understanding way with him and was a good listener. The more we chatted I felt somehow I could confide in him, so I told him. 'Why me?' I asked. 'Well, God doesn't pick and choose, you know,' was his reply – and I realized that he was correct. OK, so I had tried to look after myself all my life, I'd eaten sensibly and taken exercise but why should I think I was so special that I could avoid illness.

Instead of running in the opposite direction when he heard the news about my cancer, John stayed around and turned out to be very good to me – and for me. He sat in the house with me each evening to keep me company. We talked for hours, or just watched videos together, there was nothing more to our relationship then. Later in the evening, before he returned to his flat, he walked around the block with me when I took Shirley out for her late night constitutional.

While I was away working in Jersey, John telephoned me every night at the hotel. We had a lovely make-up designer called Lucy, who was with us over there and in the end I confided in her about John and she was really pleased for me. I also told Cathy Kirby, who was one of my favourite dressers. It was nice that a couple of the people over there with me knew about the new man in my life and although it was very hard work for me in the condition I was in, the new relationship lightened the load considerably. By the time I returned from filming in Jersey, John and I had become 'an item'.

On my return from the Channel Islands I had an appointment with an oncologist, Dr Carmel Coulter to arrange for my radiotherapy sessions. I didn't have a clue what it was going to be like and for those who have never seen a radiotherapy machine it is quite daunting, to say the least. It is an enormous piece of equipment and you have to lie on it, as if you are in a cradle. Laser lights pinpoint the exact area to be treated with the radio waves. I take my hat off to those nurses who operate the machinery because it is so incredibly accurate.

The skin on and around my breast became very tender after each treatment, it was rather like sunburn. I found that by placing a silk handkerchief inside my bra I could alleviate some of the discomfort. What I wasn't prepared for though was how tired I felt after having radiotherapy. I'd made a block booking of sessions for the afternoons. *EastEnders* were very good and allowed me to work mornings only. I used to get up for work

201

early at 5a.m., travel to Borehamwood, work all morning, travel home, have a quick lunch and then go off for radiotherapy. By the time I returned home I'd make myself a cup of tea and watch *Countdown* but unfailingly I'd fall asleep in the chair and the next thing I knew it would be around 8p.m. Then I'd have to learn my lines for the following day.

My friends were brilliant though and several of them walked Shirley for me. A number of people were very helpful and supportive, most of all John, who was a tower of strength. Trying to learn lines, go to work and then undergo the radiotherapy made me feel as if I would never reach the end of a dark tunnel. I couldn't let them down at work and the treatment was debilitating. Physically, I almost broke down. I told John I was finding it difficult to continue but then he would gently reassure me 'You can't give up now Wendy, not after everything you've already been through. You're more than half-way now, it won't last much longer.' His encouragement gave me the strength for the final hurdle.

However, when I visited Dr Coulter to discuss the progress of my treatment, she was very worried when she saw me. She insisted that I should have a break from work. I was written out of the show for two weeks, so I could get some proper rest before and after the radiotherapy sessions at Cromwell Hospital. Looking back, I do now realize it was too ambitious of me to think I could return to work straightaway because as it turned out, I was just not up to it.

The two weeks were hardly a rest though, for I was dogged with trouble throughout.

As if I did not have enough on my plate at the time, the *Sunday People* took a set of photographs of well-known people's houses. In the feature they printed a picture of my house, with a caption underneath which read: 'Wendy lives alone.' It was one of the most crass and irresponsible pieces of journalism I have ever encountered. The photograph unfortunately prompted a young man to write and say that he would be travelling to London to find me because he did not consider it correct that I should live in such a big house on my own. He'd obtained what he thought was my address – in Twickenham – from a fan magazine. Fortunately, that address was just a forwarding one, it belonged to my ex-agent.

Coincidentally, the day I finally received the letter from the man, Neil Wallace from the *Sun* rang me on my mobile. He detected there was something wrong and when I revealed to him what had happened, he told me to fax the letter to his office immediately. Straightaway he dispatched a reporter and a photographer to where the lad lived. They discovered that the walls in one room of his house were plastered with photographs of me.

Next day, two detectives arrived at my door. 'We have some very bad news for you,' one of them announced. 'I hate to have to say this but your letter writer has left home and, according to his mother, he has taken a large kitchen knife with him.'

I was petrified at the thought that this young man could soon be stalking me. The problem was, apart from seeing one photo of him in the paper, I hadn't a clue what he looked like. Whereas he had the advantage, knowing exactly who I was. It was a terrible predicament for me and I felt very scared.

The police from Marylebone station were marvellous. When I was at home, a copper in an unmarked car was parked at the end of my street day and night, watching every movement. While I was at work, I knew I was safe because of the security precautions taken there anyway. John and his mates were absolutely fabulous too. I was never once left on my own. Either he, or one of his friends, would walk with me everywhere. One Sunday morning, my friend's son, Philip was walking with me and when we arrived home there were three photographers stood on the doorstep. I was absolutely furious.

'How stupid can you be? The letter writer is still missing and you want to take more photos, here outside my house, of all places. It's because a picture of my house was published in the first place that I am in this dreadful situation now. Aren't you ashamed of yourselves? I am just getting over cancer and I'm not supposed to have this sort of stress.'

Two of them walked away. The third persisted and took a photograph. It was published next day, with a story alleging I was sheepish with photographers, which was absolute bollocks. I was not sheepish, I was furious with them! Philip was captured in the background of the picture and had his leg pulled unmercifully at the Post Office, where he works because the caption read 'Wendy's burly minder'. Well, Philip is about as burly as I am. He's tall but very slim. It was the only aspect of the whole episode that made me smile.

Then to cap it all, while I was on the supposed 'rest' from work, someone sent me a bouquet of flowers care of The Beehive pub, where I play cribbage on Sundays. I arranged to walk over and collect them. Nursie offered to come with me but I insisted I'd be fine and that I would take Shirley for company. As I was walking back a photographer suddenly leapt out from behind a tree and scared the living daylights out of me.

'Are you mad?' I shouted at him.

He took no notice and shot off several pictures of me. Next morning, one of the photos appeared in a newspaper accompanied by a story: 'Wendy leaving a pub after a knees up'.

It was an exceedingly unfair and cruel piece of 'journalism'. I was so unwell that it was taking me all my time to even stand up, let alone party. Anyway, a few days later, the stalker gave himself up to the police, thank God. So at least that was one less worry.

By then John and I had become lovers and he was staying at the house on a regular basis, although we were not yet living together permanently. It was lovely to have someone to come home to and share things with – apart from Shirley, of course! As for her, well she absolutely adored John because he made such a big fuss of her. The three of us were very happy together but our peace didn't last for long. Soon it all hit the fan because someone had informed the Press about our relationship.

One morning when I was due to leave for work, I looked outside the door for my taxi and saw a man standing in the street. I didn't take much notice of him as the taxi arrived. John kissed me goodbye and we went off to our respective jobs. Later that day, word was out. Reporters were up and down my street trying to find out about John. Once again I rang Neil Wallace at the *Sun*.

'Neil, what are you doing? You know I am not supposed to have any stress or upset during this recovery period. What on earth is going on?'

'Well, I have pictures of you with a young man.'

'So what?'

'But you are kissing him.'

'Yes, maybe but then I kiss lots of people.'

'But this one is on the lips.'

'Neil, for heaven's sake, I even kiss my dog on the lips when I want to.'

The conversation was to no avail because the *Sun* proposed to publish the most appalling story about John and his friends, which was mostly all lies. I managed to have it changed in later editions but the headline remained: 'Look who's getting friendly with Wendy.' I couldn't imagine that people would really be that interested! What upset me most was the fact that I learnt that the person who had tipped the Press off about John was known to us.

Yet again, I was betrayed by an acquaintance, this time for £3,000 apparently.

It was the first time that John that been 'exposed' in the Press and he found the whole incident distressing too. However, the one thing I can say that was a surprising bonus was when I arrived at work on the morning that the story of the kiss appeared, my street-cred seemed to have risen enormously. Me seen kissing someone in the street – the mere idea of it! I had quite a few sideways looks from the props boys, who then started whistling and making light of the story – but the ribbing was in good humour, I think they were pleased for me. Sid Owen [Ricky Butcher] found it particularly amusing and Todd Carty [Mark Fowler] looked thrilled to bits.

In July we received an invitation from theatrical agent, Johnny Mans to attend a Royal Garden Party in the grounds of Buckingham Palace, on behalf of The 'Not Forgotten' Association, a wonderful organization that represents disabled ex-servicemen. Interestingly, their party is the only occasion when visitors are allowed to take cameras into the grounds of Buckingham Palace. I gladly accepted the invite.

However, later that month I was offered work in Australia, which beside being extremely well paid, also included a free trip Down Under for John and I. The big problem was that it would coincide with the 'Not Forgotten' event. I couldn't believe the bad timing and initially it took some heart searching to decide what do to. True, I'd been to a garden party at Buckingham Palace before but John had never been there. Anyway as we are both firm Royalists, in the end, there was only one decision to be made: we went to the Palace.

I hired a limousine for 30 July to drive us to the Palace in style. When we arrived there were massive crowds outside and the main gates had not yet been opened. We stepped out of the car, I was recognized by some in the crowd and an impromptu autograph session then ensued. A policeman on the gates spotted what was going on and allowed John and I through before time.

We walked through into the Palace gardens, which are remarkable. They are so peaceful it is very hard to believe one is in the centre of London. There are trees and shrubs from throughout the world growing there, each one carefully labelled with its name and origins. John and I were very much enjoying our solitary stroll when, in the distance, we saw a Royal footman walking nine corgis. One, which I took to be the oldest, was lagging behind. Consequently we soon caught up with him but as we approached, the dog turned around and started barking loudly. That alerted the other corgis, who then all ran over to us, barking and snapping at our heels. They are probably lovely dogs and I know it was THEIR garden we were in but they certainly put the wind up John and I.

Fortunately, the footman followed in hot pursuit and as luck would have it, I recognized him from a previous party I had attended at the Palace. So we had a little chat while he calmed down the dogs. I ventured to ask him if he would take our photograph with the corgis. He gladly obliged, then John and I hastily made our way to a different part of the grounds and all was well that ended well.

The party that followed was a humbling occasion for John and I, just looking at those around us. We saw so many ex-servicemen who had been badly disabled serving their country, not just in the two World Wars but more recently in the Falklands, Northern Ireland and the Gulf. Her Royal Highness, The Princess Margaret was in attendance and during the afternoon conducted an investiture ceremony for a few of the men who had been awarded honours.

During the afternoon I had the great pleasure of meeting two lovely gentlemen who had been friends since they first joined the Army together. They had fought in World War I and one was 100 and the other 101. Despite their age, they were still very upright and sprightly, with the physique of men in their sixties. Listening to them it was quite obvious what their main pleasure was that afternoon – they were there to eye up the ladies, God bless them!

After the Palace party I had the 'infamous' corgi photograph framed and mounted with the original invitation. I had a copy of the invitation and the same photograph framed together and sent it to John's mother, Mary, in Belfast. She rang me soon afterwards to say thank you and mentioned that Jimmy, John's stepfather, had hung it on the wall.

'Good,' I replied and suggested 'Perhaps you could send Jimmy over here because John hasn't hung ours, despite my repeated requests.' [When you read this John, please note, it is STILL not up on the wall!]

As the summer of '96 progressed I felt that I needed a proper break away to further help me recuperate from the after-effects of the operation and radiotherapy. John deserved one too, for the way he had looked after me throughout, so we flew first class to Los Angeles – it was expensive but worth every penny. We had a very relaxing time which did us both the world of good and we took the opportunity to contact some US agents while we were there. In the mornings we just lazed around the pool of our hotel in Beverly Hills.

I'd stayed at the Peninsular Hotel before but had a lot of trouble from the Press, who were under the impression I was there to meet a man friend. They'd even checked a photographer into the hotel to try and get some shots. So when I went with John, I booked us in under my friend's name of Morgan. The problem was it became very confusing when we were paged for phone messages because we'd forget we were under assumed names and ignore them!

Come the afternoons and it was time for my favourite hobby – shopping! I admit that I am a shopaholic, so there was nowhere better for me to spend my time than to hit Rodeo Drive with a vengeance – much to John's annoyance!

One afternoon as we were wandering around Rodeo Drive, I spotted a beautiful Chanel suit in a window. John liked it too and suggested I should try it on. It was a very hot day and John and I were only wearing shorts and T-shirts but undeterred, we ventured into the Chanel shop. I had never been greeted by such a snooty reception in my life and – obviously because of our attire – the assistants thought I couldn't afford to buy clothes there.

'I'd like to try the suit on in the window, please?' I asked politely, ignoring the snub.

The assistant continued to treat me like dirt. 'We don't have it in your size,' he insisted point blank.

John was becoming increasingly irritated by the assistant's attitude and said it was like one of Julia Roberts' scenes in *Pretty Woman*.

At that moment a couple of Americans walked in and recognized me 'Gee but aren't you Miss Brahms from *Are You Being Served?*' With that they asked for my autograph and were, coincidentally, followed a couple of minutes later by two English fans 'Wendy, is it really you? and they too also requested my autograph. Open sesame – by that time, the previously unhelpful assistant was all over me.

'Would you like a Coke or coffee, madam? Now, although we don't have the suit in your size, we can re-make it for you without any problem.'

Suddenly nothing was too much trouble for them! It was only

because I liked the suit so much that I stayed for the re-fitting. The tailoress came down and saw me in a private fitting room and re-measured the suit to perfection. I have to say the service was getting rather good by then and although I offered to collect the suit next day, the manager insisted on delivering it personally to the Peninsular Hotel.

Needless to say, at John's insistence, we made sure we were out when he was due to arrive! Nevertheless, he still left a note in reception, saying 'how nice it had been to work with me.'

Four years on and I still really love that suit. Just as well because it cost a bomb – but it does look terrific. I wore it to Windsor Castle in April 1998 when I went to meet the Queen and Duke of Edinburgh at a reception for the arts.

While we were in LA we met up with some friends of mine, Cody and Shirley Morgan (those of the borrowed surname)! They kindly arranged a VIP tour of the Warner Brothers Studios for us which I found interesting but for me it was rather like a busman's holiday!

After LA we headed further north in California to San Francisco for another week's holiday. We met up with my friend James Gamez, whom I had last seen in London in February on the night I came home from hospital. James lives in San Francisco and had arranged for us to stay at the Sheraton on the Wharf Hotel, right down by the bay, near the Golden Gate. John and I had another lovely relaxing week there, seeing a few sights in the city and taking boat trips to Sausalito Island, which I really enjoyed.

Those two weeks in the States made me feel wonderful, I was well and truly able to put some of the trauma of my illness behind me and move on to the next stage of my life. I returned to *EastEnders* feeling fantastic, re-charged and ready to get on with my work.

*

I hope that by sharing the details of my own experience with cancer it may help others – either themselves or a loved one with cancer. I would urge any reader who finds a lump in their breast to act quickly. Do not postpone visiting your doctor. The worrying symptoms may be nothing at all but if there is something there, it is important to have treatment as soon as possible. Before I had my first mammogram, I'd been told that it was painful and that had put me off having one done. For the record, a mammogram is not painful and it can save your life.

Most of all, should cancer be diagnosed, then please keep positive. Whatever happens there is no room for negativity, never give in to it. Keep only positive thoughts in your head – they will help you fight on and overcome any problems or difficulties that may arise.

One last word, don't think I'm addressing my advice to women readers only. Remember, many men develop breast cancer too.

CHAPTER TWENTY-THREE

A Quieter Time

After all the trials and tribulations of 1996, thankfully 1997 was much quieter all round.

Pauline did have to travel to Ireland in 1997 when she discovered that she had a long-lost sister. She found an old letter from Lou to Ethel Skinner, in which Lou admitted that she'd had a daughter early in life whom she was forced to give up at birth for adoption. Pauline – with Mark, Ruth, Ian and Lucy in tow – set sail for Ireland, where the long-lost sister now lived.

I had time to take part in game shows and during the year, among other things, was asked to do *Call My Bluff* and *All Over The Shop*.

Call My Bluff, chaired by Bob Holness and featuring team leaders, Alan Coren and Sandi Toksvig with two celebrity guests on each panel, is always a hoot to do. For any readers unfamiliar with the show, it involves taking an obscure word from the dictionary, each team member gives a definition – two are false, one is true – and the opposing team have to guess the correct definition.

Alan Coren in particular is a great laugh but there's always a great deal of wit and banter flying around about the overstretched inventiveness of some of the supposed definitions. We recorded a few episodes of the show in one day at the Pebble Mill Studios in Birmingham and during one programme, I don't know what happened but for some reason, I lost my concentration. My mind started drifting as Sandi read out her explanation of a word and suddenly the camera was on me. I hadn't a clue what she had said.

'Oh, sorry, is it my go?' was all I could muster up, then quickly made the excuse, 'I thought it was Alan's turn.'

'Would you like us to read it all over again for you, Wendy?' Sandi asked.

'No, no,' I insisted and took a wild guess and by a fluke, I happened to be right but from there on, I made sure I concentrated! Apart from the fun we have making the programmes, *Call My Bluff* is a great joy for any invited guest because the whole crew and production team always make you feel very welcome.

The same can be said for *All Over The Shop*. It is hosted by Paul Ross and I did a few of the shows during 1997. The format is that three similar articles are bought from various retail outlets, ranging from High Street department stores to corner shops and the contestants have to price them up from the cheapest to the dearest. On one show I had the wonderful experience of working with Sherrie Hewson, who used to be in *Coronation Street*. Our items to evaluate were three different types of my favourite drink – champagne – although unfortunately none of them were my usual marque. They put two glasses of each in front of us and we were supposed to place the red, blue and green cards under them, according to what we considered were the dearest, middle and cheapest prices. Well I imagine that Sherrie has a low alcohol tolerance because after about four sips, she was tipsy! She started putting the glasses down on the wrong mats and in the end couldn't have cared if they were on any mats at all! Needless to say, we didn't get any of them right but at least Sherrie was very happy – and the show had only just begun!

The lovely actress, June Whitfield was on the other team and when it came to their turn, they had to taste fish cakes and place them in value order. She studied them intently and in her eloquent voice, asked 'What on earth is it?'

I think *All Over The Shop* is a very well put together show, which provides excellent light entertainment. Paul Ross is a great guy too and comes from a highly talented family. His mother, Martha is a lovely lady; she has worked as a supporting artiste on *EastEnders* for many years and she and I get on really well together. When she was a young girl Martha appeared at the Theatre Royal, Stratford and was billed as the East End's answer to Shirley Temple. I also know his brother Jonathan (who once interviewed me on his show, wearing Mickey Mouse ears!) but Paul has always been my favourite.

Talking of supporting artistes on *EastEnders*, we have had some excellent ones in our time. It was always Julia's policy to use s.a.'s on a regular basis to give credibility to the Square. Many of those in the background have been with us from the beginning and have interesting histories of their own. Like Ron Tarr, who ran the household goods stall and was one of the most striking characters in the market. Ron attended Bell Street Secondary Modern School in Marylebone from 1945–51 and by coincidence, a friend of mine – Jack Shepherd – happened to be deputy head boy at that time. Jack remembers Ron with affection because Ron looked after him, which was understandable because Ron was twice the size of Jack! At the age of 19, Ron was one of the youngest to ever swim the Channel and besides swimming, Ron's other interests were boxing and wrestling. Ron was a gentle giant and whenever there was a gap to fill in a scene, the cry always went out 'Send for Ron'. He'd also appeared in one episode of *Are You Being Served?* as a truck driver. Sadly, Ron died of cancer in October 1997 and we were all given the day off to attend his funeral. The church was packed, even crew members from previous years turned up to say their goodbyes to big Ron.

Bruce Callender was a 'floating' s.a. who was born in the West Indies. He was a very good looking, quiet and reserved man. Although he did a lot of work on *EastEnders*, Bruce was a bespoke tailor, who made silk gowns and ties for Turnbull & Asser. Sadly Bruce also died of cancer a few years ago.

Michael Leader – the milkman – is a founder member of the Laurel and Hardy fan club and often passes on messages of good will to me from Stan's daughter. His father was the famous band leader, Harry Leader – who played regularly at venues such as the Hammmersmith Palais and the Astoria – and who discovered Matt Monro.

Joan Harsant, who runs the sweetie stall, has worked in light entertainment for years and was Dame Edna's nurse for Barry Humphries. Her parents were the well-known variety act, Gatcomb and Dawson, and Joan brought in some of their playbills to show us one day. It was fascinating to see all those names from the past.

Doreen Taylor – on the bookstall – has been with us from day one. She was a club and cabaret singer, who has performed on several cruise ships.

Ulric Browne – reggae stall – is also a day oner. Ulric has appeared in many stage productions before *EastEnders* and now does occasional lines as 'Winston'.

Maggie Heald – bag stall – was a child artiste and worked with Dickie Henderson when she was just 13. She had a lead role in

Dixon of Dock Green and appeared in *Man At The Top* and *Out* with Tom Bell.

Jane Slaughter – flower stall/Queen Vic barmaid, Tracey – is another day oner and was a dancer and actress in many films and shows, including the children's shows *Ballet Shoes* and *What Katey Did*.

Ina Clare – material stall – was a Tiller girl and TV Topper and also danced in numerous films and TV shows.

Johnny Emms – whenever there is a sing-song at the Vic, Johnny is there as resident piano player.

Although we've had some excellent s.a.'s in our time, we've also had some unfortunate experiences as well. You can always tell when they are not pro's. One woman kept talking in the background, saying 'Look, look, we're on telly' (she was transfixed by the monitor on the studio floor!). With others, sometimes when you were walking on the lot, they'd stare at you as a TV personality and not a character going about your every day business!

1997 was a very sad year for us all on *EastEnders*, for that was when dear Julia Smith, our co-creator and original producer, died of cancer. I received the news of Julia's death by telephone when I was recording *Celebrity Ready Steady Cook* and felt devastated but had to carry on with the programme. I admired Julia tremendously, she was a very strong-minded person, who didn't suffer fools gladly. John and I went to her cremation service and I felt very upset by the whole occasion. The only piece of joy was to see so many other actors and crew paying their last respects to a wonderful woman. Among those who spoke at her service were the BBC's Alan Yentob and Tony Holland, co-creator of *EastEnders*. Alan said some lovely words about Julia and even referred to me and the times I'd worked with her over the years before *EastEnders* started. It made me feel even sadder, remembering. Afterwards one of Julia's friends approached me and told me 'She was very fond of you, you know, you were always one of her favourites.' I was too upset to speak to anybody after that and left the crematorium straightaway to spend time alone and reflect. Julia will be sadly missed, not just in-house at the BBC but by television viewers everywhere.

During the late summer of 1997, instead of having another long-haul flight to the US as we had done the previous year, John and I decided to go to Jersey for a couple of weeks holiday. I always love it there and we had a very relaxing time. I returned with my brain cells and batteries recharged, especially having had more than a few shopping forays around St Helier – or large doses of 'retail therapy', as I prefer to call it!

I think that Jim Davidson is one of the best all round entertainers we have left in the business. I've known him for many years and appeared on several of his TV shows. I did one towards the end of 1997 and promised Jim that we would come down to Brighton for the last night of his adult panto, *Sinderella*. Just before Christmas John and I, together with our friends, Ray and Debbie booked into a hotel in Brighton, had a few drinks and headed for the show. Jess Conrad played Prince Charming, with a sock tucked down his tights! I really like Jess and thought it was brilliant to see him laughing at his own expense.

Jim played Buttons and was fantastically funny, as usual. The only problem was half-way through the show, when Jim asked for the house lights to be put on and announced 'Ladies and gentlemen, I have a friend in the audience tonight. Wendy where are you?' I had to stand up, only to hear him say, 'Not only is this lady a fine actress but she is one of the best people in showbiz, give her a round of applause.' It brought the house down – and me with it because I was so embarrassed, but worse was to come as Jim added 'I must say, ladies and gentlemen that she is also one of the best bunk-ups I have ever had.' The audience roared with laughter and I could have died but Jim just waved and scurried off stage.

We enjoyed the evening immensely, even Jim's little joke at my expense. Listen, I know Jim well – but not that well!

CHAPTER TWENTY-FOUR

Wine in Windsor to Punch-Drunk Panel Games!

In early 1998 I was thrilled to receive an invitation from the Master of the Household at Buckingham Palace, on behalf of her Majesty the Queen. The occasion was a Reception for the Arts held by the Queen and The Duke of Edinburgh at Windsor Castle on 29 April.

It was certainly a star-studded night. There were so many faces I knew well, including Michael Caine, Kenneth Branagh, Helena Bonham Carter and Ben Kingsley among a host of others. The event was deliberately kept very low key and headlines next day referred to it as 'Cool Britannia'.

The reception was held in the magnificent St George's Hall, one of the most historic rooms in the Castle, which is associated with the Order of the Garter. The roof and east wall were seriously damaged in the fire of 1992 but they have now been splendidly restored. The shields of every Garter Knight have been re-created on the ceiling and around the room, so there could not have been a more impressive setting for the function.

I felt very excited to be a part of it all and I must confess they do serve a very good quality wine there! I was privileged to be able to speak to Her Majesty during the evening. What did we talk about? Well, the Queen Mother's love of *Dad's Army* actually!

Looking back on my career, alongside television, I have always much delighted in the work I have done on radio, *Just A Minute* being one of my particular favourites; although it is far from an easy game to play. You have to talk for sixty seconds on a given subject, without repetition, hesitation, or deviation. Right from the start I took to the programme like a duck to water and thoroughly enjoyed participating.

The person responsible for getting me on the show was the producer, Ted Taylor's, assistant, Anne Ling. She also had the task of sounding the buzzer to signal the minute was up. As I used to go there without a sensible thought in my head, I was hard pushed to keep going on anything for sixty seconds. However, at the time I had a pet cockateil called Little Henry, so at the drop of a hat I would bang on about him, whatever the subject.

In the beginning I used to sit next to Derek Nimmo but when, sadly, Kenneth Williams passed away, I felt I'd been promoted because I was placed next to Clement Freud instead. I used to shout 'what?' at Clem every time he buzzed me. One night, leaving after a recording, a very smart gentleman stopped me and said I hadn't shouted at Clem all night and he had come to the recording expressly to hear that.

One of my favourite people on the show was Peter Jones, who was one of the dearest, most charming gentlemen you could ever hope to meet. One evening, before we started the recording, Nicholas and Derek were discussing the merits and place of purchase of their silk pocket handkerchiefs. Peter disappeared for a moment and reappeared with a tiny show of pink in his top pocket. 'What do you think of my hankie, Wendy?' he asked. 'Why it's quite lovely Peter. Where did you get it?' I asked him.

'In there,' he said, pointing to the toilet. 'It's toilet paper!'

I remember, though, once walking into Broadcasting House and in one of the corridors there was a photograph of all the stalwarts from *Just A Minute*, including me. I felt as if I had really arrived – until I looked more closely and saw that they had spelt my name wrong! Hey Ho . . .

A couple of years ago, the programme converted superbly well into a television version and again, I was fortunate to be selected as a panel member. Nicholas Parsons, as always was chairman. I have known Nicholas for such a long time, since I first played his girlfriend on the *Arthur Haynes Show*. He can be rather grand at times, so one of my favourite hobbies is torturing the living daylights out of him when I am on the show! On one of the TV shows, Michael Cashman, in his minute, made a remark about Nicholas never buying a drink. So when I went on the following show, in my minute, I asked him: 'How many rounds in the show, Nicholas?' Nobody could understand why I was asking such a question because there was to be, as usual, a dozen. Until I quipped: 'Well, that is 12 more than you have bought, Nicholas!' The studio just erupted, the director was in hysterics and one of the cameramen had to walk away because he was laughing so much. But it is moments like those which make the shows just crack along, even though poor Nicholas was on a hiding to nothing after that. Doing *Just A Minute* is always such good fun and there is never any harm intended in any of the wisecracks. No wonder the radio show has survived for over forty years.

I've done more spots on radio than I can even remember, although one I do recall clearly was reading a series of stories for Radio 5's children's programmes called *The Worst Witch*. I also did the *Listening Corner* which, originally, had been *Listen With Mother*. On two occasions I have also read the *Morning Story*. One was written by Muriel Spark and was excellent and the other was a story for Holy Week. Would you believe I even received fan mail for those? I was quite taken aback, I have to admit.

Aside from the series I've worked on, I've also tremendously enjoyed my appearances as a panellist on more game shows than I would want to mention here. One though which I will never forget is *All Star Secrets*, which was hosted by Michael Parkinson. I appeared alongside Henry Cooper, Brian Johnson and Roy Kinnear. They recorded two shows of *All Star Secrets* back to back and on the first one of the evening, Oliver Reed was the surprise guest for an item concerning Henry. Unfortunately, instead of Oliver making his appearance from the side as he should have done, he went behind one of the centre panels and punched his way through the set! Parky was ashen and I don't think the rest of us were too happy either.

At first we thought it was a stunt, then we realized Reed was totally pissed. He focused on Henry, who stood up to greet him but then suddenly Reed took a swing at him, Henry ducked and I nearly took the punch for him – what a night!

Noel Edmonds' *House Party* was another show I always enjoyed – despite being Gotcha'd by him. I thought I was attending an amateur play reading for a discussion programme on Radio 4. We were in this church hall with a group of actors and after a while they started to get on my nerves, they were so bad. I was asked to comment on their performances. I told one of them I thought his performance might be bettered if he didn't use a northern accent, as the part had been tailored for Richard Briers and you could virtually hear him speaking the lines. The chap muttered, 'Well, I don't think much of your accent either.' Another wanted to dress as if for Henley, I gently explained the play was set at Christmas time, so white flannels, cravat and blazer would look out of place. He settled for a false moustache as characterization. All of a sudden people started coming in with dogs as if the hall had been double-booked. Chaos ensued. Then the door flew open and a dark man in a big fuzzy wig ran in shouting for his wife (one of the actors on stage) – he was going daft. I thought he was going to hit me and started to make a run for it, grabbing my handbag on the way. He grabbed hold of my arm and shouted, 'Look at me!' I hardly dared look him in the face and when I did, being very shortsighted and without my glasses, it took some time for the penny to drop. When I recognized Noel, I couldn't stop shaking and the make-up girl had to give me rescue remedy to calm me down.

The last time I was on the show, so was Tony Curtis. Now that man is a real star, a proper movie star. He had time for everyone, he posed for photos with just about everyone in the studio – he has such charm and charisma. He was dressed as a security guard for a gag at the start of the show. I met him walking along the corridor. 'Oh, Mr Curtis, Sir – and in a uniform, too!' I cried (a double-whammy for me – I love uniforms). 'I have to search you Madam. Up against the wall,' he said. Imagine being frisked by Tony Curtis.

Shirley has also done her fair share of TV. Apart from *Grace and Favour* she was on Steve Wright's *Auntie's TV Favourites* with me. The idea was she would walk on after me, a cut-up sausage having been placed on the desk for her. She was backstage, ready to be let off her lead on cue. Unfortunately the sausage had not been put where it should have been, Shirley came on and went straight over to the audience, amidst lots of oohs and aahs. Her logic seemed to be that someone amongst all those people must have a crisp or bit of chocolate.

She has also been on the *Generation Game* a couple of times. The last occasion was a game involving celebrity dogs, where the contestants had to match the dog to the celebrity. The dogs were brought on by handlers while we each read out some clues.

Shirley came on, again to a warm welcome, and marched around showing off all her best angles. Next up was Anthea Turner's dogs. All went well until Anthea started reading out her clues; well unfortunately Shirley joined in and didn't shut up until Anthea had finished. Gales of laughter all round. When I went on to claim Shirley, Jim was very kind, as always, and let me plug the Cairn Terrier Rescue Association. I got a lot of letters from people interested in adopting a Cairn after that show.

Shirley also gets her own fan mail. A Cairn called Holly H, who lives in Milton Keynes and goes to Guernsey for her holidays. There is another Cairn called Gi Gi Walker who lives in the north of England. Both she and Holly feature on Shirley's page on the website about me.

CHAPTER TWENTY-FIVE

All Aboard!

Later in 1998 I was invited to work on the Cunard liner *Queen Elizabeth 2* – or *QE2* as it is more popularly known. John was also invited to accompany me and on 15 September we set sail from Southampton for a ten-day cruise to the Mediterranean.

It was our first cruise and neither of us knew what to expect or even if we would enjoy it, but we felt at home as soon as we stepped aboard. What a glorious send-off we all had too: from the 100 Union Jacks adorning the ceiling of the *QE2* terminal building to the brilliant brass band that resoundingly played us out into Southampton Water and the Solent – it produced quite a lump in my throat, I can tell you.

We were given a fabulous cabin and looked after throughout the cruise by a wonderful cabin stewardess called Joanne, who came from Manchester. Unbeknown to John and I, in the cabin next to us was Jim Bowen and his wife, Phyllis. Jim was on board as one of the resident entertainers and he worked extremely hard, doing three or four shows daily, either based on his *Bullseye* game show, or playing with his jazz band.

For the first couple of days at sea I was unfortunately suffering from a terrible cough which kept me awake most of the night. I became worried that I was probably also disturbing the sleep of our neighbours in adjoining cabins and I was right. Over a drink in the bar Jim Bowen enquired of John whether it was he or I who had the terrible hacking cough. John told him it was me, to which Jim replied that I sounded terrible and he hoped I'd be OK soon.

When I heard of Jim's concern over my state of health, I wrote him a note and slipped it under his cabin door. 'Sorry, Jim and Phyllis, if my coughing has kept you awake . . . but count yourself lucky that I am not well enough to start shagging!' John told me that Jim appreciated the funny side of it and my coughing was not mentioned again.

However, a few months later I met Jim again when we were both on the *Generation Game*. 'Oh, by the way, Wendy, that note you sent me on board the *QE2* – I had it framed and it's now hung in my local Methodist hall!' I wished the ground could have swallowed me up, imagine my embarrassment, it's the last time I'll be lippy to Jim!

Another 'Jim' on board ship too was the inimitable Sir James – Jimmy – Savile. John and I were strolling around the deck on our first day at sea when we saw Jimmy go jogging by. He spotted me, did a double take and went in reverse to jog back to us. We said hello and I introduced him to John.

'There's only room on board for one good looking fella – and that's me,' he told John. Then he suggested that John would have to be thrown overboard that night and I would be so distraught, I would naturally fall into his arms instead. With that, he jogged on, good old Jimmy, always the one with a way for words with the ladies!

It was the same again the following day when we saw him on deck. 'Hi Wendy, are you going ashore today?' he asked me.

'But we are at sea all day today, Jimmy,' I pointed out.

'Well, that shouldn't be too much trouble for you, my darling,' and with that he smiled and jogged off!

Cruising is apparently one of Jimmy's favourite ways of relaxing. We were told that he'd been a passenger on the *QE2* on over thirty of her previous voyages. He is such a personality and was wonderful to the passengers, posing for photographs whenever asked and clowning around for their camcorder shots.

Another passenger on board was actor John Altman, who plays Nick Cotton. In real life John is a fantastic fellow and was accompanied on the trip by his mother, Tina. It sure was a sight for sore eyes to see the other passengers' faces as they watched the most evil man on telly walking along the deck, arm in arm with his mother and carrying her handbag, to boot! What a joy to behold.

During our second day at sea John Altman and I took part in a celebrity interview in the Grand Lounge, which comprised a question and answer session on our acting careers. It was chaired by the cruise director who, unfortunately, was American and did not appear to know too much about British television. He was supposed to be doing the interviewing but in the end, John and I side-stepped him and played it one-to-one, which appeared to go down a whole lot better with the passengers. Everyone who attended seemed to enjoy themselves, including me. When John called over to Tina 'Are you all right, Ma?' It sent shivers down my spine to hear the very same words Nick always says to Dot Cotton, in the lounge of the *QE2*, of all places.

After the interview, John and I signed some copies of an *EastEnders* book. I did it because people were interested in the book but I vowed right there and then that the next time I did a book signing it would be my own – and hopefully on the *QE2* as well!

John Altman and my John soon became good buddies and remained so throughout the cruise. One morning, however, my John popped along to the other John's cabin to see if he was ready to join us for breakfast. Apparently, there was a knock on the door and Jemson, John Altman's cabin steward walked in with his pot of morning tea. John was pulling on his trousers when suddenly Jemson spotted my John, sitting in the corner of the cabin.

'Will that be two cups, sir?' he asked nonchalantly?

'No! No! he's just going,' John splurted out, amid red faces all round and with that my John scuttled out of the cabin as quickly as he could!

I fell about laughing when they told me the story. It's very hard to embarrass either of them, let alone both of them in one go!

One of our ports of call was Barcelona. John and I were walking through one of the main streets there when a Spanish lady and her husband approached us and suddenly started humming the theme tune to *EastEnders*.

'Pauline, Pauline, I'm so pleased to meet you,' she said and then told us that in that region of Spain where *EastEnders* is televised, it is dubbed in Catalan. She informed us that Pauline has a very high-pitched, squeaky voice. Oh well! Her reaction to me was so funny but very nice, none the less.

The only downside to Barcelona for me was that in the rush to get off the ship and hit the shops, to my horror, I left all my credit cards on board. With only a small amount of cash on me, I was reduced to buying just one handbag and a holdall. Curtailing my spending produced one of the biggest's smiles on John's face of the whole trip.

I had my revenge though when we docked in Palma, the capital of Majorca, an island I have always loved – especially for the fantastic shops in Palma. There I made certain I had all my cards so I could indulge my shopping addiction to its fullest.

I nearly didn't make it to the shops at all because while we were walking near the Plaza Mayor, a builder's truck reversed and I literally had to jump sideways to avoid being hit. Yet, as luck would have it, I ended up in the doorway of a very exclusive designer boutique! John was angrily shouting at the driver of the truck, which gave me the opportunity to slip inside the shop while he wasn't looking. In there I was delighted to discover an elegant grey and black suit, plus stylish accessories of shoes, belt and handbag to accompany the outfit. My credit card took a right hammering but I still believe it was fate and no one can tell me any different!

From Palma we sailed on to Gibraltar, which I enjoyed best of all. As soon as we docked Jimmy Savile ran from the ship right up to the top of the rock. I later learned he was doing it for charity, which I thought was fantastic of him because it's a hell of a long, steep way up there and others half his age were taking the cable car to the top.

John and I visited The Trafalgar Cemetery in Gibraltar, where sailors who died in the Battle of Trafalgar are buried. We could see from the head stones that some of those who died were as young as 17. The most poignant of them all for me was the grave stone of two 19-year-old brothers, who were killed by the same bullet; it had gone through one and then into the other. I found that very distressing, thinking of how awful it must have been for their poor family. The cemetery is extremely well kept and certainly worth a visit for any tourist to the colony.

I was delighted to revisit Gibraltar after so many years and it brought back many happy memories of the time I had spent holidaying there with Robert Brown and his family when we were both in *The Newcomers*. Little would I have thought then that I would one day return and be fêted in the streets but that's what happened that day. As John and I walked around the shops, people kept walking up to me saying 'Hi Pauline, how wonderful to see you'. It was a lovely feeling so far away from home but of course, being a British colony, they receive BBC out there and are up to date on *EastEnders*. I was even persuaded into a church hall by a policeman on duty outside, there was a charity bring and buy sale in progress and he wanted me to do a few presentations. It only took fifteen minutes of our time and we did get a nice cup of tea with biscuits into the bargain, so I was more than pleased to do it.

I was sorry to bid farewell to Gibraltar again but I must say we were certainly seen off in grand style. As in Southampton, a superb brass band gave us a rousing send off as we slipped out of Gibraltar Harbour, while on deck a jazz band played and passengers danced away to its tunes. What a wonderful sight and one I will never forget.

Our last port of call was at Lisbon in Portugal and all too soon, it seemed, we were docking in Southampton again. We had made some smashing friends among crew and passengers alike during our ten-day cruise, including Esther Rantzen and her husband, the TV producer and writer, Desmond Wilcox; entertainer Stuart Hall and his wife, Hazel. Ventriloquist, Ray Allen and his wife, Jayne were also on board; along with the chirpy Lord Charles, who was kept firmly shut in a suitcase when he was not performing on stage. I found Ray Allen to be a most amusing man and we often chatted to him and Jayne in the evenings.

In Southampton we said our goodbyes amid tears, huge hugs and the taking of several last minute photographs. We'd been looked after superbly well and the only good thing about leaving the ship was that I could get back to my normal pattern of eating. I'm not usually a big eater but the bracing sea air and splendid food at breakfast, lunch and dinner in the Queens Grill had tempted even me and we were looked after exceedingly well by restaurant manager, Alex. The only part I dipped out on was the midnight buffet, thank God I was tucked up in bed by then!

After the lavish life aboard the *QE2* it was back to reality – and work – for John and I. He was working very hard at the time for an insulation firm, who were under contract to a power station. It required him working long shifts, often through the night. Now, John and I are lucky because we rarely ever argue, however, one morning he set off for work at 6.30 only to return by 8.30. I was upstairs in the bedroom, when I heard him open the front door and I called out, 'Is there anything wrong?'

'No, no, everything is fine, I've just decided to take a day off.'

'Lovely, we can spend the day together.'

With that he calmly announced, 'Oh no thanks, me and the lads are going to grab a few beers and go round to my brother-in-law's to watch some sport on television.'

He turned on his heel to go downstairs, with me screaming and shouting after him but he took no notice and carried on. Dressed only in my robe, I followed him and saw his mate, Alan in the lounge waiting for him, looking somewhat uneasy after hearing my tirade. Alan looked at me sheepishly and muttered 'Morning, Wend.'

'You can p*** off too,' I told him, which wasn't very nice but then I wasn't feeling very nice. I turned away somewhat guiltily and through the mirror could see John climbing the stairs from the kitchen, a case of lager under his arm. Something was said between them, which I couldn't hear because by then I had my hands over my face pretending to be upset – actually I could hardly stop laughing. John just looked at Alan and remarked, 'Oh take no notice of her, she's an actress and she's probably rehearsing!'

I just about kept the giggles in check as they bolted out of the house carrying the beer. So I gave it one last shot. Almost breaking down in laughter, I called after John, 'If you go now, don't bother to come back.'

Half-way through the door, he stopped in his tracks and replied, 'OK but will you still write to me?'

With that he was gone.

I don't know what his mates said to him but he returned home an hour later, looking somewhat forlorn. And painted the garden furniture!

CHAPTER TWENTY-SIX

Happy Holidays Recalled

In 1999 we were once again invited by Johnny Mans to attend a 'Not Forgotten' Association function and this time the location was St James Palace. Brian Conley, Ronnie Corbett and Bert Weedon had given their time free of charge to entertain those fine outstanding ex-servicemen. A lovely buffet lunch had been organized for us all but just before it was served John and I nipped out into an alley at the back of the Palace for a quick cigarette. We'd only just lit up when a policeman approached us with 'Are you two going to be here long?'

'I'm sorry officer but we were dying for a fag,' I explained.

'Well, you had better hurry up then, madam because the Queen and the rest of the Royal Family are in that chapel over there, for the christening of Princess Margaret's grandchild. They'll all be out in a minute and passing by this way.' Frightened of being caught, we stubbed our cigarettes out immediately, picked up the butts and cleared ORF!

We had a pleasant trip, through work, in the summer of 1999. I was delighted to be asked by the BBC's *Celebrity Holiday Memories* programme to relive my best holiday moments for a programme that was scheduled to be televised in September and hosted by Gabby Roslin.

When asked by the researchers the location of where I had spent my favourite holidays, naturally, my choice had to be Jersey because of the wonderful times I'd had in the Channel Islands with Daddy. John, however, couldn't resist remarking, 'Couldn't you pretend your father always took you to Hawaii on holiday each year?'

We flew into Jersey and were met by the programme's director, Michael Massey; cameraman, Mike; sound recordist, Bradley and the researcher, Victoria. I was four when Daddy first took me to Jersey and have returned more than a dozen times since. What I like so much about the island today is that although they have thousands of tourists every year, some lovely unspoilt parts of the island still remain. One of our first location shoots was at the German underground hospital, which had been tunnelled deep into rock by prisoners of war and built for use in the event of an attack on the island. As it turned out it was never used as such but nevertheless it still remains a most eerie place.

As Daddy and I had stayed at the Grand Hotel in St Helier, the crew co-opted an eight year old girl to portray me as a child in one of the scenes. She was asked to walk down the main stairway of the hotel and was wearing an almost identical frock to the type of dress I would have worn at her age. It felt really strange to see her recreate my own footsteps.

Even John was roped in for a scene in the hotel, Mike Massey asked him to play the part of a guest checking in at reception. John rose to the challenge and was thrilled to be filmed in his first talking part. Unfortunately for him, when the programme was televised his scene had been edited out. John was far from pleased but I was – one actor in the house is more than enough, thank you very much!

We also did some filming at the Old Courthouse Inn at St Aubin. I'd filmed there a few years previously when wicked

Willy had inveigled Pauline into spending a few days in Jersey with him.

One of my favourite haunts in Jersey was Gerald Durrell's Zoo at Trinity. I first visited there twenty-five years ago and have always thought it a fantastic place. Mike Massey wanted to film me inside the lemurs enclosure, so Bradley and Mike went in first to set up their equipment. Now lemurs are fabulous creatures who hail from Madagascar but they hate to be put on edge and unluckily that is exactly what happened because just at that moment a crowd of schoolkids walked by and frightened them. The lemurs went wild, screeching their heads off, which was enough to root Mike and Bradley to the spot!

I entered the enclosure – very apprehensively – and sat on a bench but when I pulled out some monkey nuts, I had them eating out of my hand, literally, with two on my knee and one on my shoulder. They were wonderful, with little hands that looked as if they were clothed in black velvet gloves and they just put them out so politely, there was no snatching. It reminded me of Johnny Morris – one of my favourite television programmes as a child – and his ring-tailed lemur who was called Dotty.

The next stop on our island tour was the Jersey Pottery. I take my hat off to the potters who have to work on a limited timescale with masses of people watching them. They are a far cry from my attempts at pottery in handicraft classes at school; I could never keep the clay on the wheel and it ended up flying off in all different directions. The gardens at the Pottery are a beautiful sight to behold and so is the restaurant there, with its wonderful displays of fresh lobster, crab and other delicious seafood. Sadly, I could not partake of the goodies because I have an allergy to shellfish, what a pity but at least the desserts were to die for!

One of our final scenes was on the battlements of Gorey Castle, again a location I had worked at before on the *EastEnders* Jersey episode. The holiday scene was dragging on and on as they tried to get the best shots and we were all getting tired. However, John was still buzzing around, assisting with the lighting, trying to be his usual 'helpful' self and found a ladder outside belonging to some workmen who were doing repairs.

'Couldn't you get the cameraman to climb up this ladder and shoot from over the top of the door?' he suggested to the director. The crew and I all grimaced at each other, thinking simultaneously 'Oh no, please'. I flashed John a withering look, to no avail because by then Mike had taken up his suggestion. The new camera angle added an extra hour to our workload – and I can assure you John was not the most popular person that night when we did eventually finish. I told him to keep his creative ideas to himself in future!

All in all though, we had a great time in Jersey and they were a wonderful bunch of people to work with. Despite his 'faux pas' John and I still keep in contact with the crew and meet up for a meal together occasionally.

There was one sad aspect about my return to Jersey and that was meeting up with Barbie. She and I had become friends after our first meeting in 1983 when I went to stay with John Inman. We shot a scene in Banks in which Barbie and I were looking back through old scrapbooks, which included photographs of my previous visits. The sad part was that Herbie had recently died from cancer, which saddened me greatly and it was understandably emotional for Barbie to look back an the old photographs and remember the last time when we were all together. Herbie was a great guy, a bundle of fun and one of the kindest, wittiest and most generous men I've ever met. It so happened that he was buried in the parish churchyard at St Brelade, which is where we were staying at a hotel in the bay. So one day between filming, John and I visited the church to put flowers on Herbie's grave. In one corner of the graveyard near his grave was a new bench, which Barbie had purchased in memory of Herbie. A commemorative plaque on the bench was inscribed with Herbie's usual catch phrase 'Nice to see me.'

It was Herbie's little joke at himself, pretending that he could not speak English properly, which he could. Seeing that reminded me of all the antics that Herbie was forever getting up to. We had lost one of life's great characters. It was indeed a poignant memory for me to take away from Jersey.

Just before *Celebrity Holiday Memories* was televised we found ourselves in another lovely holiday area – the county of Dorset. I am a patron of the Cairn Terrier Relief Association, a charity which raises funds to care for and rehouse unwanted Cairns. The association asked me if I would attend their annual dog show, which was to be held near Ferndown.

I was only too pleased to oblige, particularly as they had also asked Shirley to take part in the show! John's two young daughters, Jade and Shannen accompanied us on the trip, which made for a lovely drive down to Dorset one Sunday in September because they love Shirley and the feeling is mutual.

We booked into the King's Head Hotel in Wimborne, the lovely market town where my old friend Billy Burden had been born and brought up. I carry a lot of pleasant memories from there and it was nice to be back in Wimborne once more. We checked into a family room with four beds, which Shirley tried to sleep on each in turn during the night, just make sure we were all OK!

In the afternoon we made our way to the dog show and were greeted by Thelma, Chris and Philip who are all active members of the CTRA. Most of the dogs at the show were rescues and it was lovely to see them so happy with their new owners. The event was held in a farmer's field and there were a host of stalls, hot dog stands and other amusements; all was going well until the heavens opened.

I was sat in a marquee signing autographs, in return for a donation to the charity. Shannen was helping me by taking the money and was doing extremely well, until we got to the stage when people proffered a fiver for a donation – and she didn't want to give them the change. Obviously, she must have learned that from her father!

The time came round for Shirley's big moment, her début in a dog show. She had been entered for the veteran's class and at eight and a half, only just qualified. Poor Jade had to lead her out and unfortunately, as I have never taken Shirley to obedience classes, she was pulling Jade all over the place – and getting uppity with all the other dogs into the bargain! I can't remember her name being called out so often, as Jade tried, in vain, to restrain her. The rest of the entrants must have been trained by their owners because they were behaving impeccably, which made matters look worse.

Then came the judging and to my utter astonishment – and delight – Shirley came fourth! Not too bad, considering the winner was 16 years of age and had obviously had a lot of obedience training over a good many years. Despite the rain, the show was a great success and raised a lot of money for the association, so we were all pleased to have attended and helped – even Jade!

Apart from smaller events such as the aforementioned dog show, John is still quite shy when it comes to publicity, or attending some of the major charity functions that I have to go to. However, he wasn't exactly backward in coming forward when speaking to the Duke of Edinburgh, although he did show some reluctance with the Duke's daughter!

During the year John and I had attended the Variety Club

Sports Luncheon, which was held at the Hilton in Park Lane. HRH Prince Philip was guest of honour. John and I both smoke and we were stood around a table at the pre-luncheon reception, puffing away, ash tray overflowing, when Philip approached us. I curtseyed and then turned to introduce John, whom, I suddenly noticed, still had a cigarette in his hand! 'Put your fag out,' I hissed between gritted teeth. 'This is my partner, John Burns,' I told the Duke.

John shook hands with His Royal Highness, who asked him 'Good heavens, are all those cigarette ends yours?'

'No, sir,' he replied, 'Two of them are hers. Actually, it is a lack of ash trays that leads to over crowding.'

Philip laughed and rapidly moved on to the next group!

The only time I've ever known John lost for words was later that year in October when we met the Princess Royal. It was at a charity function organized by The Lady Taverners, in association with the British Sports Trust. The event was a Royal Gala Performance, starring Barbara Dixon in concert, followed by dinner in the Whitehall Banqueting Rooms. We were in the library, waiting to be presented to the Princess. Standing with us was Caroline Ratcliff, the mother of one of our friends. Suddenly Nicholas Parsons came bustling up and started to try and move Caroline further down the line. 'You can't stand there,' he fussed.

'You leave her alone, she's with us,' I insisted. Now Nicholas might well have been president of the Lords Taverners but Caroline's daughter, Jean, was chairman of the Lady Taverners – and the one looking after HRH for the evening, to boot!

When the Princess Royal walked in, Nicholas stepped forward. 'Oh, yes, I've met you before,' she said and promptly moved on to us and Caroline.

When John was presented to her, he bowed and shook her

hand. 'I expect you have got used to all these sort of occasions?' she asked him.

'Er, um, well, no, not really,' was all he could reply.

The first time that our Mr Burns has ever been at a loss for words – and it's probably the quietest I'm ever likely to see him!

John may have been struck dumb by the Princess Royal but he is rarely short of words, as Wendy well knows. So, unbeknown to Wendy, her partner, John Burns wanted to add his say to her life story. It will give you a fair idea – if you haven't gathered already – of what Wendy is really like . . .

I first got the measure of Wendy not long after I had started to go out with her in 1996. I had known her slightly for two years and already come to realise that she is one of the most unselfish people I have ever met because she takes great pleasure in being able to use her name for the benefit of those less fortunate than herself.

But what really shocked me was on 14 February 1996, the day that she had to go for her cancer tests. I was at work early that morning and watched her appearance on GMTV to promote the Variety Club's Gold Heart Campaign, in aid of underprivileged children. She was on such good form, enjoying herself in front of the cameras with Eamon Holmes, that I assumed the situation about the suspected cancer could not be as bad as she had thought. I didn't hear from Wendy again until later that afternoon, when she telephoned me to say that the tests had proved positive. She had breast cancer. Given what I had seen on television that morning, I was absolutely stunned. I couldn't believe that on the day of her worst health scare and with what she had to attend that afternoon, she had still gone out publicly raising money to help others.

I'm afraid that if I had been in that same situation, I'm sure I couldn't have done the same. I guess with me, perhaps like many others in that position, self-pity and panic would have gone into overdrive – but not with her.

Wendy has said in the past that it was myself and a few close friends who helped her get through her cancer and its aftermath but our contribution was only minor. The rest came from her extraordinary self-determination and willpower. That's what really pulled her through.

Whenever she attended her radiotherapy sessions, I accompanied her for support. I waited outside while she had her treatment and when she returned she would always talk about seeing other ladies in there who were a lot worse than her. She never spoke to me about her own treatment. That is her way and so typical of her.

I can honestly say that Wendy is generous – if not over-generous – to a lot of people, including myself. She is particularly fond of the props boys, camera crew, security guards and cleaners at the studios where she films *EastEnders* and they all receive a Christmas present from her each year. Every autumn she makes her own jars of pickled onions – and they are widely enjoyed by cast and crew alike. I tried to put a stop to it once because they stink the house out so much – and I turned out to be one of the most unpopular people at the *EastEnders* studios for a while! Needless to say, Wendy still does the pickles.

Wendy is not always the most easygoing person in the world and people who have known her closely and worked with her will vouch for that! But the point is that there is no malice in her behaviour and certainly none intended.

I've accompanied Wendy to many charity functions and the people she is due to meet and sit alongside are frequently nervous about meeting her for the first time. Yet, within five or ten minutes she will have the whole table eating out of her hand with her down to earth sense of humour and story telling – some of which could not be printed in a family book like this!

Wendy is as much at ease with bank managers, as butchers and building site workers; she has time for everyone, whatever their walk of life. She never refuses an autograph whenever she is approached by the public and still maintains the old adage that 'They pay my wages.'

Journalists frequently refer to the age gap between us both when writing stories about Wendy and I. Our age difference has never bothered her and certainly not me either. We are both very happy with each other.

Like everyone else, Wendy has her faults which are mainly brought on by tiredness owing to her hectic work schedule but she is a great laugh and such good fun to be with.

CHAPTER TWENTY-SEVEN

Pauline

It's still hard to believe that *EastEnders* celebrated its fifteenth birthday on 19 February 2000. Adam Woodyatt – who plays my nephew, Ian Beale – and I are the only original members of the cast who've been on the programme since Episode One. I've watched Adam grow from a teenage boy into a happily married man, with two lovely children of his own. It's as the years pass and you see boys like Adam grow into fine young men, you appreciate the value of the family-like friendships that develop behind the scenes at *EastEnders*. Even today he still calls me 'Aunty Wendy' or 'Aunty Pauline' off screen.

As well as a wonderful nephew, I reckon I've got the best two boys in the Square in Mark and Martin. I've watched James Alexandrou (who plays Martin) grow too – and I mean that literally – at 15 he's now a lofty 6ft 2in! James is a fabulous boy and has always had the kindness to send me a Mother's Day card each year, which is really sweet of him. One day when I asked James to sign one of his pictures for a fan, I criticised his handwriting. James' real Mum Debbie joined in. 'She's right you know, it's awful,' she said. Another cast member sat nearby asked, 'what's it like having two Mums having a go at you, James?' James just muttered under his breath and raised his eyes heavenward! Unlike Pauline, I've never had children of my own. But in Todd Carty and James Alexandrou I've two wonderful sons and I'm as proud of them as any mother would be.

Last year John bought tickets for an England cricket match at Lords and invited James, who's a keen cricket fan, to go with him. His Mum dropped James off at my house and said she'd return to collect him in the evening.

As I knew it would be a long day, I made sure John and James were fed before they set off. As they left the house, I called up the street after them 'Make sure you look after him.' The neighbours must have wondered who I meant, with James a towering 6ft plus and John . . . well, he's not! During the day I rang John several times on his mobile to make sure that James was OK, which he was and we arranged for all three of us to meet up after the match. When we did, judging by the look of John, it must have been James who'd had to look after him all day, not vice versa as I'd requested. James had to walk John home and it was obvious John had had one too many beers in the sun at Lords!

Yes, it's been a long time working with my alter ego – Pauline – and sometimes I find myself even behaving like her. I caught myself arranging fresh fruit in the bowl on my dining room table the other week and moving it off centre, as Pauline does in her house. Although it's been a decade and a half, in many ways it seems like only yesterday that I first stepped on to the set of Albert Square.

Pauline's had her ups and downs in the 1980s and 90s and the start of the new century has been no exception. This year she was worried sick about Mark's ill health. Was HIV finally taking its toll? Mark collapsed and was rushed to hospital; pneumonia was diagnosed and doctors fought to save his life.

Then there was THAT PROPOSAL from Jeff Healy and some very highly-charged emotional scenes with the death of Ethel Skinner. Tackling a controversial subject like euthanasia took its toll on all the actors and actresses involved – including me. You cannot act out such touching scenes and then just switch off immediately you leave the studio floor. Some of the misery remains with you when you return home.

It was lovely to have Gretchen Franklin – who played Ethel - back with us in 2000. She had some very long and arduous dialogues in her scenes and it can't have been easy for her at nearly 90 years old but she handled them marvellously. Everyone was very sad to bid a final farewell to her, especially because she'd been one of the originals. However, after she finished we did see her off in grand style with a lovely afternoon tea at The Ritz!

It seems as if there's been nothing but turmoil for Pauline Fowler since *EastEnders* first began but I don't think she's changed much over the past fifteen years. I know that I have though. Certainly, I think I've aged, when I look back at some of the early photos of Pauline! However, in one respect I have remained constant – and that is in striving to be a disciplined actress, especially about learning lines.

Usually we receive our scripts for *EastEnders* two–three weeks in advance. Fortunately, I've never had trouble learning lines, it is something I tried hard to perfect early on in my career. It's a much easier task if Pauline is involved in sensible conversation.

No two working days have ever been the same for me on *EastEnders* and that's why I've enjoyed it so much, variety is definitely the spice of life for me! I've tried to make my dressing room at the studios as comfortable as possible because I do spend a lot of time in there each week – sometimes there can be six or seven hour gaps between scenes.

I've put in a fridge, a radio and a kettle – it's well known my door is always open for those who fancy a quick cuppa. Even though I say it myself, I do make a blinding cup of tea (with whole milk, skimmed definitely spoils the taste!). Just to prove it, I've a photograph in my house of Colin Baker which, when we finished pantomime together, he signed 'To the best tea lady in the business' – so there!

I've also installed an electric typewriter in my dressing room and spend a lot of time, when I'm not learning lines, on answering all my own fan mail. Of course, Pauline has more than her fair share of admirers since the programme began and it's always lovely to hear from fans.

I get quite a lot of fan mail and so sometimes I get behind with it but I always try and respond myself. One lady fan, Louise Swenson, lives in Cheshire. She has been writing to me for about fifteen years, telling me about her granddaughter Becky, and her late husband Dennis and the life in Singapore. She never forgets my birthday or Christmas.

One of my younger fans is Sharon Keilty. She was always turning up at the various personal appearances I do. She writes to me at home and we have met up at birthday parties and other social events. I invited Sharon to my wedding to Paul. A lot of people think she is my daughter as we look quite similar. Sharon is married now to a very nice young man, Terry, who has his own building company.

I met up with another fan, Cody Morgan, when I was in Los Angeles on holiday and became good friends with him and his now late wife, Shirley. He sends me books on the great stars and obscure music tapes which cannot be bought here. I think he must have a record of just about every TV appearance I've ever made.

Sometimes the fan mail, especially that to Pauline, can be quite moving. For example, after we did the *EastEnders* episode in which Michelle told Pauline she was pregnant, a young schoolgirl wrote to me to say that she was expecting a baby and because of the way I reacted to Michelle, it had given her courage to tell her own mother.

Pauline

Through the years there's been a lot of Press criticism of Pauline, claiming she's miserable and that she never smiles – but they're wrong, Pauline does smile. She is the salt of the earth and a fighter, whose family counts first and foremost to her. Pauline is also a hard working mother, who has suffered a great deal.

As for the criticism that she's dowdy and wears dreadful cardigans all the time? Well, I think some journalists should take a closer look – Pauline hasn't worn a cardigan in an episode for the past seven years – and she's started to wear lipstick and eye shadow now too! OK, Pauline may not be glamorous and sometimes her clothes are dreary but for me as an actress, it certainly made a pleasant change to step out of those high heels that Miss Brahms always had to wear. I have to say though, it does feel good when I'm not playing Pauline and I can dress up again for spots on other TV shows.

There are sometimes disadvantages to being a cast member of *EastEnders*. Apart from when you're on official holiday, you are not permitted to leave the country when you're not working, just in case you have to be suddenly called back into the studio. You also have to request permission before you can appear on another television show or a charity event.

On the other hand, being a familiar face can have its advantages. Once, my very good friend Denis Compton and I were enjoying a quiet glass of champagne together, when I noticed a couple of mounted police outside the pub. 'Have you left your car on a yellow line?' I asked, which he had. I dashed out and there was the ticket on his car. Denis followed me outside, to where I was now pleading with the mounted policemen. 'How could you? This is one of our greatest living sportsmen. Don't you know who this man is?' I shouted. 'No madam,' came the reply, 'but I know who you are.' With which he got off his horse, tore up the ticket, apologized, remounted and then the pair of them rode off.

An unpleasant aspect of being so much in the public eye, is that the Press feel free to write what they want about you – stories that I believe the public are not always interested in. It's OK when you have particularly joyous news to convey, or a tragedy to speak out about. But having to air your marital problems in public is another matter. However high your profile, I feel people should be left alone and allowed to sort out those type of problems in peace.

I wouldn't want you to think I'm against the Press per se because I'm not. They do a very good job at times and certainly have been helpful to me in the past, such as when I was being pursued by the stalker. There are some journalists, such as Margaret Forward or Lynda Lee-Potter, who I admire tremendously.

But despite any disadvantages of being on *EastEnders*, I wouldn't change it for anything because the plus points count far higher. Pauline has been very good to me. She has paid my mortgage and living expenses for the past decade and a half – and bought me some of life's little luxuries too, like nice clothes and holidays abroad in good hotels. Thanks to her I can also buy fresh flowers for the house each weekend and afford to have my hair and nails done weekly. Those are the sort of things that have to go first when you are short of money. It's been a pleasure knowing Pauline – and if I had a chance to play her again for another fifteen years?

I'd say, 'Yes, thank you very much, Pauline!'

CHAPTER TWENTY-EIGHT

Reflections

The year 2000 marks my fortieth anniversary in the business. For me it has been a time to reflect on my past career. Am I resting on my laurels? – no! of course I'm not.

I've a lot to be grateful for – and many people to be grateful to. David Croft, being one in particular. I think he's the best person in the world to work for. I'm indebted to David for remembering the early work I did with him and then casting me in the role of Shirley Brahms. *Are You Being Served?* provided me with some of the happiest days of my working life.

The cast became like family and we are still firm friends today. I was always particularly close to Mollie and was very sad to hear of the death of her husband, Bill earlier this year. Fortunately, Mollie has some lovely twin sons, daughter-in-laws and grand-children, who have been very supportive of her. Mollie has been very unwell herself in recent years but hopefully, she is now on the road to recovery.

Although we finished the last series of *AYBS?* in 1985, it still has a tremendous following today, especially in the United States. They renamed *Grace and Favour* as *Are You Being Served Again? AYBS?* was first shown in the summer of 1987 on 24 Public Broadcasting Stations. Since then it has continued to be shown regularly, up to three times a day on some of the stations!

I think it's fair to say it has become cult viewing Stateside. The Americans always make a huge fuss of John Inman whenever he goes over there and in 1993 when I travelled to New York for a TV telethon to promote the programme, I was treated exceedingly well. Even on holiday in Los Angeles and San Francisco in 1996 I was regularly being recognized as Miss Brahms.

What is equally pleasing is that *Are You Being Served?* was successfully re-run by the BBC here in the UK during 1997, 1998 and 1999 – sometimes in a peak Saturday tea-time slot – and the repeats regularly attracted over eight million viewers. Not bad going, considering some of the episodes were over a quarter of a century old!

The fact that they can also be enjoyed by a new generation says a lot about the programme's harmless fun. I think *Are You Being Served?* can deservedly be called a true comedy classic.

Despite any of the criticism levelled in the early days, about the show being offensive and crude, I think it all depended on how you took the innuendos – and we always had the perfect answer to all the brickbats flung at us – viewing figures! The public loved it, despite whatever the critics said, and audiences topped more than 22 million for some episodes.

I am very fortunate to still receive around 200 fan mail letters each week. A large proportion is from the US from people who write to tell me how much they enjoy *Are You Being Served?*

I'm pleased when people write, not just to say that they admire some aspect of my work but that certain programmes I've appeared in have been helpful to them. Since 1996 for example I've received numerous letters from fellow cancer sufferers, who claim that I have been an inspiration to them. Especially after I presented the two *The Big C* programmes in 1997 which were part of the BBC's information campaign about the disease, its treatment and prevention.

Another way that fans have started to communicate with me is via the Internet. I was very flattered when a couple of years ago a guy in the States called Kurt Callaway, who is a talented computer software engineer, launched a website dedicated to me. What pleases me so much about the site is that Kurt is insistent it will not contain any derogatory comments about me. In his words: 'It's a labor of true respect; therefore if you dropped by simply seeking juicy gossip at Ms. Richard's expense, please look elsewhere – you'll find none here.' Well, that's music to my ears. The fact that Kurt has had over 32,000 visitors to his site – http://pages.prodigy.net/glc/wrhp/html/wr – since he launched it, must prove that people do like just 'good news' at times.

In July this year I was delighted to meet Kurt for the first time when he flew over to London on holiday with his wife, Carole and their two children. It gave me the chance to put a face to his name and we all had an enjoyable evening together, during which I was able to answer many of his questions so that he could update the site when he returned home.

The interest in Kurt's site has recently prompted Simon Leyland, who is a friend of ours, to launch a UK website for me and www.wendyrichard.com has already generated a great deal of interest. Simon and Kurt work in close co-operation with each other and the US site is now linked to Simon's pages in the UK. The UK website is intended as a 'meeting place' for fans. Among the pages of information, Simon is also running a question and answer section about me. Whenever he needs me to, I supply the answers myself, so that visitors to the site obtain their information 'direct from the horse's mouth', so to speak! The site has a picture gallery as well, containing photos of me with various fans. It's a slow process building up a new site but I am sure people will find it worthwhile and informative.

Looking back on my career, I've virtually no regrets. I sometimes think I might have liked to have done more films than I did. Or, I'd love to have worked with Morecambe and Wise. I think they were absolutely wonderful. Everybody loved them so much in their day and I also think their brand of comedy is timeless. I'd happily go back to comedy if the opportunity came my way and I'd even like a go at presenting but I'm very happy with my job as it is at the moment and still thoroughly enjoy playing Pauline.

I felt privileged to be invited by John and Norma Major to a reception at Number 10 Downing Street in November 1994. The photo of me being introduced to the Prime Minister and his wife has pride of place in my home. I met the couple again fairly soon afterwards, in the Dorchester Hotel, at a dinner held in his honour.

I was chatting to Norma Major at the reception beforehand and the subject of *The Archers* came up. 'Oh how are Jeffrey and Mary?' she asked.

'No, no I mean the REAL Archers,' I pointed out.

Before she could reply, John Major walked up to us. 'Hello, Wendy. How very nice to see you again,' he said.

'We were just talking about *The Archers*,' I explained.

'Yes, it's a jolly exciting storyline at the moment, isn't it?'

He knew exactly what I meant – and I quickly realised that I'd discovered a fellow *Archers* addict in Mr Major!

I've visited the House of Commons twice for receptions hosted by comedian, Jim Davidson, who is a very active and loyal Tory supporter. I met William Hague at one, plus a host of other

Conservative MPs and Whips. We have also been to the House of Lords as a guest of John Taylor, Lord of Warwick.

I've had more than my fair share of problems in my personal life but I am very happy now, with a man who I truly love and who, I believe, truly loves me. John is an extremely popular person and I've never known anyone say a bad word about him. His sense of humour and directness is a winner with all my friends and the people he's met through me at the various functions we have attended. Everyone on *EastEnders* thinks the world of him too.

John is twenty years younger than me but he has a very wise head on his shoulders and I trust his judgement. So much so, that I've now made him my personal assistant and he undertakes a huge amount of my off-screen work. He's also very helpful around the house and with driving me to work. If there is something that needs doing and he doesn't have the skills, he usually knows someone who does. One day when I was appearing on the *Richard & Judy Show* I mentioned that a friend of John's, Alan Fleming, was coming round that morning to do work in my garden. I said Alan was one of the top chefs in the country, had cooked for Mrs Thatcher, worked at the Sandy Lanes Hotel, cooked Mick Jagger's barbeque – I spoke very highly of him. When I got back from the studio, John opened the door and shook his head, 'the f***ing bastard never turned up!'. Apparently Alan's dad up in Scotland had seen my appearance, called his son and when he found out he'd let me down, went berserk at him over the phone. It was a long time before Alan and I were friends again. Mind you, I've since discovered he's brilliant at cleaning kitchens!

John is caring and considerate and tries to lighten my load at home because he knows that, even four years on from my cancer treatment, I still tire easily as a result of my busy work schedule.

We're a real partnership – and no, we haven't talked about marriage – we're happy just exactly as we are. Except we do now sometimes vie for Shirley's attentions! Whenever she has to go to our vet, Bruce Fogle, it's always me – 'the bad guy' – who has to take her in. John waits outside and then plays 'the good guy' by taking her out and she's all over him.

Apart from one occasion when she was attacked by another dog in Hyde Park and sustained a dreadful wound over her left eye. John quickly drove home and we both rushed her round to the vet. Yet again it was me who had to take her into the surgery. But when she had to have an injection that was me out of there because I can't stand the sight of needles.

'John, you'll have to go in and hold her,' I told him in a distressed state.

As soon as John disappeared inside, I broke out in a big grin, winked at the girls on reception and giving them the thumbs up, proudly announced 'Got him with the injection!'

My achievement was short-lived though for Mr Burns was not to be outdone. On the way home in the car he told me 'Well that didn't matter to Shirley because we've re-bonded now . . . I held her head under my arm while he was giving her the shot!'

Our happiness was marred in November last year after my house was burgled and the robbers stole £30,000 worth of my jewellery. It wasn't just the monetary value. What upset me most was losing special mementoes and keepsakes, some of which had belonged to my parents, some were gifts from fellow actors and some were presents from John. I also lost a gold froggy ring that Will had bought me back in the 1980s.

They were of great sentimental value to me and I was devastated at their loss. I also lost my peace of mind, it's a terrible feeling when someone has been rifling through your home and personal possessions. I kept bursting into tears for weeks afterwards and the after effects of the robbery ruined Christmas for John and I.

Despite the great loss, we've picked up our lives again and when I'm not working, neither John nor I are 'party animals' by any stretch of the imagination. Aside from what people's conception might be – about the private lives of well-known actresses – I can assure you my life is very quiet.

We do have some lovely times together. In May of this year, a friend of mine, John Scott, who is in the wine trade, took me to France with his son, Robert. We travelled to Beaune where we attended a seven hour, seven course banquet at the Chateau du Clos Vouget, seat of the Confrerie des Chevaliers du Tastevin. I was one of the few women at the banquet who was made a Dame Chevalier du Tastevin. I was presented with my somalier's silver tasting cup on a gold and orange ribbon. Quite an honour for an English woman!. The ceremony is presided over by vineyard owners who are all dressed up in their gold and orange robes. You are dubbed on the shoulder with a highly polished vine root, then there is lots of shouting and wine drinking. They had a choir of vineyard workers, dressed in their traditional work clothes who got progressively drunker as the evening wore on. They all had wonderful faces, full of character. I remember thinking David Croft could have re-cast *Dad's Army* from this lot! There was a party of Americans at our table who got quite excited when they found out Miss Brahms was seated with them.

I prefer to dress casually when I am not 'Wendy Richard, the working actress'. Usually the only occasions that I glam myself up for and hit the high spots are when I attend charity functions. I believe in doing as much work for charity, as I possibly can, spare time permitting. I think if life has been good to you, then you should put something back into life for the benefit of others.

Consequently, I am more than happy to be involved in a number of charities. Each year I am very active in the Variety Club's Gold Hearts Campaign, which was the brainchild of a lady called Marsha Rae Ratcliff. Since it started in 1991 it has raised £23 million for underprivileged children and the gold hearts, whose design changes each year, have become collectors items. I always give them a plug by wearing one when I make television appearances during the campaign month of February – and Pauline wears one on her overall or coat.

Since 1998 I've also been a member of the Lady Taverners, who raise money for disadvantaged children by purchasing vehicles, equipment and other facilities to give the kids 'a sporting chance in life'. We seek funds through a variety of means, including lunches, dinners and concerts.

Naturally I have been asked to actively support various cancer charities but I am very wary. If you encourage people to donate to a charity, you have a duty to ensure their money is being spent in the right direction. I don't always approve of the way money is used for the likes of fancy offices and bunches of flowers. I prefer to help smaller groups, who perhaps need to buy specialized equipment. I am particularly supportive of charities that campaign for breast cancer screening – I believe there should be a much wider age coverage for screening than currently exists.

I'm a great animal lover, as you will have gathered! So it's a double whammie for me to be vice patron of Dogs for the Disabled because I can help humans and animals both at the same time. I first learned of the charity in 1996 when I was asked to front an appeal for them as part of the BBC's *Lifeline* series. I was stunned by the response – viewers contributed more than £60,000 in donations. I was also highly impressed by DfD's work when we filmed part of the appeal at their headquarters. The highly trained dogs immensely improve the quality of life for their disabled owners, by undertaking some of the tasks they are unable to do. For instance, one dog partnered a lady with multiple sclerosis and if she fell, got underneath her and gradually helped her back on to her feet. Another man, who'd been paralysed had a dog who was able to switch lights on and off and change TV channels for him, he could even help with loading and unloading the washing machine!

I became DfD's vice patron in 1998 and help by showing up on their stand at major events like Crufts and signing autographed photos in return for a donation to the charity. I've also organized raffles and placed one of their charity boxes in my local. When I made a guest appearance on *Celebrity Ready Steady Cook* – partnering chef, Tony Tobin – our team beat my screen son, Todd Carty and his chef! The winning celebrity has the opportunity of donating £1,000 to the charity of their choice – and mine was Dfd.

In the past I've had shares in three greyhounds and have enjoyed the odd visit to either Walthamstow or Wimbledon greyhound stadiums. It makes for a pleasant evening, you can have a nice meal and a bit of a flutter, which is all good fun. My three dogs are retired now through ill health but happily, all are well homed – which is not always the case with greyhounds who are no longer fit for racing. So that's why I lend my support to the Retired Greyhounds Association, who do marvellous work to pay kennel fees and find homes for dogs who might otherwise end up in appalling conditions.

So when I'm not involved with charity events, how do I spend my time?

Well, I still collect frogs. I've around 3,000 of them now – all happily living together in my London home! I've no one favourite, I like them all equally.

Shopping, for frogs, or anything else come to that, remains my favourite pastime – and I've already owned up to that addiction! Selfridges and Marks & Spencer at Marble Arch are my 'corner shops.' Unfortunately, I can never bribe John to accompany me on my shopping trips. Not even with the promise of buying him something really nice because frankly, John is not a materialistic person. So I always end up shopping on my own.

I can, however, occasionally tempt him out with the promise of an Indian or Chinese meal because that is food we both thoroughly enjoy. Not that we have late nights out because usually I have lines to learn for the following day. In any case, we like to be home and in bed, in time to watch our favourite TV programme – *Frasier* on the Comedy Channel!

I have my own firm beliefs that a lot of cancer may be caused through stress. So, since my illness, I've tried to avoid stressful situations and have made more personal time for myself, by spending an hour or so a day that is definitely non work-related.

The hour may be spent working on one of my tapestries but more often than not, I can be found in deepest concentration in front of my Playstation game console! A pastime perhaps aimed more at the younger generation but surprisingly I do find it very relaxing. We've also recently bought a lap top computer and the card games on there are equally as alluring to a game addict like me!

I also enjoy a 'real' game of cards once a week and often play cribbage on Sunday lunchtime, with my friends, Philip and Tony. Sunday is still a special day for me, as it was when my parents were alive. In the morning I have my precious time listening to *The Archers* while John is out walking Shirley in Hyde Park. It's also the day I like to cook and a Sunday roast is invariably on our menu. As much as I make a smashing cup of tea, I also make wonderful gravy too, containing a generous slosh of wine!

Doing crosswords is another way in which I like to relax. When I pop into my local, one of our mates may be struggling with the clues in the *Daily Telegraph* – and I'm always willing to throw in my 'twopenny worth'.

I do lead a fairly quiet life nowadays but above all, I think I have found happiness at long last, both with John and inside myself. If the cancer taught me anything, it taught me the true value of friendship.

CHAPTER TWENTY-NINE

Wendy Richard, MBE

Since my breast cancer in 1996 I have had to go for an annual review with both the surgeon and oncologist. In February this year I went along to Harley Street for my check-up and was concerned to hear that I would have to have an ovarian and pelvic scan. This was duly arranged but after I'd had the scans done, they informed me that I had a growth on my left ovary and a fibroid in my womb. I felt my shoulders slump. Surely I was not going to have to go through all the radiotherapy and everything else that goes with cancer, all over again?

John was wonderful when I told him the bad news and kept reminding me that I'd been brave once and could be so again, if it became necessary to undergo similar treatment.

I next had to see a professor in Harley Street. Professor Campbell is the top man in his field and was a very sweet and charming gentleman. There and then I had to have another scan taken. Afterwards he sat me down and told me, to my great relief, that the cyst on my ovary was not malignant and that I did not need to have a hysterectomy, which was something I dreaded.

It had been a very dark time. The worry had caused me to lose a lot of weight, which I think is what put the thought of cancer back into my mind.

Since 1996 I have had to take the anti-cancer drug, Tamoxifen, every day. When I first started on the medication, it made my hair fall out, that's stopped now but my hair is not as thick as it used to be. But most people on Tamoxifen tend to put on weight and in May my weight went down to eight and a half stone, which is what really worried me.

Despite the latest health scare I still had to carry on work during the worrisome time, without letting people know. At work I only confided in June Brown and Roberta Taylor, with whom I am quite close. I had to ask for permission for 5 May off work, so that I could be admitted to hospital for the operation. We have a smashing lady at work called Carolyn Weinstein, who deals with all our special requests and she kindly had scenes moved about to accommodate me. I finally went into the Lister Hospital and the problem was dealt with. I had my operation on the Friday and was back at work after the weekend.

One way and another, May was a tumultuous month for me. A little while after my operation John went away on a previously-arranged holiday to Majorca with his two daughters; his sister, Mo; brother-in-law, David and their son, Glen. I came home from work one day feeling rather lonely. The house is so empty when John not there. There was just Shirley and I sitting on the sofa when my agent, Derek Webster telephoned.

'Shall I make you the happiest person in the country?' he enquired.

'Go on, surprise me,' I replied.

'I've just received a letter from No.10 Downing Street, advising you that your name is to go forward to the Queen's Birthday Honours List for an MBE'

I could not believe my ears!

'Are you sure this is not a joke?' I asked.

'No,' he assured me. 'I am sending the letter over to you by courier straightaway, so that you can sign the acceptance form.'

'But I am a Conservative and this is a Labour government,' I persisted. 'I don't know if I should accept?'

'Wendy, if you don't accept this honour, I shall personally kill you,' Derek promised. 'You are receiving this award from the Queen.'

Your first letter of notification about the award is an extremely sternly-worded letter, which makes it quite clear that you are not allowed to discuss the contents with anyone. So, the first person I told had to be Shirley – she can keep a secret!

I was longing for John to return home from his holiday, so that I could confide in him too. He was so proud and pleased for me, when I told him the news but it was a difficult time in the following few days – before the official announcement was made – in case we let anything slip to our friends, by mistake. That could have ruined it all.

In June, John and I had a trip on the cruise liner, *Arcadia*. I was doing one of the Mike Craig comedy cruises. We were delighted to see Jim Bowen and his wife, Phyllis were also aboard and we could renew our friendship from the *QE2*. Also on the trip were Paul Daniels' son, Martin, Paul Squire and his son, Ben (whom I am sure is going to be one of the greatest golfers that this country has ever turned out, so watch out for him!)

We had a lovely cabin, with a balcony and were very well looked after by the ship's officers. During the cruise we went ashore at Vigo in northern Spain, Lisbon in Portugal and Lanzarote in the Canary Islands – again I had a chance to indulge my passion of 'retail therapy'.

When we went back on board at Lanzarote, there was a note under our cabin door from Ross, one of the officers. He asked me to contact him urgently. Oh no, something must be wrong at home, I thought immediately.

Before I could find him, Ross had arrived at our cabin door, wreathed in smiles.

'Oh, Wendy I am so happy to tell you that it has just been announced that you have been awarded the MBE.'

I started to cry, as did Susan, Mike Craig's wife, who was in the cabin at the time.

We all went off to the bar for a bottle of Moet to celebrate. We called Jim and Phyllis to join us. Jim arrived straightfaced and told us 'I've just had a telephone call as well.'

'Oh yes,' we all said in chorus, expecting another honour to be announced.

'It was cancelling one of my gigs,' he replied drolly.

Mike, Paul and Ben were still ashore playing golf (as they had done in every port of call). Susan called them on her mobile phone 'Get back here, straightaway, it's urgent,' she said. The three of them came rushing up to the bar, complete with golf clubs in tow, having not dared stop on the way. Susan told them the wonderful news and they were all delighted for me. We were having our little celebration party when the ship's captain, Ian Waters appeared.

'Congratulations, Wendy, we are so pleased for you. May we announce it on the ship's PA system because this is a first for us on the *Arcadia*?'

The public announcement produced so many greetings and letters from other passengers, I was overwhelmed. It seemed everyone wanted to share in my happiness and that made a wonderful end to our cruise home.

Everyone at *EastEnders* was thrilled when I returned to work, and said they thought it was well deserved. That day we were doing a launderette scene and we had a bit of difficulty with one of the washing machines. The front machines are false and are not connected to either electricity or water. The director wanted the machine's front door open and the props boys were pressing every button in sight. To no avail – the door would just not budge.

Suddenly I noticed a piece of wire hanging down at the bottom of the machine. 'Pull that there,' I suggested. Hey presto! The door opened.

I stood up and said straight into camera 'That's what I got my MBE for! Fifteen years of these f****ing machines!'

Emma the director looked at me. 'I don't recall that in your acceptance speech!' she said.

Well, at least it made the crew laugh.

Now I am thoroughly looking forward to my investiture at Buckingham Palace on Tuesday 28 November. The citation in my honour letter says that the award is for my services to television drama.

I just knew that wearing Pauline's blue nylon overall for the last fifteen years would pay off eventually!

Wendy Richard –
Television, Film, Radio,
Stage and Music

TELEVISION:

SERIES
Are You Being Served?
Both Ends Meet
Dad's Army
Danger Man
Dixon of Dock Green
EastEnders
Grace and Favour
Harpers West One
Holly Road Rig
Hugh and I
Joe Nobody
No Hiding Place
Not On Your Nellie
On The Buses
Please Sir!
Spooner's Patch
The Arthur Haynes Show
The Fenn Street Gang
The Making of Jericho
The Newcomers
Up Pompeii!
West Country Tales
Z Cars

GUEST APPEARANCES
3–2–1
All Over The Shop
Auntie's TV Favourites

Big Breakfast
Big Night Out
Blankety Blank
Call My Bluff
Carry On Again Christmas
Celebrity Holiday Memories
Celebrity Ready Steady Cook!
Celebrity Squares
Christmas Big Break
Countdown
Cross Wits
The Bruce Forsythe Chat Show
The Dick Emery Show
Don't Turn Off The Lights
EastEnders Fighting Fit
Esther
Family Fortunes
Film Quiz
First Take
Frankie Howerd In Ulster
Funny Money
Funny Turns – John Inman
Generation Game
GMTV
Give Us A Clue
HMS Paradise
It's Only TV, But I Like It
Jim'll Fix It
Jobs For The Boys
Jonathan Ross
Just A Minute

Wendy Richard

Lifeline Appeal
The Gloria Hunniford Show
The Harry Secombe Show
The Likely Lads
Little & Large
London Wall
Monarchy – The Nation Decides
Noel's House Party
Noel's TV Quiz
Other Half Celebrity Special
Pardon The Expression
Pebble Mill
Punchlines
The Pyramid Game
Rainbow
Richard & Judy
Roland Rat
Royal Command Performance
Sammy Davis Meets The Girls
Shooting Stars
Simon King Wildlife
Telly Addicts
That Was The Day
That's Show Biz
Today's The Day
TV's Greatest Hits
Weaver's Green
West Country Tales
Whose House?
Wogan
You Bet
Zodiac Game

APPEARANCES AS PRESENTER
The Big C
History of the Circus
History of the Jack Russell
Watchdog (survey on tea)

FILMS
Are You Being Served?
Bless This House
Carry On Girls
Carry On Matron
Doctor In Clover
Gumshoe
No Blade Of Grass
On The Busses

RADIO
Cat's Whiskers
Dad's Army
Desert Island Discs
Don't Talk To Me About Kids
It's My Future
Just A Minute
Kaleidoscope
Ken Bruce Radio 2 Morning Show
The Law Game
Listening Corner
Screenplay
Some Of These Days
Trains Don't Stop Here Any More
The Worst Witch

STAGE
Are You Being Served?
Blithe Spirit
Cinderella
Let's Go Camping
No Sex, Please – We're British

RECORDS
Come Outside (with Mike Sarne 1962)
Come Outside (with Mike Berry 1986)

270

Index

275